THE
BOOK
OF
GREENS

THE
BOOK
OF
GREENS

A Cook's Compendium of 40 Varieties,
from Arugula to Watercress, with More than 175 Recipes

JENN LOUIS

with Kathleen Squires

PHOTOGRAPHS BY ED ANDERSON

TEN SPEED PRESS
California | New York

GREENS HAIKU

Writing a greens book
Lots of greens stuck in my teeth
Hazard of the trade

To the universe. You're crazy.
–J.L.

CONTENTS

RECLAIM LIST

V Vegetarian

PREFACE

I grew up in Southern California. The weather was temperate, and we always grew food. Along the side of the house were lemon, orange, and lime trees; the other side of the yard had a grape arbor, an avocado tree, and peach and plum trees, too. And in the back, close to the citrus, was a plot for growing vegetables. I ate a huge variety of foods growing up, and my siblings and I were taught that you ate what you were served. We ate vegetables with dinner, always, often starting with a salad.

At the age of fifteen I became a vegetarian: ovo-lacto, no fish. I was a competitive runner and thrived on starches, cheese, and vegetables. I quit the vegetarian diet at thirty with a hamburger; I ate the whole thing. I now label myself an "opportunivore": I eat everything. I am not picky and really love all sorts of foods and flavors. More than anything, I love to experience new cultures by exploring their food traditions, and I think that a home-cooked meal from any country or region is magic.

During college I caught the travel bug. I visited Israel in my junior year, then again after graduation, when I lived on a dairy and agricultural kibbutz. Over the next twenty years I drove the four sides of the United States, and flew to areas in between; I visited Ecuador, most of western and some of eastern Europe, South Africa, Vietnam, Canada, Mexico, and China. I was always curious about the regional cuisines in each country. I was interested in the way people ate, especially what ingredients they had to choose from and how they combined them. I discovered that most people in other countries eat a good variety of wild and cultivated greens. In Oaxaca, Mexico, for example, a guide explained to me that people with limited resources would often balance their nutrition by foraging for greens. When I visited Vietnam, I was delighted by the number of different varieties of greens in the markets, many of which I had never seen.

When I looked closer at non–North American diets, I realized just how richly and eclectically these cuisines used greens. While Westerners typically use greens in salads or side dishes—and discard edible leaves like tomato, cauliflower, broccoli, kohlrabi, and sweet potato—many cultures, especially Eastern cultures, integrate greens in so many other ways. Think soups, rice dishes, flatbreads, egg dishes, legume dishes, and more. In those cultures, greens are ever present; they are not divided into separate courses or categories. And why shouldn't we be using greens more? Their vegetal flavor is a clean and refreshing balance to richness, and they add texture and color to any dish. Greens are also incredibly nutritious, and adding them is an easy way to sneak something healthy into your meals. Greens are also full of fiber, and fiber helps keep us full and satisfied.

Americans now live in the land of farmers' markets, and really good ones at that. As a child, I ate broccoli, cauliflower, zucchini, onions, cabbage, and a few other vegetables—that was about it. Now you can find many varieties of each of these vegetables at your local grocery store, produce market, or farmers' market. It's exciting to see how many varieties of vegetables, including greens, are now available—but sometimes, the sheer number of choices is overwhelming.

Learning to buy and cook new vegetables can be intimidating. Many friends and customers have asked me, "I bought X, what do I do with it?" Or, "I bought something new, cooked it, and it didn't work out . . . ." Chefs have training, and we know how to cook all sorts of foods. So, as a lover of greens, I want to share what I know. I want not only to catalog the many varieties of greens out there but also inspire home cooks to get creative with flavors and cooking methods. There is so much more that you can do with greens than make just a salad or side (although there are plenty of those in this book, too).

When I was learning how to cook, I would shop weekly and buy something I had never cooked or eaten before. You should do this, too. Go to Asian grocery stores and marvel at the varieties that are familiar and unfamiliar. Check out every local farmers' market you can and talk to the farmers. Ask questions and buy some greens that you have never cooked before. At the grocery store, find ingredients that will complement your greens: an oil you have never used, beans, anchovies, sea salt, cured meats. Challenge yourself; that is how chefs become better at their jobs. Don't walk past some greens that look different, buy them! And at a restaurant, order the greens you have never before tried, and don't hesitate to take cues from the chef's method of preparation.

So, here's the deal: greens should be an essential part of every meal. And by greens I mean leafy greens, leaves on plants (such as tomato leaves), and herbs. (NOTE: Herbs are small leafy greens packed with intense flavor and utilized differently than other leafy greens, such as lettuces. They are typically used for their flavoring rather than bulk.) Greens are a superfood because they are so nutritious, are inexpensive to grow, and come in many varieties with a broad diversity of flavors and textures. Of course, they are superdelicious, too. Use this book as your inspiration to make a fresh start in your home kitchen with greens. Think beyond the salad bowl and begin cooking with your greens. As my old sous chef used to say: "Green means go, baby! Green means go!"

THE BASICS

You don't need a degree in botany, or even a home garden, to understand how to select, handle, and cook greens. Keep the following advice in mind when making any recipe in this book, from simple tossed salads to those that call for more elaborate methods.

BUY FRESH IN SMALL QUANTITIES

It is a given that greens at the farmers' market are going to be much, much fresher than grocery store greens. Think about it: farmers' market greens are likely coming from somewhere nearby, at least a drivable distance, and the farmers usually harvest the day before the market. The greens in conventional grocery stores have usually been shipped in from farther away, which means that by the time they are unpacked and stocked on the shelves, the greens will have some age on them. Farmers' market greens will last much longer and stay fresher longer.

There are signs of aged greens. Look at the color. If you see any browning or yellowing, that's oxidation, and that means your greens are not the freshest that they can be. And the older that a green is, the sooner it will dehydrate. If the outer leaves are soft and limp, they are dehydrated and have a lot less water in them than they had when fresh.

Smell the greens. They should smell aromatic and fresh. If their aroma is rancid, moldy, or even if there's a complete absence of aroma, the greens might not be at their freshest.

When selecting greens, don't be afraid to taste a leaf, especially at a farmers' market. Is the flavor right? Is the texture as it should be (crisp, firm, succulent, or soft, depending on variety)? Tasting food is the only way to really get to know quality and to be able to compare what is good, mediocre, and not!

BE GENTLE WITH YOUR GREENS

Greens are delicate and need to be treated delicately. So think about that whenever you are handling them—whether washing, storing, or cooking them—or even when you bring them home from the market.

Try to clean your greens as soon as you unpack them. Directions on how to clean are included in each chapter, but in general, when washing, fill your basin with cool water first, then immerse the greens. It is best to avoid spraying greens with water directly from the faucet, as the force may bruise them, though it is okay to rinse sturdy greens, especially if they have soil trapped between their leaves. Once your greens are in your basin full of water, move them around gently with loose, open fingers. It is good practice to keep your fingers loosely open, almost like palming a basketball, whenever handling greens. Loose wrists and soft fingers will prevent bruising.

Drain and dry your greens well, either with a salad spinner or by blotting with paper towels. Store greens in a lidded, plastic container, or in a ziplock bag, or wrap in plastic. If the greens are retaining a lot of moisture, store with a clean kitchen towel to absorb the excess. If the greens seem a bit dry, store with a damp clean kitchen towel, so they won't become completely dehydrated. Refresh before cooking. (Instructions for how best to do this are included in each chapter.)

DRESS AND SEASON SALADS JUST BEFORE SERVING

As soon as acid hits greens, it will start to break them down, so dress just before serving, or not too long beforehand. Use dressing sparingly at first, and add more to taste. Overdressing greens makes them droop and masks their wonderful flavors.

Always toss with your hands, not a spoon, and do it in a tumbling motion, moving the greens loosely through open fingers, making sure all of the leaves are coated very lightly with dressing. (Just as a sauce should complement, not drown, pasta, the dressing should not overwhelm the greens; it should always brighten and enlighten them!

Toss salad in a large bowl so the greens have room to move. When seasoning, sprinkle salt and pepper from up high, so they shower down. (If you season from low, the seasoning will not distribute as well.)

Dressings that include dairy, such as egg, buttermilk, or mayonnaise, and dressings with garlic in them need to be stored in the refrigerator. Vinaigrettes don't need to be stored in the refrigerator all the time, but do keep them in airtight containers and refrigerate for storage longer than three days.

EAT FRESH AND ABUNDANTLY

Eat greens raw and cooked, eat them in season, and think about incorporating them into every meal of the day. Eat them alone or combined with other foods, such as meats, grains, eggs, dairy, starches, fish, and more. You can even use them in sweets and cocktails. And no matter what you make from this book, keep in mind my main mantra: The fresher, the better.

HOW TO USE THIS BOOK

Think of this book as a reference, an encyclopedia of all the delicious leafy vegetables, leaves on vegetables, and herbs you can cook and eat. Greens are listed alphabetically, and each heading contains essential information about the green, its origin, nutritional value, varieties, and season, along with facts either essential, ancillary, or fun. Instructions on how to choose, how to store, how to clean, and how to refresh are included with each green. Use the suggested cooking methods to explore the versatility of each green and the flavor pairings as a guideline to maximize deliciousness. Recipes follow—some riff on classics, some are tied to tradition, some came out of purely creative inspiration, and some were kindly lent from friends. When cooking your way through this book, you will discover the nuances of each green, such as how tender greens might be best when eaten raw or lightly cooked or how sturdy greens can hold up to forceful methods, from stewing to braising to even cooking sous vide.

In most cases, more than one type of green can be used in a recipe. Suggestions for swapping in others follow each recipe. Use these suggestions as a springboard for experimenting with various greens.

A note about size: greens can vary in size, depending on the region, the variety, and the maturity of the green. Keep that in mind and use the cues in the recipes to cook with your gut if your greens don't seem to be done in the times noted.

TROUBLESHOOTING

Greens are easy to prepare, so you won't run into too many complications in the kitchen. Refer to these guidelines on the rare occasion that you need some extra help in coaxing out the best in your greens.

If your greens are dehydrated

Fear not: most greens that are limp and have lost some moisture can be rejuvenated and rescued (unless they are rotten and slimy—that's compost). Remove and/or discard any outer leaves that are damaged and then plunge the rest of the greens into a basin filled with cool water and ice. Gently swoosh them around, then let them sit for 15 to 20 minutes. Lift out of the water, drain, and use a salad spinner to dry them or pat them dry. This method helps your salad greens be at their perky

best and ensures that other greens will be at their prime freshness before cooking.

If your greens taste too bitter

If you have an aversion to intense bitterness in a green, like a chicory, try pairing it with fat—butter, oil, or lard—which will soften bitterness, and add acid, such as citrus or vinegar, which will brighten and soften the chlorophyll.

If your greens taste too "green"

Blanching a green first will mute its intense, grassy, chlorophyll flavor. It will also soften the texture.

HOW TO BLANCH GREENS

Bring a large pot of salted water to a boil. Add the greens. For delicate greens (like spinach), cook for about 1 minute. For sturdier greens (such as cardoons), cook for 3 to 5 minutes. Transfer the greens to an ice-water bath to cool, then drain before using.

If you overcook your greens

Toss them out. Once you've taken chlorophyll to the point where the color turns deep army green, the greens no longer taste good. Chalk it up to a learning experience. Part of learning is practice; part of practice is making mistakes.

TOOLS

The good news about greens is you don't need a lot of tools. Here are a few things that will come in handy.

Your hands

They are the best tools. I believe the more that we separate ourselves from the food that we are eating, the less we understand it, so I'm a proponent of getting right in there and using your hands. Of course, use tongs when appropriate—like for grilling and flipping meat in a hot pan. But when you're tossing salad, touch the salad. Just make sure to wash your hands before you do.

Salad spinner

This is a great way to dry your greens without bruising them.

Storage containers

Use plastic, airtight tubs or other containers or plastic ziplock bags for storing greens. Airtight tubs that stack are nice for saving space. You can also wrap the greens in plastic wrap.

Mason jars

It is easy to make and store dressings in the jars. Just shake and serve.

Also, save jars that you like from jarred foods. Take the label off with hot water and a label remover.

Good knives

You really don't need much more than a 6- to 8-inch (15- to 20-cm) French chef's knife, a serrated knife, and a paring knife. Keep them sharp, store them in a block or on a magnet, and never, ever put them in the dishwasher.

Wooden cutting board

Always have a spray bottle of diluted bleach (bleach water) for cleaning. Wash the board down with soapy water first and then bleach it. Plastic cutting boards are fine, too. Just make sure that your board is large enough so that you have the space to work comfortably.

Clean kitchen towels and paper towels

Use to dry greens after spinning, to pat dry sturdier greens, and to absorb any residual moisture when storing.

Vegetable peeler

A "Y" peeler is best for peeling woody stems and skins.

Scale

Weighing ingredients on a digital scale will yield the best results in my recipes. I recommend investing in a good digital scale that can measure in grams, and following the gram measurements in this book.

Other tools called for in this book

- Blender and/or food processor
- Microplane or other fine-rasp grater
- Handheld citrus juicer
- Immersion blender
- Mandoline
- Nonstick pans
- Oven-safe pans (cast iron is great)
- Stand mixer

TYPES OF GREENS IN THIS BOOK

ROBUST ⟶

These are strong, dense, solidly textured greens that likely need some sort of preparation before use (peeling, blanching) and should only be eaten cooked.

BEST METHOD ⟶	GREENS TO USE
PANFRIED	BROCCOLI RABE
DEEP-FRIED	BURDOCK
SAUTÉED	CARDOON
ROASTED	DOCK
GRILLED	FIDDLEHEADS
BRAISED	GRAPE LEAVES
BAKED	NETTLES
BOILED	SEAWEED
BROILED	
BLANCHED	

TENDER ⟶

These greens can be enjoyed raw or briefly cooked.

BEST METHOD ⟶	GREENS TO USE
LIGHTLY SAUTÉED	AGRETTI
WILTED IN SOUPS OR STEWS	AMARANTH
QUICKLY STEAMED	ARUGULA
QUICKLY STIR-FRIED OVER VERY HIGH HEAT WITH JUST ENOUGH OIL OR OTHER FAT TO COAT THE BOTTOM OF THE PAN	BROCCOLI GREENS
	CELERY LEAVES
	CHICKWEED
	CHRYSANTHEMUM
	DANDELION GREENS
	FAVA GREENS
	HERBS
	LAMB'S-QUARTERS
	LEMON BALM
	MINER'S LETTUCE
	MINUTINA
	MUSTARD GREENS
	PURSLANE
	RAMP GREENS
	SORREL
	TATSOI
	TOMATO LEAVES
	WATERCRESS
	WATER SPINACH
	WOOD SORREL

DELICATE →   BEST METHOD →   GREENS TO USE

DELICATE ⟶

These are the tender, thin, clean-flavored, and often (but not always) sweeter greens that should only be eaten raw; cooking will cause them to lose their integrity and flavor. These types of greens tend not to hold up to thick or heavy salad dressings.

BEST METHOD ⟶

SERVE RAW OR
PUREE RAW AND
MAKE INTO A SOUP
OR SAUCE

GREENS TO USE

MÂCHE

MIZUNA

PEA GREENS

WILD PEA GREENS

STURDY ⟶

These greens can be enjoyed raw or cooked, and they have the texture to stand up to many cooking methods. Sometimes their thicker fiber structure needs to be broken down with heat. In the case of kale, however, the fibers can be softened by massaging the new green.

BEST METHOD ⟶

BAKED

BOILED

BRAISED

ROASTED

STEWED

SIMMERED

STEAMED

SAUTÉED

LIGHTLY GRILLED

STIR-FRIED

FRIED

GREENS TO USE

BEET GREENS

BOK CHOY

BRUSSELS SPROUTS

CABBAGE

CARROT GREENS

CAULIFLOWER GREENS

CELTUCE

CHARD

CHICORIES

CHINESE CELERY

COLLARD GREENS

GAI LAN

KALE

KOHLRABI GREENS

NEW ZEALAND SPINACH

RADISH GREENS

RED ORACH

SPINACH

SQUASH LEAVES

SUCCULENTS

SWEET POTATO GREENS

TURNIP GREENS

NOTES ON COMMONLY USED INGREDIENTS

Anchovies

Fresh anchovies aren't easy to source, but there are some great anchovies that come packed in salt or oil. Anchovies packed in salt hold their flavor beautifully because they are minimally processed, but you have to fillet them. Anchovies in oil are filleted and cured in salt. I like the ease of anchovies in oil for dressings.

Cheeses

In this book, you will come across blue, feta, Fontina, Gorgonzola, Parmigiano-Reggiano, provolone, Pecorino Romano, mascarpone, and a few other cheeses. That's because cheese and greens make a great pairing. When experimenting with greens and cheese in your own recipes, keep a few tenets in mind: hard cheeses, such as Parmigiano-Reggiano and Pecorino Romano, usually add a punch of saltiness and act as a brightener to greens. Softer cheeses add creamy richness, and in some cases (ripened and blue cheese) pungency, which acts as a nice balance to bitter greens like raw dandelion and chicories. Play around to find your preferred cheese-green pairings.

Fish Sauce

Fish sauce has a deep umami flavor that really rounds out and complements bitter flavors. Red Boat fish sauce from Vietnam is my favorite. It is made from salting anchovies and letting them ferment. Look for the 40N or 50N demarcation on the label—that means higher protein levels, which contribute to a really rich, complex sauce. A little bit goes a long way to add depth and roundness to a sauce or a dish.

Lardo

When I need to add a complex layer of fat and richness to any dish, I reach for *lardo* instead of butter or oil. *Lardo* is a type of Italian cured pork fat, and I find it is a great equalizer for bitter, intense greens. Think of it as the pork version of schmaltz. It acts in much the same way. Find *lardo* in butcher shops or mail-order *salumi* shops.

Miso

This salty, traditional Japanese condiment made from fermented soybeans is (like fish sauce) another of my favorite ways to lend a punch of umami to whatever I'm cooking. It is a natural pairing for any Asian green. The most common types available are red miso and white miso. Red miso tends to have a deeper, more pungent flavor, while white miso tastes lighter and sweeter.

Oils

EXTRA-VIRGIN OLIVE OIL: I cook often with extra-virgin olive oil and prefer those from California, Italy, and Spain. The range of flavors is astounding: some are floral, some are pungent, some are spicy, and there is a whole range of tastes in between. There are different varieties of refinement. Save your best, premium extra-virgin olive oil for finishing, and use lower-grade extra-virgin olive oil for cooking and salad dressings. I always like to have that one bottle that might cost a bit extra on hand for drizzling on fish, vegetables, or greens, of course.

SESAME OIL: Toasted sesame oil is essential for Asian dishes, whether a cooked dish or a salad dressing. I use it because of its great flavor and depth. Toasted sesame oil has a nuttier flavor, a deeper brown color, and a lower smoke point than light sesame oil. You can use toasted for quick sautés, but I don't recommend it for longer frying.

OTHER VEGETABLE OILS: Good neutral vegetable oils (not Crisco!) are my go-to oils for frying because of their high smoke point. I opt for sunflower or canola oil for recipes that call for vegetable oil.

These oils are also useful for baking, dressings, and marinades. I usually fry in vegetable oil, and sometimes in olive oil if I want the extra richness.

Salt

I use basically three types of salt: kosher, fine sea salt, and flaky sea salt.

Kosher salt is the backbone basic in my kitchen. It has a clean taste, and heightens the flavor in foods. I like to use Diamond Crystal—it dissolves quickly, has a neutral flavor, and is good for consistent flavoring. You can find Diamond Crystal kosher salt in any supermarket.

Fine sea salt is more intensely salty than kosher salt, so make sure you taste as you go and season little by little until you get the feel for using it. Whenever a recipe in this book calls for fine sea salt, I recommend Trapani, which you can find online or in gourmet groceries.

Flaky sea salt is great as a finishing salt, for that last burst of flavor while adding a crunchy texture. Maldon sea salt is readily available online or in gourmet groceries, so it is my go-to salt for any recipes that call for flaky sea salt.

Spices

Keeping your pantry well outfitted with good-quality spices is a must for adding oomph to nearly anything you cook. To get the best from your spice shelf, keep a few things in mind:

1 Once opened, ground spices will lose their flavor, so it is best to use them within 1 month.

2 Consider quickly toasting spices to release their essential oils and enhance their power and flavor.

3 For sautéing, grind whole spices first, before adding them to your sauté. They will toast in the oil of the sauté.

Stocks

A good homemade chicken stock is like liquid gold. Your house will smell great and the flavor of the stock is incomparable to that of store-bought. I like to make a double-strength stock (aka double stock,

see page 299), which comes in handy for any recipe that calls for stock.

Vinegars

Every kind of vinegar is going to have a different acidity, so it is important to taste before you use it. If you find yourself with a vinegar with an acidity level that is too high, add a little water or more olive oil to balance it out when making a vinaigrette.

BALSAMIC: I don't usually use balsamic vinegar in salad dressings (the exception is the thinner, less sweet white balsamic variety, which I use on page 302). Similar to the Italians, I think of balsamic vinegar more like a condiment. The type of balsamic I enjoy in the kitchen wouldn't make for a good vinaigrette anyway. I tend to go for the high-quality, aged syrupy varieties that are wonderful when used as a finishing drizzle on everything from pasta to strawberries.

CHAMPAGNE AND WHITE WINE: I use these two types often for salad dressings. They have a great golden color, a clean flavor, and depth without being too sharp.

CIDER: Because it is made from apples, cider vinegar is a great way to add a fruity flavor to vinaigrette.

RED WINE: When searching for high acidity and sharpness in a dressing, red wine vinegar is the go-to choice.

RICE WINE: Like toasted sesame oil, rice wine vinegar is a signature flavor in the Asian pantry, especially for stir-fries or raw salads with Asian greens. Rice wine is also nice when you want a softer, sweeter vinaigrette, rather than the sharper flavor of a white wine vinegar dressing.

SHERRY: I like the sweetness and fortified strength of sherry vinegar, not just in vinaigrettes, but in sauces, too.

WHITE: Superstrong, distilled white vinegar is a good basic to use for intensely pickled items.

SEASONAL CHART

The seasonal list for each green in this book is based on North American availability. Note that many greens span more than one season. Though many of these greens are available year-round, refer to this chart for their peak times.

SPRING

AGRETTI	LETTUCES (BUTTERHEAD, CHINESE, ICEBERG, LOOSELEAF, ROMAINE)
ARUGULA	
BOK CHOYS AND OTHER CHOYS	
BROCCOLI GREENS	MÂCHE
BROCCOLI RABE	MINER'S LETTUCE
CARDOON	MINUTINA
CARROT GREENS	MIZUNA
CELERY LEAVES	MUSTARD GREENS
CELTUCE	NETTLES
CHARD	PEA GREENS
CHICKWEED	PURSLANE
CHRYSANTHEMUM	RADISH GREENS
COLLARD GREENS	RAMP GREENS
DANDELION GREENS	RED ORACH
FAVA GREENS	SEAWEED
GAI LAN (CHINESE BROCCOLI)	SORREL
HERBS	SPIGARELLO
KALE	SPINACH
KOHLRABI GREENS	SUCCULENTS
	TATSOI
	WATERCRESS

SUMMER

AGRETTI	GRAPE LEAVES
AMARANTH	HERBS
ARUGULA	LAMB'S-QUARTERS
BEET GREENS	LETTUCES
BOK CHOYS AND OTHER CHOYS	MÂCHE
BRUSSELS SPROUTS	MALABAR SPINACH
CABBAGE	MALLOW
CARDOON	MINUTINA
CAULIFLOWER LEAVES	MIZUNA
CELTUCE	NEW ZEALAND SPINACH
CHARD	PEA GREENS
CHINESE CELERY	PURSLANE
CHRYSANTHEMUM	TATSOI
FAVA GREENS	TOMATO LEAVES
GAI LAN (CHINESE BROCCOLI)	WATER SPINACH

FALL

AMARANTH	GRAPE LEAVES
ARUGULA	HERBS
BEET GREENS	KALE
BOK CHOY	KOHLRABI GREENS
BROCCOLI GREENS	LAMB'S-QUARTERS
BROCCOLI RABE	LETTUCES
BRUSSELS SPROUTS	MINUTINA
CABBAGE	RADISH GREENS
CARROT GREENS	SPINACH
CAULIFLOWER LEAVES	SQUASH GREENS
CELERY LEAVES	SWEET POTATO GREENS
CHICORIES	TATSOI
CHINESE CELERY	TOMATO LEAVES
CHRYSANTHEMUM	TURNIP LEAVES
GAI LAN (CHINESE BROCCOLI)	WATERCRESS

WINTER

BEET GREENS	KALE
BROCCOLI RABE	LETTUCES
BRUSSELS SPROUTS	MÂCHE
CABBAGE	MUSTARD GREENS
CELERY LEAVES	NETTLES
CELTUCE	RADISH GREENS
CHICORIES	SPIGARELLO
COLLARD GREENS	TURNIP GREENS
HERBS	

BOWLS 101

Here's a trade secret: a salad needs to be as thoughtfully composed as any cooked dish. It may seem like common sense, but it is often really easy to compile random and opposing ingredients that can muddle or confuse the greatness of the individual ingredients, especially the greens.

These four hard-and-fast rules will help you put together a great-tasting salad:

- Not all ingredients go together.
- Make sure your choice of base green holds up to, and won't be bogged down by, the other ingredients.
- Too many ingredients become too busy or confusing. Sometimes, it's best to take the Coco Chanel approach to salads: less is more.
- Keep these three components in mind for a delicious bowl: flavor, texture, and visual appeal.

With those four rules in mind, have fun mixing and matching. Choose from the following categories to get creative. Taste each ingredient before you add it to the mix and think about its compatibility with the other ingredients. Make sure the mouthful makes sense!

NOTE: Do not feel compelled to use items from every category!

1   CHOOSE A BASE

Any delicate, tender, or sturdy green or a combination of complementary greens that can be eaten raw.

2   ADD VARIETY

First, stick with other vegetables, raw, blanched, or roasted. Think radishes, broccoli, carrots, peas, celery, corn, asparagus. Add fresh and/ or dried fruit for sweetness.

3   ADD TEXTURE

Use grains (quinoa, barley, farro, frikeh, bulgur, couscous, pasta, rice), nuts (pine nuts, peanuts, almonds, pecans, walnuts, hazelnuts, cashews— candied or toasted), popped corn or seeds, croutons, or fine bread crumbs.

4   ADD PROTEIN

Add a hard-boiled egg, cold cuts (turkey, ham, salami), beans (chickpeas, lentils, soybeans), and/ or leftover grilled meat, Thanksgiving turkey, roasted chicken, or smoked fish.

5 + **6** + **7** + **8**

ADD SALTINESS

Add saltiness and pungency with cheese that is fresh, soft, semi-soft, firm, mild, stinky, or ripened and grated, crumbled, or sliced. Capers and olives do the trick, too.

SMOOTH IT OUT

Smooth it out with herbs.

SHARPEN IT UP

Sharpen it up with cornichons, pickles (cucumber, chiles, or giardiniera), or peppers.

DRESS IT

Use a light, vinaigrette-style dressing for delicate greens; richer and thicker dressing (such as cream or tahini based) for sturdier greens.

= Your custom-designed salad bowl.

GREENS

AGRETTI

Salsola soda

Well before it became a staple in Roman peasant food, agretti was used as an essential ingredient in glass and soap making in the Mediterranean. It wasn't until the nineteenth century, when synthetic materials replaced the green in the process, that Italians and others in the Mediterranean turned to consuming the native plant instead. Often described as a succulent-like grass, *agretti* means "little sour one" in Italian, and is also called *barba di frate*, which translates to "monk's beard." Its appearance resembles wide, grassier chives, its raw texture is lightly crunchy, and its flavor is best described as mineral, acidic, tart, and slightly salty. Because it originates in Lazio, it is prepared simply, like other vegetables native to the region; it is often served raw, boiled, or sautéed with olive oil. Though rare in the United States, its popularity rose in Europe after being featured on popular cooking shows, with a recent shortage causing a mild panic among fans in the United Kingdom, where it became particularly scarce. Agretti also makes appearances in Chinese cuisine and in Japan, where it is known as "land seaweed."

Also called opposite-leaved saltwort and roscana, agretti is a good source of vitamins A, C, and K and of iron, fiber, and calcium. Traditional Chinese medicine hails it as a blood purifier and natural laxative.

VARIETIES SALTWORT

SEASON Late spring to early summer

HOW TO CHOOSE Agretti should be vibrant and sprightly, not wilted. There should be a crisp "bite" to its texture. Avoid limp greens and any with discoloration, slime, or mold.

HOW TO CLEAN Trim off the roots, immerse in cold water, and wash thoroughly, rinsing off sand and grit by agitating with fingers. Drain; spin or pat dry.

HOW TO STORE Store in an airtight plastic bin or ziplock bag or wrap in plastic wrap. In the crisper drawer of the refrigerator, the greens will keep for 2 to 3 days.

HOW TO REFRESH Immerse in ice water for 15 minutes. Drain; pat or spin dry.

COOKING METHODS Use raw in salads or cook by boiling, steaming, sautéing, or stir-frying. Mix into pasta and risotto or use as a topping for crostini, bruschetta, or pizza.

PAIRINGS Olive oil, garlic, lemon, vinaigrette, poultry, fish, lamb, bacon, eggs, cheese, tomatoes, arugula, escarole, radicchio.

AGRETTI WITH LEMON

My favorite way to serve agretti is with fish, though it makes a fitting side dish for poultry and lamb. Steamed and then tossed with a little bit of lemon is the perfect, simple preparation. Agretti's long, thin, grassy tendrils are attractive on the plate, too.

SERVES 6 AS A SIDE DISH

12 ounces [340 g] agretti, roots and tough stems removed

Juice of ½ lemon, or as needed

2 tablespoons olive oil

Bring a large pot of salted water to a boil. Add the agretti and cook at a medium simmer for 5 to 8 minutes, until tender. Using a slotted spoon, remove the agretti from the water and toss with enough lemon juice and the olive oil to brighten the greens but not make them sour. Serve warm or chilled.

OTHER GREENS TO TRY dandelion greens, mâche (omit simmering)

AGRETTI WITH MUSHROOMS

Button mushrooms, especially when thinly sliced, have a neutral flavor and a delightfully delicate texture. Add agretti and a little of my bagna cauda sauce and the combination becomes a salad. What I find particularly appealing about this mixture is that it blends a somewhat rare ingredient, the agretti, with the very common mushrooms

SERVES 6 AS AN APPETIZER OR SIDE DISH

12 ounces [340 g] agretti, roots and tough stems removed

½ cup [120 ml] bagna cauda (page 295), warmed

4 ounces [115] button mushrooms, thinly sliced on a mandoline (¾ cup)

1 hard-boiled egg (page 293), chopped

Kosher salt and freshly ground black pepper

1 lemon, cut into 6 wedges

Bring a large pot of salted water to boil. Add the agretti and cook at a medium simmer for 5 to 8 minutes, until tender. Using a slotted spoon, remove the agretti from the water, draining well, and transfer to a bowl. Dress with the bagna cauda, add the mushrooms and egg, toss well, and season with salt and pepper. Divide among six plates and serve with a lemon wedge on each plate.

OTHER GREENS TO TRY raw chicories (chopped Belgian endive), salicornia

Agretti with Lemon

AMARANTH

Amaranthus spp.

Its name is derived from the Greek *amarantos*, which means "unfading," because the plant was believed to be immortal. Living up to its name, it has thrived on nearly every continent, especially in its native lands of North and Central America. Amaranth is believed to have originally been cultivated in Mexico, where it is known as *quintoniles*. The Aztecs and Incans used the seeds for religious rituals and ate the greens for sustenance.

Its immortal nature has impressed scribes throughout history, appearing in everything from *Aesop's Fables* to Milton's *Paradise Lost* to poems by Samuel Taylor Coleridge and Percy Bysshe Shelley.

Also known as African spinach, bush greens, Chinese spinach, Indian spinach, Joseph's coat, and yin choy, amaranth can range in color from bright green to green with red or purple, depending on variety.

The flavor is akin to spinach; the texture is sturdier, holding up well to stewing. Amaranth leaves are currently eaten across Asia in China, Malaysia, the Philippines, Indonesia, and Vietnam, where it is often stir-fried and used in soups. In India, it is used to bolster curries and dal and across Africa, it is stewed and sautéed. Across the Caribbean, it is especially popular in Jamaica, where it stars in its signature dish, callaloo; in Trinidad, the leaves are known as *bhaji*. In Europe, the Greeks are most likely to eat it with olive oil and lemon, alongside fish. The greens are rich in protein; in vitamins A, C, and folate; and in calcium, iron, manganese, and dietary fiber.

VARIETIES AUSTRALIAN, AFRICAN, BIGELOW'S, BONE-BRACT, BROWN'S, CALIFORNIA, CARELESS WEED, CHIHUAHUAN, CRISPLEAF, FLORIDA, FRINGED, GREEN, GREENSTRIPE, GREGG'S, JOSEPH'S COAT, LARGE FRUIT, LOVES-LIES-BLEEDING, MAT, MEXICAN GRAIN, PALMER'S, PENDANT, POWELL, PRINCE-OF-WALES FEATHER, PRICKLY, PRINGLE'S, PROSTRATE, PURPLE, RED, ROUGH-FRUIT, SANDHILL, SLENDER, SMOOTH, SOUTHERN, SPINY, SPLEEN, SPREADING, TALL WATERHEMP, TASSEL FLOWER, THORNY, TIDAL MARSH, TORREY'S, TUMBLE PIGWEED, WATSON'S, WRIGHT'S, WHITE PIGWEED

SEASON Summer to midfall

HOW TO CHOOSE Choose perky amaranth greens with bright, uniform coloring. Avoid slimy, wilted greens with dark spots. Also, avoid greens that are starting to flower, a sign of age.

HOW TO CLEAN Slice off woody stems; immerse greens in cool water and agitate with fingers. Drain; spin or pat dry.

HOW TO STORE Store in an airtight plastic bin or ziplock bag or wrap in plastic wrap. In the crisper drawer of the refrigerator, the greens will keep for 2 to 3 days.

HOW TO REFRESH Immerse in ice water for 15 minutes. Drain; pat or spin dry.

COOKING METHODS Use raw in salads or cook by stir-frying, sautéing, braising, boiling, steaming, simmering, or stewing. Toss with noodles, use as a pizza topping, or simmer the stems in soups and stews.

PAIRINGS Garlic, cumin, cilantro, chiles, butter, onions, coconut, raw or cooked fish, poultry, corn, zucchini.

AMARANTH FALAFEL

Falafel is a Middle Eastern street food that is now appreciated around the globe. It is a great snack to have on-the-go, tucked in a pita. But it is also nice to sit down and savor, too. And there are few better ways to enjoy chickpeas than when they are mashed and fried. Amaranth adds a fresh quality to this dish and an extra dose of nutrition to boot. Be sure to use dried chickpeas. Do not sub in canned chickpeas, which will throw the texture off.

MAKES 20 SMALL BALLS, SERVES 4 AS AN ENTRÉE

1½ cups [300 g] dried chickpeas

½ bunch cilantro, including stems

½ bunch curly parsley, including stems

½ bunch dill, including stems

30 g amaranth leaves

1 small yellow onion, grated on a box grater

1 to 2 jalapeño chiles, stemmed and seeded (heat will vary among chiles)

4 cloves garlic

1 teaspoon baking powder

2 teaspoons ground cumin

1 teaspoon ground coriander

Kosher salt

3 tablespoons white sesame seeds, toasted

4 cups [960 ml] neutral vegetable oil

Put the chickpeas in a large bowl and cover with water by 4 inches [10 cm]. Soak overnight at room temperature.

The following day, drain the beans. In the bowl of a food processor, combine the beans, cilantro, parsley, dill, amaranth leaves, onion, chiles, garlic, baking powder, cumin, and coriander. Grind together, stopping to scrape down the sides of the bowl as needed to ensure a fine grind, but not a puree.

Scrape into a large bowl, season with 2 teaspoons salt, and stir in the sesame seeds.

Preheat the oven to 200°F [95°C]. Set a wire rack on a sheet pan. Gently heat the oil in a heavy pot to 350°F [180°C].

Shape the chickpea mixture into walnut-size balls. Working in batches, fry the balls in the hot oil, turning once, for about 3 minutes per side, until crispy on the outside and tender and warm on the inside. Be sure not to crowd the balls in the pot or they will not cook evenly. Transfer the cooked falafel to the prepared rack and keep warm in the oven. Fry the remaining balls the same way and sprinkle the falafel with salt before serving.

NOTE: The falafel are delicious served with lettuces dressed with pomegranate molasses vinaigrette (page 301), pita bread, and muhammara (page 299). They can also be wrapped in lettuce leaves or tucked into a pita with the lettuce leaves as an accompaniment.

For a brighter flavor, add finely chopped preserved lemon (page 294) to the falafel mixture.

OTHER GREENS TO TRY nettles, spinach

AMARANTH SPANAKOPITA, STRUDEL-STYLE

The Greek word *spanakopita* translates to "spinach pie." My first memory of this iconic dish dates from my vegetarian days, when I was about fifteen years old. I had gone with my parents on a summer vacation to Canada, and it was in a tiny Greek restaurant in a remote mountainous area that I enjoyed my first spanakopita. I thought it was just crazy delicious because of the fresh, salty feta, the flakiness and butteriness of the dough, and the rich green layers of spinach—a nice hearty meal for a vegetarian.

My version swaps out the traditional spinach for amaranth, which is a good choice as the flavor difference is not great. Amaranth also takes well to my addition of fresh dill and oregano to amp up the flavor.

1 pound [455 g] amaranth leaves

¼ cup [60 ml] olive oil

1 large yellow onion, diced

¾ cup [230 g] feta, crumbled

2 eggs

1 cup [230 g] large-curd cottage cheese

¼ cup [15 g] finely chopped fresh dill, including stems

2 tablespoons coarsely chopped fresh oregano

Zest of 1 lemon, finely grated on a Microplane

Freshly grated nutmeg

Kosher salt and freshly ground black pepper

24 (9 by 12-inch/23 by 30.5-cm) sheets phyllo dough from 1 (1-pound/455-g) package, thawed according to package directions

1 cup [230 g] unsalted butter, melted

Bring a large pot of lightly salted water to a boil over medium-high heat. Add the amaranth and cook, stirring often, until completely wilted, about 4 minutes. Drain well, wrap the leaves in a clean kitchen towel, and wring out the excess moisture with your hands. Chop the amaranth coarsely and set aside to cool.

Warm the olive oil in a large sauté pan over medium-high heat. Add the onion and cook, stirring often, until translucent, about 4 minutes. If the onion starts to brown, decrease the heat. Remove from the heat and let cool.

In a large bowl, combine the cooled onion and amaranth, feta, eggs, cottage cheese, dill, oregano, lemon zest, and a few gratings of nutmeg. Season lightly with salt and pepper and stir to mix well.

Preheat the oven to 425°F [220°C]. Line a large sheet pan with parchment paper.

Unroll the phyllo dough on a work surface, keeping a shorter side parallel with the edge of the work surface. Peel off the top sheet from the stack and place it on the work surface, again with a shorter side parallel to the edge of the work surface. Cover the stack of phyllo sheets with a clean, dry kitchen

towel and always keep it covered when you are not removing a sheet. Brush the sheet with some of the melted butter, then top it with a second sheet and brush it lightly with butter. Continue layering sheets until you have stacked eight sheets total, lightly buttering each sheet except for the final one. Spoon 1½ cups [365 g] of the amaranth mixture into a rough sausage shape about 3 inches [7.5 cm] in from the short edge of the stack nearest you and extend it right and left to the edges of the stack. Starting at the edge nearest you, fold the phyllo stack over the filling and then continue to roll to the opposite end, forming a tight, even log. Generously brush the top of the log with butter, then transfer it to the prepared sheet pan. Repeat this process two times, using the remaining 16 sheets of phyllo dough and the rest of the filling. You will have three logs total. Refrigerate them, uncovered on the sheet pan, for 15 minutes.

Bake for 22 to 23 minutes, then rotate the pan back to front and continue baking for 22 to 23 minutes longer, until the strudel filling is set and the pastry is flaky and golden. If the pastry becomes too dark before it is ready, turn down the heat to 375°F or 400°F [190°C or 200°C].

Remove from the oven and let cool on the pan. Cut into slices 2 to 3 inches [5 to 8 cm] thick and serve immediately. The strudel does not store well in the refrigerator.

OTHER GREENS TO TRY spinach, chard

ARUGULA

Eruca sativa

This ubiquitous salad green may seem ordinary and common today, but in ancient Rome, where it was first cultivated, arugula was known as an aphrodisiac. Virgil, in his poem "Moretum," pointed out that arugula "excites sexual desire of drowsy people." Indeed, it was believed so potent that it was often mixed with less powerful greens in order to temper longing, and it was forbidden to be grown in monasteries.

Its strong, pungent, peppery flavor—in sharp contrast to its delicate texture—makes it easy to see why arugula was once deemed so powerful. Whether they call it rocket, *rucola*, *roquette*, *ruchetta*, or Italian cress, what many don't realize about this "ordinary" salad green is its versatility beyond the salad bowl. It is added to pastas in Italy, tossed with boiled potatoes or into soups in eastern Europe, mixed into omelets in the eastern Mediterranean, and used to make *rucolino*, a digestif favored by Neapolitans. Even its seeds are valued in northern India, where they are pressed to make an oil used for both pickling and cooking. Arugula contains vitamins A, B, C, and K and potassium, zinc, copper, iron, calcium, phosphorus, and manganese, protein, and dietary fiber.

VARIETIES APOLLO, ASTRO, ASTRO II, BABY, BUCKINGHAM, DRAGON'S TONGUE, EVEN STAR, FRESCA, GARDEN, ITALIAN, ROCKET, ROQUETTE, RUCOLA, RUNWAY, RUSTIC, SURREY, SELVETICA, SEL ORTOLANI, SPRINT, SYLVETTA, WASABI

SEASON Late spring to early fall

HOW TO CHOOSE Look for perky leaves that have a vibrant green color. Avoid arugula with wilted, yellowing, slimy, or browning leaves.

HOW TO CLEAN Immerse greens in cool water. Agitate with fingers. Drain; spin or pat dry.

HOW TO STORE Store in an airtight plastic bin or ziplock bag or wrapped in plastic wrap. In the crisper drawer of the refrigerator, arugula will keep for up to a week.

HOW TO REFRESH Immerse in ice water for 15 minutes. Drain; pat or spin dry.

COOKING METHODS Use raw in salads and sandwiches or as the main ingredient in pesto. Toss in pasta, use as a pizza topping, or use as a garnish on soups and stews.

PAIRINGS Olive oil, vinegar, lemon, olives, nuts, potatoes, watermelon, peaches, plums, pears, grapes, cheese, anchovies, berries, poultry, cured meats, veal, beef, pork, mild white fish.

ARUGULA SALAD WITH RED GRAPES, FETA, AND DUKKAH

Dukkah, an Egyptian spice blend that usually includes hazelnuts, has a an earthy flavor that goes great with greens, especially arugula. Salty and cumin-forward, it delivers an intense depth of flavor that makes a perfect pairing with the pepperiness of arugula and the sweetness of the grapes. Make extra and use it on fish, pork, or vegetables. This easy salad calls for only a few elements in addition to the spice blend. If you like, exchange the grapes for plums, peaches, or even apples or pears.

SERVES 4

8 cups [160 g] packed arugula leaves

32 seedless red grapes, halved

4 ounces [115 g] feta, crumbled

¼ cup [30 g] dukkah, homemade (page 297) or store-bought

Lemon vinaigrette (page 300)

Kosher salt

In a bowl, gently toss the arugula, grapes, feta, and dukkah. Dress with the lemon vinaigrette and season to taste with salt. Dukkah has salt in the mix, so taste the salad before seasoning and adjust as preferred. Serve immediately.

OTHER GREENS TO TRY Little Gem lettuce, frisée

BORANI ESFANAAJ (PERSIAN GREENS DIP)

Visiting Israel turned me on to the joys of herbal purees, spreads, and condiments. They are a great way of adding another element to a dish. Even a dollop on a piece of grilled meat can bring out all of the dormant elements in the meat. This Persian dip is usually made with spinach. I wanted to see what arugula would do to it, and I was thrilled with the results—it is bright, herbal, and light and perfect with crudités, or on fish, chicken, or pork, or simply slathered on a piece of bread.

This recipe works best with young arugula leaves, which are smaller, less peppery, and less astringent than more mature greens.

MAKES 3 CUPS [720 ML]

¼ cup [60 ml] olive oil, plus more to finish

1 yellow onion, diced

2 large cloves garlic

12 cups [240 g] packed arugula leaves, preferably young

Stems from 1 bunch mint (about ½ ounce/15 g)

Tender stems from 1 bunch flat-leaf parsley (about 1½ ounces/40 g)

1 cup [140 g] pistachios, lightly toasted

Zest of 2 lemons, finely grated

2 teaspoons kosher salt

Dukkah, homemade (page 297) or store-bought, for garnish

Warm the olive oil in a large pan over medium-high heat. Add the onion and garlic and cook until translucent and tender, 2 to 4 minutes. Stir often. Add the arugula and cook, stirring, until the arugula is wilted and mostly dry, 2 to 3 minutes. Place on a tray and cool completely in the refrigerator, 10 to 15 minutes.

Put the cooled arugula in a blender with the mint and parsley stems, pistachios, lemon zest, and salt. Process until pureed. Store in an airtight container, refrigerated, for up to 3 days.

To serve, place the dip on a plate or in a bowl, sprinkle with dukkah, and drizzle with olive oil.

NOTE: Serve this dip with hard-boiled eggs (page 293), on bread, with roasted summer vegetables, or with roasted chicken.

OTHER GREENS TO TRY chard, spinach

Borani Esfanaaj (Persian Greens Dip)

CIABATTA PANZANELLA WITH CHERRIES, MINT, BASIL, AND FETA

Bing, Rainier, Lambert—any sweet cherry will work with this offbeat *panzanella*. The peppery arugula and herbal edge of the mint and basil really bring the bright sweetness to the fore. Some salty feta balances out all of that intensity. What I love most about any *panzanella* is the texture, and the fact that my leftover bread doesn't go to waste. Bread has a life like a banana: a banana has something like eight levels of ripeness, and bread does too. So instead of throwing bread away, a good cook thinks of how to use it in different parts of its life.

SERVES 4

4 cups [120 g] cubed ciabatta (1-inch/ 2.5-cm cubes)

2 tablespoons olive oil

Kosher salt

1 cup [240 ml] white balsamic vinaigrette (page 302), or more as needed

1½ cups [210 g] cherries, pitted and halved

10 large basil leaves, sliced into ribbons

10 large mint leaves, sliced into ribbons

2¾ cups [55 g] packed arugula leaves

½ cup [75 g] crumbled feta

Freshly ground black pepper

Preheat the oven to 325°F [165°C].

In a bowl, toss the ciabatta cubes with the olive oil and lightly season with salt. Put the cubes on a sheet pan in a single layer and bake until completely dry and lightly golden, 20 to 30 minutes. When done, cool on the pan at room temperature. Once the croutons are cool, they can be held for 1 to 2 days in an airtight container.

In a large bowl, toss the cooled croutons with ½ cup [120 ml] of the vinaigrette. Allow the croutons to soak up the vinaigrette for 2 to 3 minutes, until semisoft but still crunchy. Add the cherries, basil, mint, arugula, and feta. Season with salt and pepper and add a drizzle of the remaining vinaigrette. Toss to combine. Add more dressing as needed to lightly coat all of the ingredients.

OTHER GREENS TO TRY pea tendrils, watercress

ARUGULA ZEPPOLE WITH ARUGULA PESTO

Zeppole are basically Italian doughnuts. I used to make sweet zeppole at one of my restaurants. But then I thought about making a savory version, so I took out the sugar and added lemon zest and arugula. Arugula has a peppery quality that pairs especially well with lemon, but the best thing about these fritters is that their personality changes with different dipping sauces. Arugula pesto intensifies their peppery flavor, but they are also great with muhammara (page 299), which adds a little heat, or with yogurt sauce, which cools them off.

MAKES 2 CUPS [480 ML] BATTER, SERVES 8 TO 10

1 pound [455 g] fresh ricotta

4 eggs

Kosher salt

1 tablespoon baking powder

Zest of 3 lemons, finely grated on a Microplane

¼ cup [30 g] finely grated Parmigiano-Reggiano

1 cup [140 g] all-purpose flour

8 ounces [230 g] arugula leaves, chopped

¼ cup [55 g] pitted and coarsely chopped oil-cured black olives

Neutral vegetable or olive oil, for frying

½ cup [115 g] plain Greek yogurt

Arugula pesto (recipe follows), for serving

In a stand mixer fitted with a paddle attachment, beat together the ricotta and eggs on medium speed until well mixed. Add 1 teaspoon salt, the baking powder, the lemon zest, and the Parmigiano-Reggiano and mix beat a smooth, homogeneous mixture forms. Add the flour and continue to mix just until combined. Using a rubber spatula, gently fold in the arugula and olives.

Pour oil to a depth of 4 inches [10 cm] into a heavy pot and heat to 350°F [180°C]. Set a wire rack on a sheet pan and place near the stove.

When the oil is ready, working in batches, gently drop the batter by the tablespoon into the hot oil, being careful not to crowd the pan. Fry until golden and cooked through, 3 to 4 minutes. Using a slotted spoon, transfer the zeppole to the prepared rack to drain. Repeat until all the batter is used.

Sprinkle the fritters with salt and serve hot with the yogurt and pesto for dipping.

OTHER GREENS TO TRY: mâche, spinach

ARUGULA PESTO

MAKES 1 CUP [240 ML]

6 ounces [170 g] arugula leaves

1 small clove garlic

½ cup [120 ml] olive oil

Kosher salt

Combine the arugula and garlic in a food processor and process until the arugula is broken down into small pieces. With the motor running, slowly drizzle in the oil and process until a thick dip consistency forms. Season with salt.

BOK CHOY

Brassica rapa subsp. *chinensis*

Choy translates to "vegetable" in Chinese. The global embrace of Chinese cuisine has popularized its star, bok choy, while other varieties have been trickling into Chinatowns and Asian groceries across the United States. Asians, like Europeans, have a tradition of purchasing food on a daily basis to consume it, so choys in Asian markets tend to have great turnaround, meaning they are particularly fresh and meant to be eaten right away. These markets don't tend to stockpile nearly ripe fruit or vegetables that are almost prime. The freshness ensures the vibrant and complex natural flavors of choy: sometimes mild, sometimes peppery, sometimes sweet, and always clean, crunchy, and vegetal. Choys are historically cited as a supremely healthy food, rich with vitamins A and C, potassium, and beta-carotene and known for their immune-boosting properties.

VARIETIES A CHOY, AA CHOY (CELTUCE, SEE PAGE 69), BABY YUE CHOY MUI, BABY BOK CHOY, BOK CHOY, CAI BE XANH, CANTON BOK CHOY, CHOY SUM (YAU CHOY), DWARF BOK CHOY, EN CHOY (AMARANTH, SEE PAGE 23), GAI CHOY, ONG CHOY (MORNING GLORY), PENNY WORT, ROSETTE BOK CHOY, SHANGHAI BOK CHOY, SHEN CHOY, SHER LI HON CHOY, TAKKOU CHOY, TATSOI (SEE PAGE 267), TAIWAN BOK CHOY, YU (YUE) CHOY

SEASON Spring to fall

HOW TO CHOOSE Make sure that stems are crisp and firm with tight heads. All bok choys should have vibrant green leaves without any dark or yellow spots.

HOW TO CLEAN Trim off dirty or oxidized root ends. Immerse greens in cool water. Agitate with fingers. Drain, shake off excess moisture, and pat dry.

HOW TO STORE Store in an airtight plastic bin or ziplock bag or wrap in plastic wrap. In the crisper drawer of the refrigerator, bok choy will keep 3 to 5 days.

HOW TO REFRESH Immerse in ice water for 15 minutes. Drain; pat or spin dry.

COOKING METHODS Use raw in salads or cook by stir-frying, braising, grilling, roasting, blanching, or simmering in a soup.

PAIRINGS Garlic, ginger, black beans, miso, oyster sauce, fish sauce, mushrooms, beef, pork, poultry, fish.

BRAISED BOK CHOY WITH APPLES AND BACON

Juicy and crisp, bok choy is one of the most refreshing vegetables. And apples happen to be one of the most refreshing, juicy, and crisp fruits. Drawing that parallel inspired me to create this dish. Adding bacon, candied ginger, chile, rice wine vinegar, and soy sauce strikes the perfect sweet, salty, sour, and smoky balance. This makes a wonderful side dish to meaty main dishes like pork or chicken, but it is also great on its own with jasmine rice and a poached egg.

SERVES 4 AS A SIDE DISH

¼ cup [60 ml] soy sauce

¼ cup [60 ml] rice wine vinegar

¼ cup [45 g] firmly packed light brown sugar

2 tablespoons, candied ginger, cut into thin strips

1 serrano chile, thinly sliced

½ cup [120 ml] neutral vegetable oil, plus more as needed

1 pound [455 g] bok choy, large or small heads halved or quartered lengthwise

Fine sea salt

2½ ounces [70 g] bacon (about 2 slices), cut into matchsticks

1 yellow onion, cut into large dice

2 crisp apples, such as Braeburn, quartered, cored, and thinly sliced

In a small bowl, combine the soy sauce, rice vinegar, brown sugar, candied ginger, and chile. Stir well to dissolve the sugar. Set aside.

Place a large sauté pan over medium-high heat and warm the oil. Add the bok choy, cut side down, and sear each side, turning once, until golden and becoming tender, 2 to 4 minutes per side. Decrease the heat if the greens are cooking too quickly or becoming too dark without becoming tender. Season lightly with salt. Remove the greens from the pan and reserve on a plate.

If pan has become dry, add a thin layer of oil to coat the bottom. Over medium-high heat, add the bacon, onion, and apples. Cook, stirring occasionally, until the onion is translucent, the bacon is becoming crisp, and the apples caramelize, 3 to 4 minutes. Return the bok choy to the pan and decrease the heat to medium. Add the reserved soy sauce mixture and simmer gently until the sauce is slightly reduced but not thick, about 2 minutes. Lightly season with salt, if needed, and serve immediately.

OTHER GREENS TO TRY gai lan, radicchio

TENDER BOK CHOY SALAD WITH CHICKEN AND ORANGE

My version of a Chinese chicken salad gets a lot of its flavor and texture from raw bok choy. The bok choy is full of water, so the sensation becomes like the watery crunch of celery in a regular old chicken salad, but with a much more powerful greenness in flavor.

SERVES 4 AS A MAIN DISH

4 (5-ounce/140-g) boneless, skinless chicken breasts

Double chicken stock (page 299)

12 ounces [340 g] young (baby) bok choy

1 small shallot, thinly sliced

4 oranges, peeled and segmented

½ cup [70 g] roasted cashews

Kosher salt

Miso vinaigrette (page 300)

Place the chicken breasts in a pan and add enough chicken stock to just cover. Bring to a very gentle simmer over high heat, then decrease the heat to low, so that the stock doesn't bubble, and gently cook the breasts. After about 3 minutes, when the breasts are firm on the outside but still tender on the inside, remove from the heat. Keep the breasts submerged for an additional 1 to 2 minutes, until firm and cooked through.

Cut the white stalks of the bok choy crosswise into pieces ¼ inch [6 mm] wide; keep the green leaves whole. Combine the bok choy in a bowl with the shallot, orange segments, cashews, and chicken. Season with salt and dress with the miso vinaigrette before serving.

OTHER GREENS TO TRY broccoli rabe, romaine lettuce varieties

PORK AND KIMCHI SOUP WITH TOFU AND BOK CHOY

This is based on my friend and food writer Kristin Donnelly's spin on *jigae*, a comforting, rainy-day soupy stew common on Korean tables. The important thing about this recipe is to taste as you go, balancing the kimchi with the broth to your liking, and adjusting the seasoning, keeping in mind the power of salt and spice in the kimchi itself. Serving this dish over rice gives it a bit more substance.

SERVES 8 TO 12

4 cups [785 g] kimchi, homemade (page 81) or store-bought

3 tablespoons grapeseed or other neutral vegetable oil

2 pounds [900 g] boneless pork shoulder, cut into 1-inch [2.5-cm] pieces

1 tablespoon light brown sugar

4 cups [960 ml] double chicken stock (page 299)

1 to 3 tablespoons gochujang (Korean chile paste; available at Korean and other Asian markets)

1 pound [455 g] firm silken tofu, cut into ¾-inch [2-cm] cubes

1 large head bok choy (not baby bok choy), green leaves separated from the white stalks, both thinly sliced crosswise

2 teaspoons toasted sesame oil

Soy sauce, for seasoning

Kosher salt

Steamed rice, for serving (optional)

Dark green parts of green onions, thinly sliced on the diagonal, for garnish

Set a large sieve over a bowl. Add the kimchi and let stand, stirring occasionally, for 10 minutes, so the liquid drips into the bowl.

Meanwhile, in a large pot or enameled cast-iron casserole, heat the grapeseed oil over medium-high heat. Add half of the pork in a single layer and cook, turning as necessary, until deeply golden all over, about 8 minutes. Transfer the browned pieces to a plate. Repeat with the remaining pork.

To the same pot set over medium-high heat, add the drained kimchi and the brown sugar and cook, stirring and scraping up browned bits from the bottom of the pan, until the kimchi is quite dry and darkens slightly, about 15 minutes. Add the kimchi liquid and the chicken stock, scraping up any remaining browned bits, and then stir in 1 tablespoon of the gochujang. Return the pork and any accumulated juices to the pot and cover. Turn down the heat to low and simmer until the pork is very tender, 1 to 1½ hours.

Add the tofu, bok choy stalks, and sesame oil to the pot and cook until the stalks are crisp-tender, 2 to 3 minutes. Season the stew with more gochujang and with soy sauce and salt, if necessary. Stir in the bok choy leaves. Serve in bowls or over rice, garnished with the green onions.

OTHER GREENS TO TRY gai lan, broccoli rabe

BROCCOLI RABE

Brassica rapa var. ruvo

Some people have issues with broccoli rabe, aka raab, rabe, or rapini, because of its intense bitterness. But here's a tip: the fresher it is, the less bitter it will taste, so search it out in farmers' markets instead of grocery stores. Blanching before cooking will reduce its pungency as well. Broccoli rabe is also called Italian turnip, which is actually a more accurate name, as it is botanically much closer to turnips than it is to broccoli—like first cousins versus third cousins thrice removed—though they all belong to the big Brassicaceae family. Other greens, like different varieties of sprouting broccoli and cabbage, are also harvested for their sprouting flowers after the winter and are referred to as rapini. A stalky green, broccoli rabe's small florets make it distinctive. Though its history is vague, we do know that it appeared in Italian cookbooks in the fourteenth century, that it is a staple especially in southern Italian cuisine, and that the Portuguese, Spaniards, and Chinese have also been eating it for generations. High in fiber, broccoli rabe is known to aid digestion, while its high folate content lends anti-inflammatory properties. It also contains high levels of vitamins A, C, and K and of potassium and manganese.

VARIETIES BROCCOLI RAAB SPRING, BROCCOLI RAAB FALL, RAPA, RAPPONE

SEASON Fall through spring

HOW TO CHOOSE Look for broccoli rabe with bright green coloring throughout its stalk, leaves, and florets. Avoid any that are wilted, yellowing, or have dark blemishes or mushy patches. Broccoli rabe with thinner stems tend to be more tender than ones with thicker stems.

HOW TO CLEAN Immerse in cold water. Agitate with fingers. Drain, shake off excess moisture, and pat dry. Trim off the base of the stem and discard.

HOW TO STORE Store in an airtight plastic bin or ziplock bag or wrap in plastic wrap. In the crisper drawer of the refrigerator, broccoli rabe will keep for up to 3 days. Keep in mind that this green will become more bitter as it ages.

HOW TO REFRESH Immerse in ice water for 15 minutes. Drain; pat or spin dry.

COOKING METHODS Cook by blanching, steaming, broiling, stir-frying, braising, sautéing, roasting, or grilling. Toss with pasta or use as a pizza topping.

PAIRINGS Garlic, chiles, lemon, anchovies, or pork.

BREAD GNOCCHI WITH BROCCOLI RABE

One core tenet of traditional cooking of any culture is never to waste. In Italy, for example, if you have stale bread, you don't throw it away. You repurpose it. In the north of Italy, the stale bread is used as the main ingredient in dumplings. While researching my book, *Pasta by Hand*, I learned that these dumplings, which are similar to the *canederli* of the alpine regions, originated because of a short growing season. Townspeople would bake bread four times a year in communal ovens. They would eat the bread fresh, then dry out the leftovers and use the bread crumbs to make their dumplings, a great way to feed a family during the winter season. I enjoy them in soup, or even just dressed with butter, as they are here, and eaten as an entrée.

NOTE: Taste for salt when seasoning, as the saltiness of prosciutto can vary by brand.

SERVES 6

2 tablespoons olive oil

7 ounces [200 g] prosciutto, ground or finely chopped

1 yellow onion, finely diced

1 carrot, peeled and minced

2 bay leaves

8 ounces [230 g] broccoli rabe, chopped into ¼-inch [6-mm] pieces

1 large tomato, cut into 8 pieces

Kosher salt

1 teaspoon freshly ground black pepper

8 ounces [230 g] crustless fresh bread, cut into 1-inch [2.5-cm] cubes

⅔ cup [160 ml] whole milk

2 eggs, lightly beaten

1 cup [30 g] lightly packed finely grated Parmigiano-Reggiano, plus more for serving

4 cups [560 g] all-purpose flour

¾ cup [170 g] unsalted butter, for serving

In a large sauté pan, warm the olive oil over medium-high heat. Add the prosciutto, onion, carrot, and bay leaves and cook, stirring often, until the vegetables are tender, about 4 minutes. If the vegetables begin to turn golden, decrease the heat. Add the broccoli rabe and cook for 2 to 3 minutes, just until tender. Add the tomato and cook for another 3 to 4 minutes, pressing a spoon against the tomato pieces to break them up as they soften. Season lightly with salt and add the pepper. Remove the gnocchi filling from the pan, discard the bay leaves, and cool the mixture in the refrigerator until chilled.

Combine the bread, milk, and eggs in a large bowl and, using a spoon, mash until the bread is wet and broken down into a not-quite-homogenous mash. Add the cheese and the chilled cooked filling and stir to combine. Taste and adjust the seasoning as needed. The mixture will be wet.

Line a sheet pan with parchment paper, generously dust with flour, and set aside. Put the remaining flour in a large bowl. Scoop up large walnut-size portions of the gnocchi mixture and roll into balls. Roll the balls in the flour to coat well, then place on the sheet pan. Continue until all of the mixture is formed into balls, making about 36 gnocchi total. (Smaller gnocchi, or gnochetti, can also be shaped). Chill the gnocchi, covered with a piece of parchment paper, then wrapped in plastic wrap, for at least 4 hours, or up to overnight, to set. Turn the gnocchi over halfway through resting to make sure no wet spots form. Add a dusting of flour as needed to coat. The coating should not be heavy, but it should be evident because it will form a thin "noodle" around the dumpling.

Bring a large pot of salted water to a simmer.

Heat the butter in a small sauté pan over low heat, season lightly with salt, and remove from the heat as soon as it is melted. Shake off any excessive flour from the gnocchi and add to the simmering water. Simmer for 2½ minutes; do not boil hard or the dumplings may fall apart. Remove from the water with a slotted spoon. Place on plates, dress with the melted butter, and sprinkle with grated Parmigiano-Reggiano.

NOTE: Gnocchi can be frozen on a sheet pan, then stored in an airtight container for up to 1 month. If frozen, do not thaw before cooking. Cook frozen gnocchi as directed, but increase the cooking time to 8 minutes, or until the center of each dumpling is no longer cold.

OTHER GREENS TO TRY roasted radicchio, pan di zucchero

BROCCOLI RABE PESTO

Pesto is one of the most common and easy to make of all Italian sauces. It is also among the most versatile. Depending on the greens and herbs used, it can be deeply vegetal or bitter or even sweet. I love what broccoli rabe does to pesto—it lends just the right amount of bitterness, earthiness, and fibrous texture to the sauce. Spread this pesto on sandwiches, add a dollop to liven up polenta, slather on hard-cooked eggs (page 293), toss with pasta, or spoon over meats such as roasted pork or chicken. Even a teaspoon in a bowl of minestrone or potato soup will add depth.

MAKES 2 CUPS [480 ML]

1 pound [455 g] broccoli rabe

¼ cup [35 g] pine nuts, lightly toasted

2 cloves garlic

2 cups [60 g] lightly packed finely grated Parmigiano-Reggiano

½ cup [120 ml] olive oil

Zest of 1 lemon, finely grated on a Microplane

Fine sea salt

Fill a large bowl with ice water and bring a large pot of salted water to a simmer.

Submerge the broccoli rabe in the simmering water and blanch until tender, about 3 minutes. Drain and immediately submerge in the ice water to cool the greens rapidly.

Once chilled, remove the greens from the ice water and, using a clean, dry kitchen towel, blot excess moisture.

Chop the broccoli rabe into 1-inch [2.5-cm] pieces and combine in a blender with the pine nuts, garlic, cheese, olive oil, and lemon zest. Process until mostly homogenous, working quickly so the broccoli rabe does not become warm. Warmth will cause the greens to become dark and the flavor to turn very vegetal.

When the puree is smooth, season with salt. Use immediately or, using a plastic spatula, scrape the pesto into a small airtight container and store for up to 3 days, refrigerated.

NOTE: Add more olive oil, tablespoon by tablespoon, to desired consistency when using this pesto as a pasta sauce; keep thicker for spreading, as on the doubles (page 49).

OTHER GREENS TO TRY see pesto variations (page 46)

TESTAROLI WITH BROCCOLI RABE PESTO

When I was in Italy researching my book *Pasta by Hand*, I learned about *testaroli*, one of the most ancient forms of pasta—basically a crepe. The crepes are made by spreading a batter thinly in a superhot pan. Once you have made the crepes, they can be served two different ways: Traditionally they are cut into diamonds or strips, briefly immersed in hot water (a step I skip here), and finally tossed with pesto. But you can also leave them whole and spread them with pesto. The first time I had them was in a little restaurant in Rome, where I learned about their history as one of the pastas made before extrusion and rolling came into fashion. Broccoli rabe pesto brings a bitter energy to the crepe.

NOTE: If you are cutting the crepes into strips, make sure the batter is slightly thicker than if serving the crepes whole.

SERVES 8 AS AN APPETIZER

1 cup [160 g] semolina

1 cup [140 g] all-purpose flour

½ teaspoon kosher salt

2 cups [480 ml] water

Olive oil, for cooking

1½ to 2 cups [360 to 480 ml] Broccoli Rabe Pesto (page 43)

Finely grated Parmigiano-Reggiano, for serving

In a bowl, combine the semolina, flour, and salt. Whisk in the water until smooth and cover the bowl with plastic wrap. Set aside for 1 hour.

In a 7-inch [17-cm] nonstick skillet, heat 1 tablespoon olive oil over high heat. When the oil is hot, add 4 to 6 tablespoons [60 to 90 ml] (about a ladleful) of testaroli batter, remove the pan from the heat, and spread the batter thinly with the side of a spoon. If the batter does not spread easily and sticks to the bottom of the pan, try again without using oil in the pan. The pan must be hot to spread the batter evenly and thinly and for it to adhere to the bottom. Cook until the batter is set and there are a few spots of golden color, 2 to 3 minutes. Flip, cook briefly, about 1 minute, on the second side, and remove from the pan. As the testaroli are ready, stack them on a plate and cover them with a kitchen towel. Repeat with the remaining batter.

Serve cut into diamonds or strips and tossed with the pesto or leave whole and spread with pesto. Top with a sprinkle of Parmigiano-Reggiano.

OTHER GREENS TO TRY see pesto variations (page 46)

PESTO 101

One of the greatest uses of greens is making pesto. The classic Genoese sauce is made with basil, nuts, garlic, and Parmigiano-Reggiano cheese. But it's not just for basil. You can use countless greens to make a pesto, and it's a great way to add fresh flavors to anything from pasta to soup to flatbreads.

Just keep in mind a few things:

- Always use oil.
- Add lemon juice of vinegar for brightness.
- Use garlic to taste.
- Bitter greens can work well as long as they are properly balanced with fat and acid.
- For the best texture, stick to the less-watery types that I have suggested.

NOTE: I've aligned my favorite flavor combinations (i.e., cilantro + pumpkin seeds + Cotija cheese), but feel free to mix and match!

① CHOOSE A GREEN	+ ② ADD CRUNCH AND TEXTURE	+ ③ ADD CHEESE OR DAIRY	+ ④ ENHANCE WITH
Cilantro	Pumpkin seeds	Cotija cheese	Roasted jalapeños
Garlic scapes	Almonds	Feta	Orange zest
Flat-leaf parsley, watercress, chives, and sorrel	Chopped hard-cooked egg	Buttermilk and sour cream	Lemon juice
Basil	Walnuts	Parmigiano-Reggiano	Dried or fresh tomatoes
Sage, basil, and mint	Pistachios	Mascarpone	Lemon juice
Flat-leaf parsley and mint	Capers	Pecorino Romano	Anchovies and chiles
Arugula and basil	Smashed croutons	Small pieces of fresh mozarella	Lemon juice
Basil, oregano, and mint	Cornichons	Provolone picante	Capers and anchovies
Fennel fronds, flat-leaf parsley, and mint	Pine nuts	Mascarpone	Chile flakes and red wine vinegar

FOLLOW THIS BASIC RECIPE, AND YOU HAVE PESTO.

Combine ½ cup nuts, 2 cloves garlic, and 1½ teaspoons salt in a food processor and pulse until finely chopped. With a rubber spatula, scrape down the sides of the bowl, then add the greens, ½ cup [120 ml] of olive oil, and the cheese or dairy. Continue to pulse, stopping occasionally to scrape down the sides of the bowl, until the greens are coarsely chopped. Turn the processor back on and add another ¼ cup [60 ml] olive oil and any remaining ingredients, processing until the mixture is finely chopped but not fully pureed. Turn the food processor off and scrape down the sides of the bowl several times during the process. The ingredients should be fully incorporated, with enough oil to hold the sauce together without being runny.

To store, transfer to an airtight container and drizzle just enough oil over the top to cover. This will prevent the pesto from oxidizing and turning brown. Use immediately, refrigerate for up to 4 days, or freeze for up to 1 month. To thaw, place in the refrigerator overnight or until fully thawed.

DOUBLES WITH BROCCOLI RABE AND SLOW-ROASTED PORK

In Trinidad, the popular street food known as doubles consists of two puffy flatbreads wrapped around a chickpea curry to make a sandwich. I don't know why these snacks are typically relegated to "breakfast food," as they are delicious anytime. I make my doubles with a single bread, but the result is just as tasty. You can stuff them with anything—even distinctly Italian ingredients, as I do here. Broccoli rabe gives this sandwich a bitterness that pairs perfectly with fatty pork.

SERVES 4

1 pound [455 g] broccoli rabe

½ cup [120 ml] olive oil

4 cloves garlic, finely chopped

6 cornichons, sliced into thin rounds

4 teaspoons sherry vinegar

4 anchovy fillets packed in oil, finely chopped

Zest of 2 lemons, finely grated on a Microplane

Fine sea salt and freshly ground black pepper

4 tablespoons [60 g] Dijon mustard

4 doubles flatbreads, freshly cooked (recipe follows)

8 ounces [230 g] slow-roasted pork loin (page 274), thinly sliced

Fill a large bowl with ice water and set aside. Bring a large pot of salted water to a simmer.

Blanch the broccoli rabe in the simmering water until tender, about 3 minutes. Immediately remove from the pot and plunge into the ice water to stop the cooking. When chilled, remove the broccoli rabe from the water and gently pat dry with a clean towel.

Coarsely chop the broccoli rabe into about ½-inch [12-mm] pieces, then combine in a bowl with the olive oil, garlic, cornichons, vinegar, anchovies, and lemon zest. Stir to mix and then season with salt and pepper.

To assemble the sandwiches, spread 1 tablespoon of the mustard on each flatbread. Top with one-quarter of the pork and then one-quarter of the rabe salad. Fold over and enjoy while the bread is hot.

OTHER GREENS TO TRY arugula, chard, spinach

DOUBLES FLATBREADS

MAKES 4

1½ cups [210 g] all-purpose flour

2 teaspoons baking powder

½ teaspoon kosher salt, plus more to season

¾ cup [180 ml] water, plus more as needed

Neutral vegetable oil, for frying

In a bowl, mix together the flour, baking powder, salt, and water. Knead the dough in the bowl until it is cohesive, soft, and no longer sticky, 1 to 2 minutes. Add more water, a tablespoon at a time, if the dough does not come together. Shape into a ball, wrap in plastic wrap, and set aside to rest for 1 hour.

Fill a 10-inch [25-cm] or larger pot half full with vegetable oil and warm over medium heat to 350°F [180°C]. Line a platter with paper towels.

Meanwhile, divide the dough into four equal pieces, lightly flour the pieces, and then roll out each piece into a round ⅛ to ¼ inch [3 to 6 mm] thick. One at a time, fry the rounds in the hot oil, gently pressing on them with a large spoon to submerge them, until lightly golden on both sides but still soft, 1 to 2 minutes. The breads should be tender and pliable, with a bit of crispiness in areas.

Drain the breads on the prepared platter. Lightly season with salt and keep warm until serving.

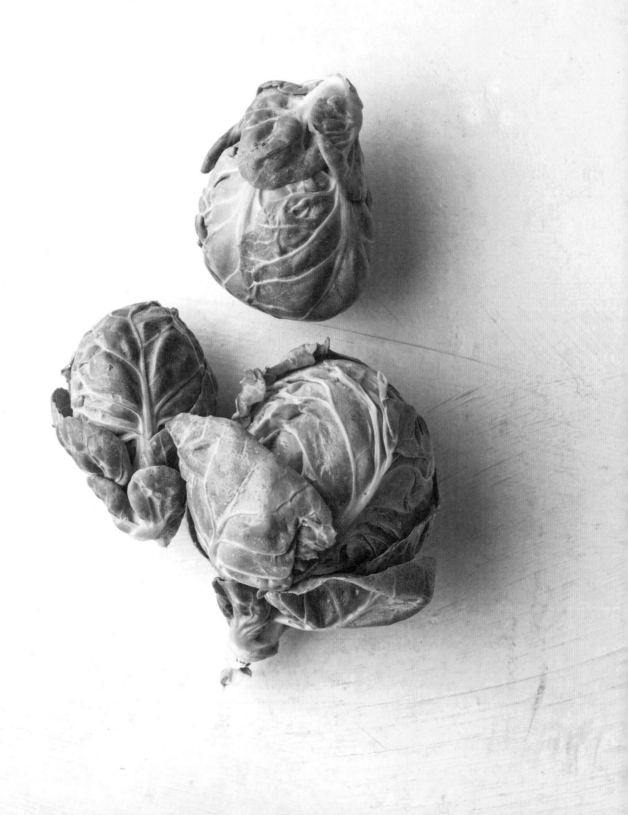

BRUSSELS SPRO

Brassica oleracea L. var *gemmifera*

Though they earned their name because of their massive popularity in Belgium during the Middle Ages, brussels sprouts likely originated in Italy during the days of the Roman Empire. The vegetable didn't arrive in the United States until the 1800s, along with relatives broccoli and cauliflower, though its look-alike cousin, the cabbage, was already established in North America by the sixteenth century.

Often described as "mini cabbages," brussels sprouts pack a lot of flavor in their tiny heads. Sharp with notes of mustard, brussels sprouts have the unfortunate reputation of emitting a foul odor during preparation—partly undeserved because the sprouts tend to reek only when cooked too long. Overcooking releases the vegetable's sulfur content, which is actually more helpful than it sounds. According to dozens of studies, it is the sulfur content that helps prevent and fight cancer, particularly bladder, breast, colon, lung, prostate, and ovarian cancers. In addition to that famous sulfur content, brussels sprouts are loaded with vitamins B, C, and K and are a good source of beta-carotene, iron, magnesium, and dietary fiber.

VARIETIES ALBARUS, BRODIE, BUBBLES, CATSKILL, CHURCHILL, CONFIDANT, DAGAN, DIABLO, DOMINATOR, EARLY HALF TAIL, EVESHAM, FALSTAFF, GRONINGER, JADE CROSS, GUSTUS, ICARUS, IGOR, KRYPTUS, LONG ISLAND, LONG ISLAND IMPROVED, OLIVER, PRINCE MARVEL, MEZZO NANO, RED BULL, ROODNERF, RUBY CRUNCH, RUBINE, SEVEN HILLS, TASTY NUGGETS, VANCOUVER

SEASON Late summer through winter

HOW TO CHOOSE If you see brussels sprouts on the stalk, grab them! That means they are as fresh as can be and will last longer than those sold loose. Either way, the heads should be tight and firm, never soft, with a bright, uniform color—no dark spots or yellowing. Give them a sniff: they shouldn't have any odor when raw.

HOW TO CLEAN If on the stalk, cut the heads from the stem with a paring knife. Trim any brown spots and peel off any loose or damaged leaves (but reserve them to make Brussels Chips, page 52). Wash well under cold running water and pat dry.

HOW TO STORE Keep loose heads in a ziplock bag or plastic airtight container in the refrigerator for up to 1 week. If the sprouts are on a stalk, do not remove from the stalk until you are ready to use them. Stored in a plastic bag and refrigerated, brussels sprouts on the stalk can last for up to 2 weeks.

HOW TO REFRESH Immerse in ice water for 15 minutes. Drain and pat dry.

COOKING METHODS Use raw in salads or cook by boiling, steaming, stir-frying, grilling, sautéing, roasting, or baking.

PAIRINGS Butter, bacon, lard, vinegar, mustard, brown sugar, chiles, cheese, nuts, squash, beef, pork, poultry, fish.

ACORN SQUASH WITH KIMCHI BUTTER, POACHED EGG, AND BRUSSELS CHIPS

Here is a substantial, one-of-a-kind dish where no one element is overly complicated.

SERVES 4

6 tablespoons [85 g] kimchi butter (page 292)

2 acorn squashes, halved lengthwise and seeded

Fine sea salt

4 eggs, poached (page 293)

Flaky sea salt

¾ cup [180 ml] tahini sauce (page 296)

1 cup [30 g] Brussels Chips (recipe follows)

4 teaspoons dukkah, homemade (page 297) or store-bought (optional)

Preheat the oven to 350°F [180°C]. Place 1½ tablespoons of the kimchi butter in each squash cavity and place the squash halves, cut side up, on a sheet pan. Sprinkle the cut side with the fine salt. Roast, basting the exposed squash meat with the melted butter from the cavity every 15 minutes, until the squash is tender and beginning to caramelize, 45 to 60 minutes.

Remove the squash from oven, place each half in a bowl, and place a warm egg in each cavity. Sprinkle with the flaky salt and top each egg with 3 tablespoons of the tahini sauce. Pile the chips atop the sauce and finish with the dukkah.

BRUSSELS CHIPS

These chips are a great use of the sprouts' outside leaves. They make a great snack or appetizer or a crisp garnish for a thick pureed soup.

SERVES 4 AS A SNACK

4 cups [960 ml] neutral vegetable oil

8 cups [200 g] brussels sprout leaves, separated from their cores, from about 12 ounces [340 g] whole brussels sprouts

4 teaspoons crack spice mix (page 296)

Heat the oil in a heavy pan to 350°F [180°C]. Fry the sprout leaves in batches until crispy, 1 to 1½ minutes per batch. Using a fine-mesh sieve, remove each batch from the oil and gently shake the excess oil back into the pot. Place the leaves in a bowl and season with the crack spice. Serve immediately.

OTHER GREENS TO TRY mustard greens, kale

BRUSSELS SPROUTS AND PARSNIPS WITH LARDO

Here, kimchi syrup lends brussels sprouts a funky sweet-and-sour flavor, while the lardo adds creaminess and the parsnips deliver sweetness.

SERVES 4

2 cups [200 g] brussels sprouts, trimmed and halved

8 baby or 4 large parsnips, peeled and cut into 2-inch [5-cm] pieces

2 tablespoons olive oil

Kosher salt

1 tablespoon whipped lardo spread (page 298) or coconut oil

1 tablespoon kimchi syrup (page 293)

1 teaspoon fresh lemon juice

2 teaspoons peeled and finely grated fresh horseradish root

Preheat the oven to 425°F [220°C]. In a bowl, toss the brussels sprouts and parsnips with the oil and season with salt. Place on a sheet pan and roast until charred and tender, about 20 minutes.

Melt the lardo in a small pan over medium-low heat. Drizzle over the roasted vegetables and then toss together with the kimchi syrup, lemon juice, and salt. Place on a large platter and garnish with the horseradish.

OTHER GREENS TO TRY cabbage wedges

Acorn Squash with Kimchi Butter, Poached Egg, and Brussels Chips

CABBAGE

Brassica oleracea capitata

Derived from the French *caboche*, slang for "head," cabbage is a crisp, pungent crucifer known for its bitter—and sometimes sweet—flavor and its substantial, crunchy texture. In a recent study, researchers at Stanford University noted that sulforaphane, a leading nutrient in cabbage and in its relative, brussels sprouts, boosts cancer-fighting enzymes. Such contemporary scholars are not the first to recognize the vegetable's medicinal properties, however; in ancient Greece, cabbage was used as a laxative and as a liniment for healing bruises and sties, while the Romans swore by its hangover-curing properties. During World War I, the British used cabbage to treat trench foot. Cabbage is packed with nutrients: it is a good source of calcium, iron, magnesium, phosphorus, and potassium and a very good source of dietary fiber, manganese, and vitamins B, C, and K.

VARIETIES CANNONBALL, CHINESE, EARLY JERSEY WAKEFIELD, JANUARY KING, MAMMOTH RED ROCK, NAPA, PORTUGAL, RED, SAVOY, WALKING STICK, WINNINGSTADT

SEASON Late fall through winter

HOW TO CHOOSE When shopping for all types of cabbage, make sure the leaves form a tightly packed head—the leaves should not be loose or separating—and the texture is crisp and firm. Select heads with no visible bruising or insect damage on the exterior. They should not have a strong odor and should feel dense and hefty, though density will vary by variety. A head of common American green cabbage, for example, will feel denser than a head of Savoy or of red cabbage, which has more room between its leaves and a looser head structure.

HOW TO CLEAN Before using, cut around the thick core at the bottom and remove. Then remove any wilted or damaged outer leaves. Often cabbage heads are tight and are not dirty, so they don't always need to be washed.

HOW TO STORE Wrap cabbage in plastic wrap or seal in an airtight plastic container or ziplock bag. In the crisper drawer of the refrigerator, a properly stored cabbage will keep up for up to 1 month.

HOW TO REFRESH Immerse in ice water for 15 minutes. Drain and pat or spin dry.

COOKING METHODS Use raw and shredded in salads and slaws and to garnish soup; pickle; or cook by baking, broiling, braising, sautéing, steaming or stir-frying.

NOTE: Different cabbages have different moisture levels. If using a high-moisture cabbage, you may want to pour off any excess water while cooking.

PAIRINGS Curry, garlic, ginger, beets, tofu, and rich meats such as beef, pork, veal, and lamb.

CHARRED CABBAGE WITH MISO AND LIME

I love the simplicity of this recipe: there are not many ingredients, yet they all bring out the sweetness of the cabbage. Searing the cabbage in a hot pan gives it a smoky depth, and the miso butter enhances the sweetness even more. A squeeze of lime cuts through it all, adding brightness. This is the sort of recipe that is so simple that you can practically taste the innate nutrition of cabbage.

NOTE: Different cabbages give off different ammounts of water during cooking. If water is released, it needs to be poured off.

SERVES 4 AS A SIDE DISH

> 2 tablespoons unsalted butter, at room temperature
>
> 2 tablespoons red miso
>
> ½ cup [120 ml] neutral vegetable oil, plus more as needed
>
> 1 green cabbage, about 1¼ pounds [570 g], cut into 8 wedges with core intact
>
> Kosher salt
>
> 1 lime, cut into wedges
>
> Flaky sea salt

Preheat the oven to 400°F [200°C].

In a small bowl, mix the butter and miso until combined. Set aside.

Over high heat, warm ¼ cup [60 ml] of the oil in each of two large cast-iron or other ovenproof sauté pans. When very hot, place half of the cabbage wedges, cut side down, in each pan. Do not overcrowd the pans. Leave the cabbage wedges in the pans without turning until the cut sides are charred and lightly blackened, about 3 minutes. If the oil is absorbed by the cabbage and the pan appears dry, add more oil, 1 tablespoon at a time, until the pan is lightly coated. When lightly charred, turn the cabbage wedges cut side up and spread the miso butter on the cut sides, dividing it evenly.

Cook for about 3 minutes, or until the color matches the first side. When seared on both sides, place the pans with the cabbage in the preheated oven. Using a spoon, baste every 5 minutes with melted butter from the bottom of the pan. After 10 minutes, season lightly with kosher salt on both sides. The total roasting time should be about 20 minutes, and the cabbage should be very tender and charred. Remove the cabbage from the oven, sprinkle with the flaky salt, and squeeze the lime wedges over the top. Serve immediately.

OTHER GREENS TO TRY halved brussels sprouts, romaine lettuce, pan di zucchero

OKONOMIYAKI WITH BRINED CABBAGE

Okonomiyaki are one of my favorite things to make. At first, I made the pancake traditionally, with raw, shredded cabbage. But then I tasted chef Hillary Sterling's fermented cabbage salad in New York City. I asked her to teach me how to make that salad, and I immediately thought that the funky, fermented flavor would add complexity to the pancakes. And that it does: these are tangy, briny, and bright, with a lot of depth. This recipe is based on what she taught me. Once you have brined cabbage, this dish is fast and easy to make. Keep an eye on the batter—it should be loose and thickly pourable, somewhere between a biscuit batter and thickened cream.

SERVES 4

1 cup [240 ml] brined cabbage liquid (from following recipe), cold

2 tablespoons water

4 eggs

3 cups [455 g] drained brined cabbage (recipe follows)

1 teaspoon baking powder

2 cups [280 g] all-purpose flour

4 tablespoons [60 ml] toasted sesame oil

8 ounces [230 g] bacon, cut into 16 slices

Neutral vegetable oil, for frying

Fish sauce aïoli (page 293) or Kewpie brand mayonnaise, for finishing

2 tablespoons shichimi togarashi or mustard green furikake (page 297)

Preheat the oven to 400°F [200°C].

Whisk together the cabbage brine liquid, water, and eggs in a bowl. Stir in the cabbage, then stir in the baking powder and flour. (If the batter is too thick, add water, 1 tablespoon at a time, to loosen it.)

In an 8-inch [20-cm] nonstick ovenproof skillet, warm 2 tablespoons of the sesame oil over medium heat. Add 4 slices of the bacon and cook just until the fat begins to render from the bacon, 3 to

4 minutes. Top with one-quarter of the batter and cook undisturbed until the sides are set and are crispy, 3 to 4 minutes. Carefully lift the pancake to make sure the bacon is crisp and the pancake is crispy. Flip the pancake so the bacon is on top and the bottom of the pancake can cook. Drizzle a tablespoon of vegetable oil around the pancake, allowing it to drip between the pan and the bottom of the pancake to help the underside become crispy. Cook until crisp, 2 to 3 minutes. Finish cooking the pancakes in the oven for 3 to 4 minutes, until set. Remove from the pan and keep warm. Repeat with the remaining batter and bacon to make four pancakes total.

To serve, place on individual plates, drizzle with the aïoli, and sprinkle with the shichimi togarashi.

OTHER GREENS TO TRY brussels sprouts, romaine

BRINED CABBAGE

MAKES 2½ QUARTS [2.4 L]

2 quarts [2 L] warm water

2½ ounces [70 g] sugar

4 ounces [115 g] kosher salt

5 red Fresno chiles, stemmed

5 cloves garlic

1 medium head green cabbage, cored and cut into 1-inch [2.5-cm] squares

To make the brine, in a large plastic or glass container, whisk together the water, sugar, and salt until the sugar and salt dissolve.

In a food processor, pulse the chiles and garlic until coarsely pureed. Add to the brine. Let cool completely, then add the cabbage. Press down with two heavy plates to submerge the cabbage, then cover the container with cheesecloth. Leave the container at room temperature for 3 to 5 days, until the cabbage ferments and smells a little funky. Replace the cheesecloth with an airtight lid and store in the refrigerator. Brined cabbage, fully submerged, will keep in the refrigerator for 3 months.

Cabbage Rolls with Arborio Rice, Pork, and Nutmeg

CABBAGE ROLLS WITH ARBORIO RICE, PORK, AND NUTMEG

Cabbage rolls are labor-intensive, but they are worth the work. This recipe is a great way to use the outer leaves of cabbage, something some cooks throw away.

SERVES 6

 3 tablespoons unsalted butter

 ½ large yellow onion, finely diced

 2 cloves garlic, thinly sliced

 2-inch [5-cm] spig rosemary, leaves only

 ½ teaspoon dried red pepper flakes

 12 large green cabbage leaves

 1 cup [200 g] Arborio rice

 1 pound [455 g] ground pork shoulder

 ½ cup [15 g] lightly packed finely grated Parmigiano-Reggiano

 Freshly grated nutmeg, for seasoning

 1 tablespoon kosher salt

 1 teaspoon freshly ground black pepper

 Butter and fresh tomato sauce (page 235)

 ½ cup [120 ml] crème fraîche or sour cream, for serving

Preheat the oven to 375°F [190°C]. Melt the butter in a skillet over medium-high heat. Add the onion, garlic, rosemary, and red pepper and cook until translucent and tender, about 8 minutes. If the onion begins to brown, decrease the heat. When translucent, transfer the mixture to a plate and chill completely.

Fill a large bowl with ice water and set aside.

Bring a large stockpot filled with salted water to a boil. Add the cabbage leaves and cook for 3 to 4 minutes, until very tender. Remove the cabbage from the water and place in the ice water. When fully chilled, remove the cabbage leaves from the ice water and pat dry with a clean dish towel. Using a paring knife, remove the thick rib from the center of each leaf. Set the cabbage aside.

Bring a small pot of salted water to a simmer, add the rice, and cook until al dente, 4 to 5 minutes. Drain the rice into a fine-mesh sieve and hold the rice under cool tap water until no longer warm. Place the rice in a large bowl and add the chilled onion mixture, pork, cheese, a healthy grating of nutmeg, the salt, and pepper. Stir gently until fully combined.

Lay a cabbage leaf on a work surface and place ⅓ cup [65 g] of the rice filling on the top third of the leaf. Fold the sides of the cabbage leaf over the filling and, starting with the stem end, roll up the cabbage to enclose the filling. Repeat with remaining leaves and filling.

Transfer the stuffed cabbage leaves, seam side down, to a baking dish and pour the tomato sauce over them. Cover with aluminum foil and bake until cabbage is very tender, about 1 hour.

To serve, place two cabbage rolls on each plate, spoon the tomato sauce over the rolls, and drizzle the crème fraîche over the sauce.

OTHER GREENS TO TRY: chard, collard greens, fig leaves, grape leaves

KIMCHI SODA

This recipe is super polarizing—some people hate it and some people love it. It can also be boozed up with whiskey or vodka.

SERVES 1

 2 ounces [60 ml] kimchi syrup (page 293)

 1 ounce [30 ml] fresh lemon juice

 1 ounce [30 ml] fresh grapefruit juice

 1 ounce [30 ml] fresh lime juice

 1 ounce [30 ml] fresh orange juice

 Ice

 Soda water, to fill glass

Mix the kimchi syrup, lemon juice, grapefruit juice, lime juice, and orange juice in a pint glass. Stir and top with ice and soda water.

CARDOON

Cynara cardunculus

It looks like a celery plant with silvery leaves, yet it tastes like an artichoke (a relative). Cardoons have been a rare delicacy since the times of the ancient Greeks and Romans and are believed to have originated in Sicily. In the United States, cardoons were cultivated primarily in the South from the Civil War era through World War I, before the vegetable faded in popularity. Today in New Orleans, cardoon stems continue to be battered and fried and placed on altars on St. Joseph's Day, in keeping with Sicilian tradition. The vegetable is also commonly eaten in Italy, Spain, Algeria, and Tunisia.

Cardoon is an especially multitalented green. It is not only used to flavor an *amaro* (herbal liqueur) called *cardamaro,* but is also a source of vegetable rennet in cheese making in Spain and Portugal and is being studied as a source of biodiesel fuel. In the diet, cardoons are rich in fiber, vitamin C, folate, calcium, iron, magnesium, potassium, copper, and manganese.

NOTE: For most preparations, before cooking, cardoon stalks should be boiled for 30 minutes to tenderize them and to mute their bitterness. If using the leaves, blanch separately for about 5 minutes. (See general blanching instructions on page 6 and sidebar on preparing cardoons on page 64.) Blanching and boiling can be done a day ahead, with cardoons drained and stored in the refrigerator.

VARIETIES BOUVIER, CARDON DE TOURS, COMMON, GIRARD, GRELLET, RED

SEASON Spring to early summer

HOW TO CHOOSE Look for firm stalks with silvery leaves. The stalks and leaves should be free of black spots and not at all limp. Look for whole cardoon plants at farmers' markets.

HOW TO CLEAN Wear gloves when handling because cardoons have tiny spikes. Peel cardoon stalks with a vegetable peeler or knife. Rinse under cold, running water. Pat dry.

HOW TO STORE Separate leaves and stems and store in an airtight plastic bin or ziplock bag or wrap in plastic wrap. In the crisper drawer of the refrigerator, cardoons will keep for about 2 days.

HOW TO REFRESH Immerse in ice water for 15 minutes. Drain; pat or spin dry.

COOKING METHODS Blanch stalks first for 2 to 4 minutes to tenderize, then braise, bake, sauté, fry, simmer in a soup or stew, or puree in a soup. In Italy, cardoons are often served with a fondue-like dip known as *bagna cauda* (page 295) or used as a bruschetta topping. In North Africa, they are often included in tagines.

PAIRINGS Citrus, dairy, anchovies, mayonnaise, aioli, olive oil, beef, chicken, eggs, risotto, fish.

STEAMED WHITE FISH WITH CARDOONS AND LEMON IN PARCHMENT

Cooking en papillote, which is steaming in parchment paper, is one of the simplest, easy-to-clean methods around, and it is especially great for cooking fish. It is pretty fail-safe in terms of overcooking, and it imparts flavors and moisture wonderfully. You basically pile the fish and vegetables in the parcel, cook, and voilà, even a sauce is rendered in the packet.

NOTE: The cardoon needs to be blanched or it will oxidize, so don't skip that step.

SERVES 4

4 (6-ounce/170-g) fillets delicate white fish, such as halibut, flounder, or sole

Fine sea salt

1 cup [115 g] sliced and blanched cardoon stalks (see sidebar)

⅔ cup [115 g] cooked flageolet or other small white beans

½ teaspoon finely chopped preserved lemon (page 294)

4 green onions, green and white parts, trimmed and cut into quarters lengthwise

4 thin slices fresh lemon

2 sprigs thyme

4 sprigs flat-leaf parsley

8 green olives, pitted and coarsely chopped

¼ cup [55 g] unsalted butter

½ cup [120 ml] dry white wine

Preheat the oven to 425°F [220°C].

Place four 12-inch [30.5-cm] squares of parchment paper on a work surface and center a fish fillet on each square. Season the fish with salt and divide the blanched cardoon stalks, beans, preserved lemon, green onions, fresh lemon, thyme, parsley, olives, and butter among the fish portions, piling the ingredients on top of the fish. Finish with the white wine and season with salt.

Fold the parchment squares to seal the fish and liquid in the paper so no juices will leak out during baking. Place the packets on a sheet pan and bake until the fish is cooked through, depending on thickness. Plan on 10 to 12 minutes for fillets 1 inch [2.5 cm] thick and about 15 minutes for fillets 2 to 3 inches [5 to 7.5 cm] thick.

Place the packets on individual plates and serve immediately. Make sure your guests are careful when opening their packets, as very hot steam will escape.

OTHER GREENS TO TRY celery, Chinese celery

PREPARING CARDOONS

1 One plant will yield 4 cups [700 g] cooked greens and 8 cups [735 g] cooked stalks (in ½-inch/12-mm pieces).

2 The stalks will oxidize once cut. When preparing them, place any cut pieces into a bowl of water with a lemon squeezed into the water to prevent browning.

3 The leaves of the cardoon plant are too bitter for many people. To break down some of the intensity, I blanch the greens and then braise in a bunch of butter and use a bit of them in things like a frittata or a pasta with cream. I also serve creamed cardoon greens on toast with a bit of preserved lemon (page 294).

Peel the cardoon stalks with a vegetable peeler to remove the thick, fibrous outer layers. Cut the stalks into ½-inch [12-mm] slices and blanch in salted water, court bouillon (wine and vegetable stock), or any stock for 2 minutes. Drain and discard the blanching liquid. The cooked stalks are now ready to cook with and will not turn brown (oxidize). They will keep for about 4 days, refrigerated.

Cardoon Gratin

BRAISED CARDOON GREENS

I like to describe the flavor of cardoons as "angry." Because of their intense nature, I don't recommend eating cardoon greens on their own. When braised, they can add a forceful counterpoint to rich dishes such as creamy pastas, frittatas, or a panino with a pungent or triple cream cheese.

MAKES ABOUT 4 CUPS [960 ML] GREENS

- 1 cardoon plant, leaves and stalks/separated and stalks reserved for another recipe
- 1 pound [455 g] unsalted butter
- 1 cup [240 ml] olive oil
- Juice of 1 lemon
- Fine sea salt

Fill a large bowl with ice water and set aside.

In a large pot of salted boiling water, blanch the cardoon leaves until just tender, 4 to 5 minutes. Immediately transfer the cooked leaves to the ice water to cool completely. When cool, remove the leaves from the ice water and wring with your hands until mostly dry.

Over medium heat, melt the butter in the olive oil in a large sauté pan. Add the blanched cardoon leaves and cook slowly until very tender and dark green, 30 to 45 minutes. Season and top with lemon juice and salt. Serve hot.

NOTE: Serve over toast and top with a rich, creamy cheese like robiola. Or use in the following gratin recipe.

CARDOON GRATIN

I bought a whole cardoon plant when I came up with this recipe, and I was hell-bent on using both the stalks and the leaves. Some people will think I am crazy for including the incredibly bitter leaves in this dish, but I like bitter flavors, and frankly, it is food! You are not going to eat a pile of them, because they are that intense. In other words, a little goes a long way, so you need to use a restrained hand. The cardoons are a great balance to the richness of the dairy in this cheese and cream laden gratin.

SERVES 4 TO 6 AS A SIDE DISH

- 1 tablespoon olive oil
- ½ yellow onion, diced
- 2 cloves garlic, thinly sliced
- 2 fresh sage leaves
- 3 heaping cups [390 g] sliced and blanched cardoon stalks (see Preparing Cardoons, page 64)
- 2 heaping tablespoons finely chopped blanched cardoon leaves (see Preparing Cardoons, page 64)
- 1½ cups [360 ml] heavy cream
- ¾ cup [45 g] shredded Pecorino Romano
- ¼ teaspoon freshly grated nutmeg
- ¼ teaspoon ground cayenne pepper
- Kosher salt

Preheat the broiler.

Heat the olive oil in an 8-inch [20-cm] cast-iron skillet over medium-high heat and add the onion, garlic, and sage. Cook until translucent, 2 to 3 minutes. Add the blanched cardoon stalks and leaves and stir to combine. Add the cream, ½ cup [30 g] of the Pecorino Romano, the nutmeg, and the cayenne and stir to combine. Season lightly with salt and stir again. Simmer over medium-low heat until the cardoons are tender and the cream has thickened—this should be a slow process—30 to 45 minutes. Top the gratin with the remaining ¼ cup [15 g] cheese and place the pan under the broiler, on the top rack, for 2 to 4 minutes to caramelize the top. Serve immediately.

OTHER GREENS TO TRY celery, Chinese celery

CELTUCE

Lactuca sativa angustana

A native of China, this variety of stem lettuce became a staple of Chinatown groceries across the United States in two waves: first, courtesy of Mennonite horticulturist Jacob B. Garber, who cultivated the plant in Lancaster County, Pennsylvania, in the 1850s, and then again thanks to its inclusion in the Burpee seed catalog in 1942, via a missionary who brought back an abundance of seeds from China. Contrary to what the name might lead one to believe, this green is not a celery-lettuce hybrid. It is also called AA choy, stem lettuce, asparagus lettuce, celery lettuce, *wosun*, *woju*, and Chinese lettuce and is traditionally stir-fried in Sichuan cooking. Prized for its woody stem, which looks like a thick asparagus stalk or wasabi root, celtuce has a nutty, cucumber-esque flavor. The leafy tops are also edible and are lightly bitter and sweet. Celtuce is high in vitamins A and C and potassium.

VARIETIES MAX GREEN

SEASON Late spring to early summer

HOW TO CHOOSE Choose celtuce with a sturdy stem (bumps are okay) and with sprightly dark green tops. Don't buy if the stem or leaves are limp. Also avoid celtuce that is yellowing or has dark spots on the stem or leaves.

HOW TO CLEAN Peel the stalk with a vegetable peeler, then cut into rounds or planks before cooking. Immerse the leaves in water and agitate with fingers. Drain; spin or pat dry.

HOW TO STORE Cut off the tops and keep separate from the stems. Store the stems and leaves in separate ziplock bags or airtight plastic containers. In the crisper drawer of the refrigerator, celtuce will keep for 2 to 3 days.

HOW TO REFRESH Immerse in ice water for 15 minutes. Drain and pat or spin dry.

COOKING METHODS For the leaves, see 20 Things to Do with Root, Fruit, and Vegetable Greens (page 212) for the best preparation tips. Cook stems as you would asparagus: stir-fry, roast, grill, braise, steam, or sauté. The stems are a great candidate for pickling, too.

PAIRINGS Dairy, nuts, tomatoes, vinaigrette, eggs, fish.

CELTUCE WITH CHERRY TOMATOES, GOAT MILK FETA, AND ALMONDS

Celtuce stems are like broccoli stems. They are firm and fibrous, so they need to be peeled before use. When shaved, they are crunchy are like celery, which makes this salad a textural gem.

SERVES 4

- 10 ounces [280 g] celtuce stem, peeled and cut into 2-inch [5-cm] pieces, then shaved on a mandoline
- 24 cherry tomatoes, halved
- 1 small shallot, cut into matchsticks
- 3 tablespoons fresh flat-leaf parsley leaves, cut into ribbons
- ¼ cup [10 g] mint leaves, cut into ribbons
- ¼ cup [30 g] almonds, coarsely chopped
- 1½ tablespoons finely chopped preserved lemon (page 294)
- Kosher salt and freshly ground black pepper
- Feta vinaigrette (page 300)

Combine the celtuce, tomatoes, shallot, parsley, mint, almonds, and preserved lemon in a large bowl and season with salt and pepper. Dress lightly with feta vinaigrette, divide among four plates, and serve immediately.

OTHER GREENS TO TRY blanched cardoon stalks, celery

PICKLED PEPPER PANZANELLA WITH MUSTARD SEED AND CELTUCE

Here is something a little spicier than your basic cucumber, tomato, and bread *panzanella*. Celtuce provides the cool, crunchy, juicy counterpoint to the croutons, while the vinaigrette and peppers bring some punch. The eggplant puree smooths it all out.

SERVES 4

- 8 cups [320 g] croutons (page 293)
- ¾ cup [180 ml] pickled mustard seed vinaigrette (page 301), plus more to serve
- 2 ounces [55 g] provolone cheese
- 6 tablespoons [60 g] pickled peppers, from escabeche (page 265) or store-bought
- ¾ cup [130 g] thinly sliced bell peppers
- 3 ounces [85 g] celtuce stem, peeled and cut into 2-inch [5-cm] pieces, then shaved on a mandoline
- Kosher salt and freshly ground black pepper
- ¾ cup [195 g] eggplant puree (page 73)

Combine the croutons and vinaigrette in a large bowl. Toss to combine and set aside for 5 minutes or so to let the croutons absorb the vinaigrette. Add the cheese, pickled peppers, bell peppers, and celtuce. Season with salt and pepper and toss to combine.

Place a dollop of eggplant puree on each plate. Put the salad on top, drizzle with additional vinaigrette, and serve.

OTHER GREENS TO TRY blanched cardoon stalks

Celtuce with Cherry Tomatoes, Goat Milk Feta, and Almonds

Celtuce Frittata

EGGPLANT PUREE

MAKES 5 CUPS [1.3 KG]

6 tablespoons [90 ml] plus 2 cups [480 ml] olive oil

Kosher salt

2 medium globe or bell eggplants, stemmed and halved lengthwise

¾ cup [180 g] tahini

5 small cloves garlic (about ½ ounce/15 g)

Zest of 2 lemons, finely grated

2 tablespoons fresh lemon juice

Preheat the oven to 400°F [200°C].

Pour 6 tablespoons [90 ml] of the olive oil on a sheet pan, sprinkle 1 tablespoon salt over the oil and place the eggplants, cut side down, on top of the seasoned oil. Bake the eggplants until very tender but not mushy, 15 to 20 minutes. Remove from the oven and let cool.

Peel the skin from the eggplants and discard. Using a blender or food processor, and working in batches, puree the eggplant flesh with the remaining 2 cups [480 ml] oil, and the tahini, garlic, lemon zest, and lemon juice. When each batch is smooth, scrape into a bowl using a rubber spatula. Season with salt. Pack into pint containers and refrigerate for up to 5 days.

CELTUCE FRITTATA

A frittata is one of the simplest egg dishes you can make. It takes on another dimension when you add an interesting green, like celtuce, with its mild asparagus-like flavor and crunchy texture. It mingles particularly well with tarragon in this easy recipe.

MAKES 1 (7-INCH/17-CM) FRITTATA, SERVES 1 OR 2

3 eggs

1½ tablespoons heavy cream

1 tablespoon unsalted butter

2 ounces [55 g] celtuce stem, peeled and cut into 2-inch [5-cm] pieces, then shaved on a mandoline

1 tablespoon fresh tarragon leaves

Kosher salt

1½ tablespoons finely grated Parmigiano-Reggiano

Preheat the oven to 375°F [190°C].

In a bowl, beat together the eggs and cream until combined; set aside.

Over medium heat, melt the butter in a 7-inch [17-cm] nonstick ovenproof sauté pan. Add the celtuce and sauté until just tender but still with a crunch, about 2 minutes. Add half of the tarragon leaves and lightly season with salt. Pour the egg mixture over the celtuce and sprinkle the Parmigiano-Reggiano over the egg. Lightly season with salt and the remaining tarragon.

Bake until the frittata is just set, slightly risen, and still pale yellow with little caramelization, about 8 minutes. Tilt the pan to release the frittata onto a plate and serve immediately while warm, or cool to room temperature and serve.

OTHER GREENS TO TRY blanched cardoon, celery

KULCHA WITH CELTUCE

A cousin of naan, *kulcha*, the north Indian Punjabi flatbread, is less well known, but it is easier and simpler to make because it doesn't include yeast. Kulcha is ideally served with spicy beans, dals, and (most famously) chole masala, which is spice-braised chickpeas. Ideally made in a tandoor oven, *kulcha* can be made on a griddle on the stove top or on the flat top of a wood-burning grill. If you develop the right touch, you can even make them using your broiler.

I serve *kulcha* with everything I can think of: as a flatbread for shashlik (a form of shish kebab), in the place of tortillas for *tacos al pastor*, and rolled around grilled sausage with peppers and onions.

This is an adaptation of Andrew Zimmern's recipe. I like his version because of the abundance of chiles in it. I added greens, which makes the bread a little fatter and a little more substantial.

MAKES 8 FLATBREADS

3 cups [420 g] all-purpose flour

1 tablespoon sugar

Fine sea salt

½ teaspoon baking powder

⅛ teaspoon baking soda

½ cup [120 g] plain yogurt

½ cup [120 ml] water, plus more as needed

¼ cup [60 ml] neutral vegetable oil

1 large shallot, minced

1 green onion, green and white parts minced

2 tablespoons minced serrano chile with seeds

1 teaspoon peeled and minced fresh ginger

1 teaspoon white sesame seeds, toasted

¼ teaspoon ground fennel

¼ teaspoon ground cumin

¼ teaspoon dried oregano

1½ cups [60 g] loosely packed celtuce leaves, thinly sliced

Ghee or clarified butter, for brushing

In a large bowl, whisk the flour with the sugar, 1 teaspoon salt, the baking powder, and the baking soda. Using a wooden spoon, stir in the yogurt, water, and oil until the dough starts to come together. Add additional water, a tablespoon at a time, as needed until the dough comes together (2 to 3 tablespoons more). Using your hands, knead the dough in the bowl until it is mostly smooth, soft, and tender without being sticky. Wrap the dough in plastic wrap and let rest at room temperature for 2 hours.

In a bowl, mix together the shallot with the green onions, serrano, ginger, sesame seeds, fennel, cumin, oregano, and celtuce.

Unwrap the dough and cut into eight pieces. Roll out one piece of dough into an 8-inch [20-cm] round. Spoon one-eighth of the shallot mixture onto the center of the round, then season the mixture lightly with salt. Roll up the round into a cylinder. Now, starting at one end, coil the cylinder into a spiral reminiscent of a snail shell. Flatten the spiral gently with your hand and then roll out the filled dough into a 7-inch [17-cm] round.

Preheat a large cast-iron skillet or griddle over medium-high heat. Melt 1 to 2 tablespoons ghee in the skillet, then carefully lay a kulcha in the pan. Decrease the heat to medium and cook, turning once, until the flatbread is puffed and charred in spots, about 4 minutes total. The dough should be golden and cooked through and the outside of the flatbread should be crispy. Add 1 tablespoon additional ghee to the pan to cook the second side and raise the heat slightly if the flatbread does not become crisp. Transfer to a plate. Repeat with the remaining pieces of dough and shallot mixture. Serve warm.

OTHER GREENS TO TRY amaranth, mustard greens

CHARD

Beta vulgaris subsp. *cicla*

Sturdier than spinach and more delicate than kale, chard boasts two great components: its dark leaves are both tasty and nutrient rich, and its ribs and stalks are uniquely flavored, pleasantly crunchy, and wonderfully colorful, whether red, pink, golden, purple, orange, yellow, or white. Despite being labeled "Swiss," chard is native to the Mediterranean. In Italy, it is known as *bietola*. Another misnomer is "rainbow" chard, which is not a variety of its own but rather a compilation of varieties with colorful stems. Chard is a relative of beets and spinach, and it is thought that its name stems from cardoon, from the French *carde,* as the Gauls used the same term for both plants. One undisputable fact about chard is that it is a nutritional powerhouse, rich in vitamins A, B, C, E, and K, as well as in magnesium, manganese, iron, and potassium. It is also a great source of dietary fiber, calcium, phosphorus, protein, pantothenic acid, zinc, and selenium. In more good news on the health front, recent studies have shown that the unique flavonoid phytonutrients in chard can aid in blood sugar regulation.

VARIETIES BIETOLA, BRIGHT LIGHTS, BRIGHT YELLOW, BURGUNDY, CRAB BEET, FORDHOOK GIANT, GENEVA, LUCULLUS, MANGOLD, PERPETUAL, RED, RHUBARB, RUBY, SEA KALE BEET, SILVERADO, SILVERY, SPINACH BEET, WHITE LEAF BEET, WINTER KING

SEASON Spring through summer

HOW TO CHOOSE Look for perky, vivid green leaves without any brown or yellow spots. The stalks and ribs should be firm and crisp, without any blemishes.

HOW TO CLEAN Immerse greens in cool water. Agitate with fingers. Drain; spin or pat dry.

HOW TO STORE Store chard in an airtight plastic bin or ziplock bag or wrap in plastic wrap. In the crisper drawer of the refrigerator, chard will keep for 5 to 7 days.

HOW TO REFRESH Immerse in ice water for 15 minutes. Drain and spin or pat dry.

COOKING METHODS Use the leaves raw in salads or cook by sautéing, blanching, steaming, or stir-frying. Chop the stems and toss them into a salad, layer them in a sandwich, serve them with charcuterie, use as a hot dog topping, pickle them, or sauté them with the greens.

PAIRINGS Garlic, lemon, dairy, eggs, beef, pork, poultry, veal, lamb, fish, mushrooms.

PICKLED CHARD STEMS

The sturdy stems of chard make colorful, potent pickles. Serve as a companion to hard-boiled eggs (page 293), on a sandwich with ham and Brie, as a garnish for braised beef short ribs, or as an accompaniment on a charcuterie plate.

MAKES 4 CUPS [960 ML]

> 6 ounces [170 g] chard stems, cut into ½-inch [12-mm] pieces
>
> 1½ cups [360 ml] white wine vinegar
>
> 1 cup [240 ml] water
>
> 2 tablespoons sugar
>
> 1 tablespoon kosher salt
>
> 3 cloves garlic, halved
>
> 1 tablespoon yellow mustard seeds
>
> 1 tablespoon caraway seeds
>
> 3 bay leaves
>
> 2 sprigs thyme
>
> 7 ounces [200 g] shallots, sliced (about 2 cups)

Place the stem pieces in 1-quart [1-L] jar or container.

Combine the vinegar, water, sugar, salt, garlic, mustard seeds, caraway seeds, bay leaves, and thyme in a pot over high heat. Bring to a simmer, then add the shallots. The simmer will die for a moment when shallots are added; wait for the simmer to begin again and simmer for 30 seconds.

Remove the pot from the heat and spoon the shallots into the jar with the chard stems. Pour the spices and picking liquid over the chard stems and shallots. Allow to cool at room temperature for 20 minutes, then cover and chill completely. Pickled chard will be ready to eat after 24 hours; it tastes even better after 1 week. Store, refrigerated, for up to 1 month.

OTHER GREENS TO TRY celery, celtuce stems

SWISS CHARD FRITTATA

The element of surprise in this recipe is brought to you by Swiss chard, kimchi-style. The fermented green really punches up the flavor in this frittata, while the fat from the pancetta fries away some of its pungency. The sesame seeds add a toasty finish.

MAKES 1 FRITTATA, SERVES 1 AS A MAIN OR 2 AS AN APPETIZER

> 1 (¾-ounce/20 g) slice pancetta
>
> 2 eggs
>
> 3 tablespoons heavy cream
>
> ½ cup [100 g] Italian-Style Chard Kimchi (page 81)
>
> 4 teaspoons crème fraîche or sour cream
>
> ¼ teaspoon white sesame seeds, toasted

Preheat the oven to 425°F [220°C].

Sear the pancetta in a 7-inch [19-cm] nonstick ovenproof pan over high heat for 2 to 3 minutes, until golden. Be careful not to overcook. Set the pancetta to the side. Do not discard the fat. Decrease the heat to medium-high. Whisk together the eggs and cream to make a custard. Spread the kimchi evenly over the bottom of the pan, then cover with the custard. Top the frittata with the crème fraîche, spacing the teaspoons evenly. (You should have four distinct spots of crème fraîche.) Set the pancetta on top.

Bake for 6 minutes, until the custard is set but not too brown. Plate and then sprinkle with the sesame seeds.

OTHER GREENS TO TRY green varieties of cabbage, brussels sprouts

Italian-Style Chard Kimchi (page 81)

Swiss Chard Polenta

ITALIAN-STYLE CHARD KIMCHI

MAKES 1 GALLON [3.8 L], WITH LIQUID

 1 pound [455 g] Swiss chard with white stems, ribs cut into 1-inch [2.5-cm] ribbons (leaves reserved for another use)

 7 tablespoons [105 g] fine sea salt

 ½ cup [100 g] plus 2 tablespoons sugar

 4 cups [960 ml] water

 20 cloves garlic, minced

 20 slices fresh ginger, peeled and minced

 7 teaspoons dried red pepper flakes

 ¼ cup [60 ml] fish sauce

 ½ cup [25 g] green onions, green and white parts, cut into 1-inch [2.5-cm] pieces

 1 orange, peeled, halved, and thinly sliced

Toss the chard with 2 tablespoons of the salt and 2 tablespoons of the sugar in a large bowl. Let sit for at least 4 hours or up to overnight in the refrigerator.

Mix the water with the remaining 5 tablespoons [75 g] salt in a large bowl to make a brine. Add the garlic, ginger, red pepper, fish sauce, and the remaining ½ cup [100 g] sugar and stir until the sugar dissolves. Stir in the green onions and orange. Add the brine to the salted chard and stir to combine. Cover and refrigerate. The kimchi is ready to eat immediately but will continue to develop more complex flavors over the next couple of weeks. Kimchi will keep for up to 6 months in the refrigerator.

SWISS CHARD POLENTA

Blanching the greens, shocking them in ice water, and keeping them cold in the refrigerator is essential here. Also, the stock needs to be cold. Otherwise, the polenta will turn an unpleasant army green. I enjoy this for breakfast with an egg and bacon, but it is also really nice with braised or roasted meats or with mushrooms, rosemary, and prosciutto.

SERVES 4

 5 cups [1.2 L] double chicken stock (page 299), chilled

 1 cup [140 g] polenta

 Leaves from 1 bunch chard (about 6 ounces/170 g)

 2 tablespoons unsalted butter

 2 tablespoons olive oil

 2 ounces [55 g] Fontina Val d'Aosta, grated

 Kosher salt

Combine 4 cups [960 ml] of the chicken stock and the polenta in a pot over medium heat and stir until the polenta begins to simmer. Turn down the heat to low and cook, stirring occasionally, until the polenta grains are cooked and tender and the polenta has a very thick consistency, 30 to 45 minutes.

While the polenta is cooking, fill a large bowl with ice water. Bring a large pot filled with salted water to a simmer, add the greens, and cook until tender, 2 to 3 minutes. Using a slotted spoon or tongs, transfer the greens to the ice water to chill quickly. Drain, then using your hands, wring out the greens until mostly dry. Chill the greens in the refrigerator.

When the polenta is almost done, combine the greens with the remaining 1 cup [240 ml] cold stock in a blender and puree until smooth.

Decrease the heat under the polenta to low and add the butter, olive oil, and Fontina. Stir to combine. Add the pureed greens, season with salt, and gently warm over low heat. Serve immediately.

OTHER GREENS TO TRY arugula, kale

SWISS CHARD WITH GARAM MASALA AND COCONUT MILK

There are a million recipes for creamed spinach in the world, so you don't need another one from me. Instead, here is something a little different that fills that same creamy green niche, but with tons more flavor. It has texture, thanks to the pistachios, and sweetness, thanks to the sultanas (golden raisins). It is rich because of the coconut milk. And the foundation of the exotic flavor is thanks to the garam masala.

SERVES 4 TO 6 AS A SIDE DISH

1 pound [455 g] Swiss chard, leaves and stems

3 tablespoons coconut oil

1 red onion, halved and thinly sliced

3 large cloves garlic, thinly sliced

2 tablespoons garam masala

1 teaspoon ground cayenne pepper

1-inch [2.5-cm] piece fresh ginger, peeled

1 (13½-ounce/400-ml) can coconut milk, shaken before opening

1 cup [240 ml] double chicken stock (page 299) or vegetable stock

½ cup [60 g] raw pistachios

½ cup [70 g] golden raisins

1 lime, halved

Kosher salt

Cooked basmati rice, for serving

Separate the chard leaves from the stems and cut the leaves into ¼-inch [6-mm] ribbons. Then cut the stems crosswise into slices ¼ inch [6 mm] wide. Set aside.

In a saucepan, melt the coconut oil over medium heat. Add the red onion, garlic, garam masala, and cayenne and cook, stirring often, until the onion is translucent and soft and the spices are fragrant, stirring often, 2 to 3 minutes. If the spices begin to darken, decrease the heat so they do not burn. Using a fine-rasp grater, grate the ginger into pan, then add the chard and stir to combine. Add the coconut milk and chicken stock and bring to a simmer. Cook until the sauce slightly thickens and the chard becomes tender, 2 to 4 minutes. The sauce should be loose and not thick. If needed, add a couple of tablespoons of water, one at a time, to adjust the texture. Stir in the pistachios and the raisins, squeeze the lime juice into the pan, and season with salt.

Serve with basmati rice.

OTHER GREENS TO TRY Malabar spinach, nettles, spinach

CHARD PANEER

Chard is not the green that you usually see with paneer, a type of curd cheese commonly used in Indian cuisine. Spinach is its typical companion, however, so chard slides into this recipe as a seamless substitute. Store any leftovers in the refrigerator, then reheat gently on the stove top and serve with basmati rice.

SERVES 4

1 pound [455 g] chard leaves

¼ cup [60 ml] neutral vegetable oil

1 large yellow onion, diced

6 garlic cloves, thinly sliced

1-inch [2.5-cm] piece fresh ginger, peeled and finely chopped

½ teaspoon ground cumin

½ teaspoon ground coriander

½ teaspoon fenugreek seeds

1 teaspoon garam masala

¾ cup plus 2 tablespoons [420 ml] tomato
puree

8 ounces [230 g] paneer (recipe follows),
cubed

Kosher salt

Bring a large pot of lightly salted water to a boil
over medium-high heat, add the chard, and blanch
until wilted, 1 to 2 minutes. Drain into a colander
and hold under cold running water until cool.
Wrap the leaves in a clean kitchen towel and wring
out the excess moisture with your hands. Chop
finely and set aside.

Warm the oil in in a large cast-iron skillet or other
heavy pan over medium heat. Add the onion, garlic,
ginger, cumin, coriander, fenugreek, and garam
masala and cook, stirring occasionally, until the
onion is translucent, 3 to 4 minutes. If the onion
begins to brown or the spices begin to darken too
much, decrease the heat. Add the tomato puree,
stir well, and bring to a simmer. Add the chard and
paneer and stir gently to mix, being careful not to
break up the paneer. Cook just until the chard and
paneer are heated through, season with salt, then
serve immediately.

OTHER GREENS TO TRY amaranth, Malabar spinach

PANEER

MAKES ABOUT 1 POUND [455 G]

3 quarts [2.8 L] whole milk

6 tablespoons [90 ml] fresh lemon juice

Pour the milk into a large, heavy pot, place over
medium-high heat, and bring just to a boil, stirring
with a wooden spoon so the milk does not form a
skin on the bottom of the pot. Turn down the heat to
medium-low, stir in the lemon juice, and continue to
stir over medium-low for about 2 minutes, until
curds begin to form. You will see the white part of
the liquid start to coagulate (the curds) and
separate from the yellow part of the liquid (the
whey). If curds do not form, continue to heat over
low heat until they start to take shape. Remove the
pot from the heat and let sit for 15 minutes, until
the curds have fully separated from the whey.

Line a colander with cheesecloth and place it over
a large bowl. Pour the curds and whey into the
colander, capturing the whey in the bowl. Reserve
the whey for another use, such as using it as the
liquid for cooking polenta. Gather together the
edges of the cheesecloth to form a bag, squeeze
gently, and run the bag briefly under cool water
to release any excess whey.

Tie kitchen string around the top of the bag to
secure it closed, hang the bag from the sink tap,
and leave to drain for a few hours. Transfer the bag
to a sheet pan, place a second sheet pan on top, and
top the second pan with several heavy food cans.
The cans will weight down the paneer, pressing out
any remaining moisture. Refrigerate the pan setup
to drain for 2 to 3 hours. The paneer is ready when
it is firm enough to cut with a knife.

The paneer will keep well wrapped in plastic wrap
or in an airtight container in the refrigerator for up
to 1 week.

CHICKWEED
Stellaria media

This European native is named as such because the chicks love it—literally, baby chickens can't get enough of it. It is clear why: chickweed is mild, grassy, and extremely palatable. What is interesting about something so mild mannered is that it apparently has superpowers. It has been used in traditional Chinese medicine as an anti-inflammatory, a digestive aid, and to treat skin ailments for thousands of years. It has also been promoted as a tonic for a healthy liver and kidneys in folklore. That is likely because of chickweed's high content of vitamin C, beta-carotene, calcium, iron, magnesium, niacin, potassium, riboflavin, thiamin, and zinc.

VARIETIES CHICKENWORT, COMMON, FIELD, JAGGED, MISCHIEVOUS JACK, MOUSE EAR, STAR, STARWEED, STARWORT, STICKY, UPRIGHT, WINTERWEED

SEASON Late winter through spring

HOW TO CHOOSE Look for leaves that are perky and vivid green without any spots, browning, or yellowing.

HOW TO CLEAN Immerse greens in cool water. Agitate with fingers. Drain; spin or pat dry.

HOW TO STORE Store in an airtight plastic bin or ziplock bag or wrap in plastic wrap. In the crisper drawer of the refrigerator, chickweed will last for 2 to 3 days.

HOW TO REFRESH Immerse in ice water for 15 minutes. Drain and spin or pat dry.

COOKING METHODS Use raw in salads or cook by sautéing, simmering in soups and stews, stir-frying, or baking in a casserole or a quiche. Can be steeped to make tea.

PAIRINGS Lemon, curry, scallops, firm-fleshed fish, pork, mild cheese, egg.

AREPAS WITH EGG, FETA, AND CHICKWEED

This style of *arepa* (a masa flatbread typical of several South American cultures with varying styles of preparation) is Colombian, from the Caribbean side of the country. When you drop these into the fryer, the dough puffs up just enough so that you can cut a slit in it, put an egg inside, then toss it back in the fryer to cook the egg. The chickweed salad adds a clean and bright flavor to the richness of the egg and fried *arepa*. These flatbreads also pair wonderfully with Carrot Greens Salsa Verde (page 295).

SERVES 4

1 cup [115 g] precooked white corn flour, preferably Masarepa

Kosher salt

1 cup [240 ml] warm water

3 tablespoons plus 2 teaspoons canola oil, plus more for frying

¼ cup [40 g] crumbled feta cheese

4 eggs

2 ounces [55 g] chickweed

½ apple, cored and thinly sliced

Freshly ground black pepper

Red wine vinaigrette (page 301)

½ cup [115 g] butternut squash puree (page 298)

Pickled chiles (page 294), for topping

Mix the corn flour and ¾ teaspoon salt in a bowl. Stir in the water and 2 teaspoons of the oil and knead in the bowl until smooth, about 2 minutes. Divide the dough into four equal balls.

Place a wire rack on a sheet pan and set aside. Pour oil to a depth fo 2 inches [5 cm] into a 6-quart [5.7-L] saucepan and heat to 325°F [165°C].

Flatten each dough ball into a round 5 inches [12 cm] in diameter and about ¼ inch [6 mm] thick. Working in batches, fry the rounds, flipping once, until puffed, 2 to 3 minutes. Transfer to the rack to drain.

Increase the oil temperature to 375°F [190°C]. Make a 3-inch [7.5-cm] incision horizontally into an arepa without cutting all the way through, to make a pocket. The outer layer of the pocket will be thin; gently pry the opening apart without tearing the outer layer. Place 1 tablespoon of the feta into the pocket, then crack 1 egg into the pocket. Place the arepa in the oil and fry until the egg is set, about 2 minutes. Drain on the rack and season with salt. Repeat with the remaining arepas, feta, and eggs.

Combine the chickweed and apple in a large bowl, season with salt and pepper, and dress lightly with the vinaigrette. Divide the arepas among four plates. On each warm arepa, smear 2 tablespoons of butternut squash puree and sprinkle with pickled chiles. Top with the chickweed salad. Serve immediately.

OTHER GREENS TO TRY mâche, miner's lettuce

Belgian endive

Frisée

Escarole

Radicchio

CHICORIES

Chicory has been around as long as civilization itself. The University of California documents archaeological evidence of chicory dating back to the Bronze Age. It is also apparently one of the "bitter herbs" cited in the Bible to be eaten for Passover, and the ancient Greeks and Romans consumed it copiously. Native to Europe, North Africa, and West Asia, the aggressive flavor and versatility of these bitter lettuces certainly made an impression wherever they spread, whether the hardy magenta leaves of radicchio, the crisp stems of puntarelle, or the roots used to stretch out coffee in France during the Napoleonic era and in the United States during the Civil War. Chicory even has a history with the Founding Fathers: Thomas Jefferson was one of the country's first chicory farmers, cultivating seeds given to him by George Washington. Overall, chicories are powerfully nutrient rich, packed with vitamins A, B, C, and K, as well as calcium, copper, iron, potassium, manganese, zinc, and dietary fiber.

BELGIAN ENDIVE
Cichorium endivia

This white, oblong-shaped leaf curves into light yellow tips at the end. Also called French endive or witloof chicory, Belgian endive has a waxy texture on the surface and a light crispiness when bitten into. Because of its shape, it is a great spoon-like vehicle for dips or hors d'oeuvres. Endive is one of the mildly bitter, juicy chicory varieties.

ESCAROLE
Cichorium endivia

Dark green, leafy, and assertively bitter, escarole is an Italian favorite, appearing often in soups, as a companion to beans, or as a side dish. Also called Batavian endive, scarole, and broad-leaved endive, it's the greenest leaf of the chicory bunch.

FRISÉE
Cichorium endivia

Like the name suggests, these are those greens with the "frizzy" heads. Sometimes called curly endive, curly chicory, or chicory endive, these have a crunchy stem, light frilly leaves, a yellowy-green color, and a sharp, bitter flavor very much like its relative, escarole. (The darker green edges of heads that are usually trimmed away are great to use when making Lettuce Jam, page 155).

PAN DI ZUCCHERO
Cichorium intybus

Literally "sugar loaf," *pan di zucchero* is among the sweeter varieties of chicory. Its light green-and-white appearance and hardy, crisp texture is similar to romaine, which makes it a great candidate for a Caesar-like salad and grilling.

PUNTARELLE

Chicorium intybus

A fleeting winter favorite, this chicory is marked by thin, light green stems. Sharp, bitter, and crispy, it is a favorite in Rome when prepared with anchovy and lemon. The dark green leaves, which stand out in contrast to the light stems, have a softer texture but an equally powerful flavor.

RADICCHIO

Chicorium intybus

Its red color makes it the flamboyant, nonconformist member of the chicory clan, while its bitter-sweet flavor, wide availability, and versatility—it can be served raw, grilled, sautéed, or roasted—make it one of the more common types to find on the plate. It also goes by Chioggia, red chicory, and red Italian chicory.

OTHER VARIETIES BIANCA DI MILANO, CASTELFRANCO, CATALOGNA FRASTAGLIATE, CATALONA GALATINA, CATALONA GIGANTE DI CHIOGGA, DA TAGLIO BIONDA FOGLIE, ITALIKO ROSSO, PUNTARELLE STRETTA, SPADONA, TARDIVO, TREVISO, VERONA

SEASON Fall through winter

HOW TO CHOOSE Chicory leaves and stems should be perky and firm, not wilted, and free of dark spots and browning.

HOW TO CLEAN Wash chicories thoroughly under cold running water. Pat or spin dry. When preparing, avoid cutting chicories with a knife because the cut area will oxidize and turn brown. Tear leaves with your hands instead.

HOW TO STORE Store in an airtight plastic bin or ziplock bag or wrap in plastic wrap. In the crisper drawer of the refrigerator, most chicories will last for 3 to 5 days.

HOW TO REFRESH Immerse greens in ice water for 15 minutes. Drain and pat or spin dry.

COOKING METHODS Serve raw in salads, pickle, or cook by sautéing, steaming, stir-frying, baking, braising, grilling, or simmering in soups or stews.

PAIRINGS Olive oil, garlic, anchovy, citrus, honey, chile, dairy, grains, pork.

ENDIVE AND FENNEL WITH DUNGENESS CRAB AND TARRAGON VINAIGRETTE

This has come to be my New Year's salad, as Dungeness crab happens to be in season then. I love the varying textures of the soft crab and the crisp chicories. The tarragon vinaigrette is aïoli based, so it binds the crab and the greens, while the shallot adds an herbal flavor. Sometimes I add a sliced tangerine for a sweet-and-sour element.

SERVES 6

3 heads Belgian endive, halved crosswize, cored, and leaves separated

1 small fennel bulb, thinly sliced

1 small shallot, thinly sliced

Kosher salt and freshly ground black pepper

Tarragon vinaigrette (page 302)

12 ounces [340 g] Dungeness crabmeat

Fresh lemon juice, for serving (optional)

Combine the endive, fennel, and shallot in a large bowl, season with salt and pepper, and mix gently. Add the vinaigrette, making sure that the salad is well coated but not overdressed. Add the crab and mix gently. Adjust the seasoning with salt, pepper, or lemon juice if needed. Serve immediately.

OTHER GREENS TO TRY mizuna, tender pea tendrils

FRISÉE, ESCAROLE, AND PAN DI ZUCCHERO SALAD WITH LAMB BACON AND POACHED EGG

A spin on the classic *frisée aux lardons*, this combination of chicories melds the richness of an egg yolk with the bright acid of vinaigrette and the salty, fatty loveliness of bacon. I love it with smoked lamb bacon, though pancetta or pork bacon works equally well. Hemp seeds add a little soft, nut-like texture.

SERVES 4

4 ounces [115 g] smoked lamb bacon or pork bacon

8 ounces [230 g] assorted chicory leaves, such as frisée, escarole, pan di zucchero, radicchio, and Belgian endive

½ shallot, thinly sliced

¼ cup [40 g] hemp seeds (optional)

Sherry vinaigrette (page 301)

Flaky sea salt

4 eggs, poached (page 293)

Place a pan over medium-high heat and cook the bacon until golden but not crispy, 3 to 4 minutes.

Chop the bacon, transfer to a bowl, and add the chicories, shallot, and hemp seeds (if using). Dress with the vinaigrette and season with salt. Divide among four plates and garnish each salad with a warm poached egg. Serve immediately.

OTHER GREENS TO TRY mixed chicories

PANZEROTTI WITH FRISÉE, LEMON, ANCHOVY, AND DIJON MUSTARD

Panzerotti are savory pies that hail from central and southern Italy. In Puglia, they are like mini-calzones and are fried instead of baked. It is fun to play with the fillings of these. When you think of calzones, you think of cheese, maybe some meat. But what about greens? It's a glaring omission, but frisée happens to make the perfect filling. If you leave out the anchovy, you can sub in some chopped prosciutto for the same salty effect, or a rich cheese like Taleggio or Fontina or robiola would work well. The moistness of the dough is the most important factor in this recipe. The dough should be smooth and soft but not sticky. Adding as much water as possible, little by little, helps strike the right consistency. Without the moisture, the dough becomes too much like a cracker.

Continued

MAKES 12

Dough

2 cups [420 ml] water, at room temperature, plus 5 to 7 tablespoons [80 to 105 ml] more as needed

2 tablespoons active dry yeast

5 cups [710 g] all-purpose flour

1 teaspoon fine sea salt

1 teaspoon sugar

2 tablespoons olive oil, plus more for the bowl

Filling

½ cup [120 ml] olive oil

1 yellow onion, diced

6 cloves garlic, thinly sliced

1 lemon, halved lengthwise and then crosswise, seeded, and very thinly sliced

2 large sprigs rosemary

1½ pounds [680 g] escarole hearts, all dark and damaged leaves and stems removed, and frisée leaves, cut into ¼-inch [6-mm] pieces

Fine sea salt

¼ cup [10 g] lightly packed finely grated Parmigiano-Reggiano

Kosher salt and freshly ground black pepper

2 tablespoons Dijon mustard

12 anchovy fillets packed in oil

Olive or neutral vegetable oil, for frying

To make the dough, combine the water and yeast in the bowl of a stand mixer and whisk to combine. Fit the machine with a dough hook attachment and add the flour, salt, sugar, and olive oil. Mix on medium-low speed until the dough is shaggy. Add 5 to 7 tablespoons [80 to 105 ml] additional water as needed, tablespoon by tablespoon, until the dough becomes a cohesive mass. The dough should be as soft and hold as much water as possible without being sticky. Knead on medium-low for 5 minutes, until the dough is smooth and soft.

Pour olive oil into a metal or glass bowl and turn to coat the lower third of the inside of the bowl. Place the dough in the bowl, cover with a piece of plastic wrap, and gently tuck the plastic around the sides of the dough.

Allow the dough to rise in a warm spot until doubled in size, 1½ to 2 hours. Meanwhile, make the filling.

To make the filling, warm the olive oil in a large sauté pan over medium heat. Add the onion, garlic, lemon, and rosemary and cook until the lemon is tender and the onion is translucent, 4 to 5 minutes. Add the escarole and frisée and decrease the heat to medium. Cook, stirring often, until the greens are wilted and no longer raw, 2 to 3 minutes. Season with sea salt and cool completely. When chilled, discard the rosemary sprigs, stir in the cheese, and season with kosher salt and pepper.

Lightly flour the work surface as needed. To assemble, roll out the dough to a thickness of ⅛ to ¼ inch [3 to 6 mm] and cut into twelve (3-inch/7.5-cm) circles.

Smear ¼ to ½ teaspoon mustard on the top of a dough round, leaving a ¼-inch [6-mm] border around the edge. Lay 1 anchovy on top of the mustard, then top with 2 tablespoons of the chilled escarole mixture. Fold the dough round in half over the filling to form a crescent and crimp the edges to seal. Start on one end of the crescent and turn the edge of the dough over on itself to make a seal.

Fill a saucepan half full with olive or vegetable oil. Heat the oil to 350°F [180°C]. Set a wire rack on a sheet pan or line a plate with paper towels. Slip 2 or 3 panzerotti into the oil and cook, flipping once or twice, until the dough is golden and the filling is warm, 3 to 4 minutes. Remove from the oil and drain on the rack or towel-lined plate. Serve immediately or at room temperature later.

OTHER GREENS TO TRY mixed chicories

PUNTARELLE ALLA ROMANA

I had *puntarelle* for the first time when I was in Rome's Jewish Quarter. It was just before I wrote *Pasta by Hand*, and I was touring Italy. It was spring, and I went to the market and saw puntarelle there. Immediately afterward, I saw it on a menu at a restaurant and ordered it. It was served very traditionally, in a lemony, garlicky anchovy vinaigrette. I was startled by its brightness and loved the crunchy, celery-like texture.

SERVES 6

2 heads puntarelle (about 1 pound/455 g)

1 large clove garlic

Coarse sea salt

4 anchovy fillets packed in oil

2 teaspoons white or red wine vinegar

4 teaspoons olive oil

Freshly ground black pepper

To prepare the puntarelle, remove the skinny outer leaves, which you won't need for this salad (reserve to sauté with garlic in olive oil or use in soup). Pull or cut apart the fat, hollow stems at the core of the head. These are white on the bottom, with pale green asparagus-like tips.

Next, cut off the tough bottom part of the stems. Slice the stems in half lengthwise, then slice each half into long, thin strips.

Fill a large bowl with ice water and submerge the sliced puntarelle stems in the water. Let them soak for a good hour. After about 30 minutes, they will begin to curl.

After an hour, drain the puntarelle in a colander, then pat them dry with a clean kitchen towel or paper towels. (At this point, you can either dress them with your anchovy vinaigrette or put them in a bag and store them in the refrigerator for a couple of hours.)

To make the vinaigrette, on a cutting board, finely chop the garlic, then add a pinch of coarse salt and smear the garlic with the side of your knife until a paste forms. Add the anchovy and continue to make a paste of the three ingredients. Transfer the garlic-anchovy paste to a small bowl, stir in the vinegar and mix well. Dribble in the oil and stir until well combined.

Drizzle the dressing over the puntarelle and season with a generous grinding of black pepper. Toss to combine and serve immediately.

OTHER GREENS TO TRY escarole, frisée, or radicchio sliced into long strips or torn into bite-size pieces; soak whatever greens you use in ice water, which will give them extra crunch and curl.

RADICCHIO, ENDIVE, AND FRISÉE SALAD WITH BLOOD ORANGE, APPLE, AND PECANS

There is more available in the winter at your farm stand than you might think, and this salad makes use of the best fruits and vegetables found during the colder months. It has crunch. It has sweetness. It has tartness. And it is a little bitter. Pecans add the crunch; apples, a nice juiciness; and tarragon, an herbal punch. It is a really nice textural salad for a season when people think there is nothing growing.

SERVES 4

1 head radicchio, halved, cored, and sliced into ⅛-inch [3-mm] ribbons

1 small head frisée, dark leaves trimmed, core removed, and separated into fronds

1 small shallot, sliced into thin half-moons

Leaves of 1 sprig tarragon

½ crisp apple, such as Braeburn or Gala, cored and thinly sliced

¼ cup [30 g] pecans, lightly toasted

Kosher salt and freshly ground black pepper

Red wine vinaigrette (page 301)

1 blood orange, peeled, sliced into thin wheels, and seeded

Combine the radicchio, frisée, shallot, tarragon, apple, and pecans in a large bowl. Season with salt and pepper and dress with the red wine vinaigrette. Divide among four plates and garnish with slices of blood orange. Serve immediately.

OTHER GREENS TO TRY mixed chicories

BRUSCHETTA WITH ESCAROLE AND GORGONZOLA DOLCE

Bruschetta is basically a toast that has a really good char on it. Usually seen with tomato and basil on top, it is eaten in Italy as a light meal, sometimes topped with an egg and prosciutto. This recipe features a few dynamic flavors on each piece of toast. There is the escarole, with a bitterness that cuts through the intense richness of Gorgonzola dolce cheese. A drizzle of balsamic brightens everything. When preparing, make sure the Gorgonzola is at room temperature. And choose a high-quality, aged balsamic for the drizzle for a nice, rounded flavor that's less harsh than cheaper, unaged varieties.

SERVES 4

4 slices rustic artisanal bread

½ cup [120 ml] olive oil, plus more for finishing

12 ounces [340 g] escarole hearts, inner leaves intact with stems, from about 4 small escarole heads

Fine sea salt

6 ounces [170 g] Gorgonzola dolce

Aged balsamic vinegar, for drizzling

Flaky sea salt

Preheat the oven to 400°F [200°C].

Place the bread on a sheet pan and set aside.

Place a large ovenproof sauté pan over medium-high heat. Add the olive oil, and while it is heating, cut the escarole hearts in half lengthwise. Add the escarole hearts to the pan, and sear until dark golden brown, 2 to 4 minutes. Lightly season with fine sea salt, then flip and lightly season the other side. Place the pan with the escarole in the oven and roast until the greens are tender, 3 to 4 minutes. When tender, remove the pan from the oven and set aside to cool.

Turn the oven to broil and toast the bread, turning once, until golden on both sides, 2 to 3 minutes total, watching carefully so it does not burn. When toasted, smear each piece with one-quarter of the cheese. Top with a pile of the roasted escarole, then drizzle with the finishing oil and the balsamic vinegar and sprinkle with the flaky sea salt. Serve immediately.

OTHER GREENS TO TRY mixed chicories

RADICCHIO HAND PIES WITH QUINCE PASTE AND BLUE CHEESE

Hand pies can be sweet or savory. These are a little of both, with the sweetness of quince mingling with the pungent blue cheese and the slightly bitter radicchio. Thyme injects a smooth herbal quality that meets the sweet and savory halfway.

MAKES 6 PIES

Single-crust batch cream cheese pastry dough (page 292)

3 tablespoons olive oil

1 head radicchio, halved through the core

Kosher salt

2 tablespoons quince paste or strawberry jam

1½ ounces [40 g] blue cheese, crumbled

2 sprigs thyme

Freshly ground black pepper

1 egg

1 tablespoon heavy cream

Preheat the oven to 400°F [200°C]. Line a sheet pan with parchment paper. Using a rolling pin, roll the pastry dough disk into a rectangle ⅛ inch [3 mm] thick. Cut the rectangle into six equal smaller rectangles and place on the prepared sheet pan. Store in the refrigerator until ready to use.

To make the filling, heat the oil in a large ovenproof sauté pan over medium-high heat. Place the radicchio cut side down in the olive oil. Cook until the cut surface of the radicchio is golden and caramelized, 3 to 4 minutes. Using tongs, turn the radicchio over and season lightly with salt. Place the pan in the oven and roast until the radicchio halves are very tender when gently pressed with a finger, 15 to 20 minutes.

Allow the radicchio to cool, then cut one of the halves into narrow ribbons. Reserve the other half for another use.

Remove the pastry from the refrigerator and place a small pile of roasted radicchio in the center of each rectangle. Top each pile with one-sixth each of the quince paste and the blue cheese, then garnish with leaves picked off the thyme sprigs. Sprinkle with salt and add a few grinds of pepper.

In a small bowl, mix the egg and cream until blended. Using a pastry brush, paint a ¼-inch [6-mm] border of the egg mixture around each of the pastries. Flip the far end of the dough over the filling to its opposing side while gently using your thumbs to push the filling toward the center. Using the tines of a fork, gently press around the edges of the hand pies to make a seal. Trim any rough edges with a paring knife. Refrigerate for 30 minutes.

Brush the tops of the hand pies with the remaining egg wash, then bake in the preheated oven for about 20 minutes, rotating halfway through baking, until the pastry is flaky and golden.

Let cool before eating.

NOTE: You will have ½ head radicchio left over from this recipe. Eat it as a side dish with a steak, on a bruschetta with tarragon vinaigrette (page 302) or use it to make Salt-Roasted Yukon Gold Potatoes with Radicchio and Crème Fraîche (page 99).

OTHER GREENS TO TRY mixed chicories

PAN DI ZUCCHERO AND APPLE TART WITH TARRAGON AND HONEY

Just because this is an apple tart doesn't mean it is a dessert, even though the Italian green *pan di zucchero* translates as "sugar loaf." It is an escarole-like chicory, not too bitter, which lends a very vegetal flavor to this recipe. The roasted apples do add a lovely, sweet counterpoint, while the whole assemblage is smoothed out by a cream cheese crust.

SERVES 6 TO 8 AS AN APPETIZER, 4 AS A LIGHT ENTRÉE

Single-crust batch cream cheese pastry dough (page 292)

1½ cups [360 ml] olive oil, plus more for finishing

½ large head pan di zucchero

1 large crisp red apple, such as Gala or Braeburn, quartered and cored

Fine sea salt

8 ounces [230 g] mascarpone or cream cheese, at room temperature

1 tablespoon coarsely chopped fresh tarragon leaves

2 teaspoons fresh coarse-ground black pepper

Zest of 1 orange, finely grated on a microplane

2 to 3 tablespoons honey

1 to 2 teaspoons aged balsamic vinegar

Flaky sea salt and freshly ground black pepper

Line a 13¾ by 4½ by 1-inch [35 by 11 by 2.5-cm] fluted tart pan with the cream cheese pastry dough. Chill for 20 minutes in the freezer.

Preheat the oven to 400°F [200°C].

Place the pastry-lined tart pan on a sheet pan and cover the pastry with aluminum foil or parchment paper. Place loose dried beans or rice on the foil or parchment paper to weight down the dough as it bakes.

Place the entire sheet pan, with the tart pan on top, in the oven for 20 minutes, rotating it 180 degrees halfway through baking time. Peel back the covering to check the crust. When the crust is beginning to turn golden, remove the weights and foil or parchment and pierce with the tines of a fork in eight to ten places evenly distributed along the crust. Decrease the heat to 350°F [180°C] and return the crust to the oven until it is golden and crisp, about 10 minutes more. Cool to room temperature.

To make the filling, return the oven temperature to 400°F [200°C]. Warm the olive oil in a large ovenproof sauté pan over medium-high heat. Add the pan di zucchero, cut side down, and sear until golden. At the same time, add the apple quarters, cut side down, to the same pan. When golden, flip the pan di zucchero and place the entire pan in the oven until the apples are tender and the greens yield gently to the touch, about 30 minutes. (If the apples cook more quickly than the greens, remove them from the pan with a spatula and let cool to room temperature.) When the greens are very tender and lightly golden, remove from the oven and cool to room temperature. Season the apples and greens lightly with fine sea salt on both sides when done.

In a small bowl, mix together the mascarpone, tarragon, ½ teaspoon fine sea salt, coarse black pepper, and orange zest. Gently spread in an even layer in the baked tart shell. Slice the apples and lay them on top of the mascarpone. Separate the golden pan di zucchero leaves and fit as many as possible on the top to decorate. (All the leaves will not be needed, so reserve the additional roasted leaves for a salad or serve warm with bagna cauda, page 295.)

Garnish the tart with a drizzle of honey, aged balsamic vinegar, and olive oil and a generous sprinkling of flaky sea salt and a few grinds of black pepper.

OTHER GREENS TO TRY radicchio, romaine lettuce

Salt-Roasted Yukon Gold Potatoes with Radicchio and Crème Fraîche

SALT-ROASTED YUKON GOLD POTATOES WITH RADICCHIO AND CRÈME FRAÎCHE

A couple of recipes in this book call for just half a head of radicchio. These cute little potatoes make a great use of that other half. Though tiny, these potatoes are rich, the perfect balance for the bitterness of the radicchio. They are easy and quick to make, and they look really spiffy because of the melted cheese on top. They are the perfect accompaniment to a steak, and they make nice little hors d'oeuvres, too.

MAKES 8 SMALL STUFFED POTATOES

4 tablespoons [60 ml] olive oil

1 head radicchio, halved through the core

Kosher salt

8 small Yukon gold potatoes

½ cup [120 ml] crème fraîche or sour cream

1 green onion, green and white parts, thinly sliced into rings

1 teaspoon freshly ground black pepper

3 tablespoons finely grated Parmigiano-Reggiano

Worcestershire sauce, for drizzling

Preheat the oven to 400°F [200°C].

Heat 3 tablespoons of the olive oil in a large oven-proof sauté pan over medium-high heat. Place the radicchio, cut side down, in the pan and cook until the cut surface is golden and caramelized, 3 to 4 minutes. Using tongs, turn the radicchio over and season lightly with salt. Place the pan in the oven and roast until the radicchio halves are very tender when gently pressed with a finger, 20 to 25 minutes. Remove from the oven and allow to cool.

Place the potatoes in a bowl and toss with the remaining 1 tablespoon olive oil and 1 tablespoon salt. Toss so each potato is well coated with salt. Place the potatoes on a sheet pan and bake until tender, about 30 minutes.

Finely chop half of the roasted and cooled radicchio. Mix in a small bowl with the crème fraîche, green onion, black pepper, and a light sprinkling of salt. The roasted potatoes will be quite salty, so not much is needed for the filling.

Cut an X in the top of each potato and, holding the bottom of each potato with your thumbs and forefingers, press to open each X. Divide the radicchio filling evenly among the potatoes, then top with the Parmigiano-Reggiano.

Place the potatoes on a sheet pan and bake until hot and the cheese is melted and golden, about 15 minutes. Drizzle with Worcestershire and serve immediately.

NOTE: You will have ½ head radicchio left from this recipe. Eat it as a side dish with steak or use it to make the hand pies on page 95 or substitute for chickweed in arepas (page 85).

OTHER GREENS TO TRY frisée, pan di zucchero

BANH XEO BLT

If you want to impress dinner guests, serve this. I promise you'll get ooohs and aahhs all around. There are a few tricks to pulling off this recipe, but when done correctly, it's such a likeable dish, flavor-wise and texture-wise, because of some nontraditional ingredients. A *banh xeo* is a savory pancake, one of the best things I ate when I traveled to Vietnam. Typically it includes pork, shrimp, and sometimes chicken in the batter. I change things up a little by using bacon instead of pork and adding some ingredients you wouldn't usually see in Vietnam, like frisée. I like the frilly loftiness that the frisée brings to this dish. That frilliness holds nice texture and volume, playing off the crispiness of the crepe.

Using a good nonstick pan is key to the success of this recipe. The crepe needs to be seared until crispy, yet it needs to slide off the pan easily. Another key is to let the batter sit overnight, so

Continued

that the rice absorbs moisture and the batter becomes thicker and more conditioned.

MAKES 6 PANCAKES

¼ cup [55 g] dried mung beans

½ cup [120 ml] coconut milk, stirred before using

1 cup [140 g] white rice flour

½ cup [70 g] cornstarch

2 cups [480 ml] water

4 green onions, green and white parts, thinly sliced

½ teaspoon ground turmeric

Kosher salt

36 fresh mint leaves

36 fresh basil leaves

36 Sungold cherry tomatoes, halved

1 cucumber, peeled, halved, seeded, and thinly sliced

6 shishito peppers, thinly sliced

2 heads frisée, leaves separated, dark leaves discarded

Neutral vegetable oil, for frying

1 white onion, halved lengthwise and thinly sliced

12 thin slices bacon

Nuoc cham (recipe follows), for serving

2 heads red leaf lettuce, separated into individual leaves, for serving

In a small bowl, soak the mung beans in hot water until softened, about 30 minutes. Drain the beans and transfer them to a blender. Add the coconut milk and puree until very fine, 3 to 4 minutes. Transfer the mung bean puree to a large bowl and whisk in the rice flour, cornstarch, water, half of the green onions, and the turmeric; season with salt. The batter should be very smooth. Let the banh xeo batter rest at room temperature for at least 30 minutes or refrigerate up to overnight.

In a large bowl, combine the remaining green onions, the mint, basil, tomatoes, cucumber, peppers, and frisée. Toss to combine and set aside.

Over medium-high heat, warm 1 tablespoon vegetable oil in a 14-inch [35.5-cm] nonstick skillet. Scatter a few white onion slices around the pan, then lay the slices of bacon equidistant from each side of the pan. After 3 to 4 minutes, when the onion is golden and the bacon renders its fat, stir the batter and ladle ⅔ cup [160 ml] of it into the pan. Tilt and swirl the pan to coat the bottom with a very thin layer of batter. Drizzle 2 teaspoons vegetable oil around the edges of the crepe, allowing the oil to reach between the bottom of the pan and the crepe. Cover the skillet and cook until the bottom of the crepe is golden and crisp, about 2 minutes. Slide the crepe onto a plate and top with one-sixth of the vegetable salad. Gently fold the the crepe in half over the vegetables. Repeat with remaining ingredients to make six crepes.

Serve the nuoc cham in individual dipping bowls. To eat, tear off a piece of the crepe with the salad filling and place in a lettuce leaf. Dip into the nuoc cham and eat immediately.

OTHER GREENS TO TRY butter lettuce for wrapper, chickweed as filling

---

NUOC CHAM

MAKES 2⅓ CUPS [560 ML]

1 cup [240 ml] hot water

½ cup [100 g] sugar

½ cup [120 ml] fresh lime juice

⅓ cup [80 ml] fish sauce

2 cloves garlic, minced

1 small bird's eye chile or 1 serrano chile, thinly sliced

In a small bowl, whisk together the water and sugar until the sugar dissolves. Add the lime juice, fish sauce, garlic, and chile and stir to combine. Use immediately or store in an airtight container in the refrigerator for up to 3 days.

SLOW-ROASTED COPPA PORCHETTA WITH ESCAROLE

Coppa is the solid muscle of pork shoulder. Here it is butterflied and stuffed with a fennel and garlic. But it is the insertion of cooked escarole that adds a very delicate bitterness to the coppa. When you slice this roast it reveals a beautiful cross-section of the stuffing at the center.

SERVES 10

2 teaspoons olive oil, plus more if needed for serving

½ head escarole, chopped (about 4 cups/ 80 g)

½ yellow onion, finely diced

Kosher salt and freshly ground black pepper

1 pork coppa or boneless pork shoulder, about 5 pounds [2.3 kg]

1 teaspoon fennel pollen

Leaves of 2 sprigs rosemary (about 2 teaspoons)

½ cup [20 g] fresh bread crumbs from ciabatta or other soft, light-colored rustic bread

4 large cloves garlic, thinly sliced

In a large sauté pan, heat the olive oil over medium-high heat. Add the escarole and onion and sauté until wilted and lightly browned in places, 3 to 4 minutes. Season lightly with salt and pepper. Cool to room temperature.

Place the coppa on a cutting board. Using a sharp knife, and starting from a long side, cut horizontally through the center of the meat, stopping just short of the opposite side. Open the coppa flat like a book and then make deep, long slits through any thick areas, being careful not to cut through to the outside. Season the meat on both sides with 1 tablespoon each salt and pepper, rubbing them into the slits. Cover the cut side with the fennel pollen, rosemary leaves, bread crumbs, garlic, and escarole mixture, distributing them evenly and leaving a ½-inch [12-mm] border on all sides.

Starting from a long side, roll up the coppa, keeping all the fillings inside. Truss tightly so the roast is an even thickness. Wrap the coppa in two layers of aluminum foil, making a tight wrap with no gaps. Place in the refrigerator and marinate for 2 days prior to cooking.

Preheat the oven to 200°F [95°C].

Place the roast, still in its foil wrapping, in a glass or metal baking pan with 2-inch [5-cm] or higher sides. The roast should fit snugly in the pan, with space (about 1 inch/2.5 cm) on all sides. Roast for about 9 hours, until a thermometer reads 180°F [85°C]. Start checking the temperature after 5 hours, then every 15 or 30 minutes. When piercing the roast to check the temperature, juices will run into the pan. The pan juices are delicious, so do not discard. Allow the coppa, still wrapped, to cool at room temperature for about 1½ hours.

When unwrapping the roast, do so gently and let all of the juices run into the pan. Skim the fat from the juices. If once you snip the strings and slice the roast it is no longer warm enough to serve, heat a small amount of olive oil in a sauté pan over medium heat. Add the pork slices and heat until warm and slightly crisped. Reheat the pan juices; if they taste too salty, add a bit of chicken stock or water to balance the flavor. Serve the juices spooned over the pork slices.

OTHER GREENS TO TRY mixed chicories

CHINESE CELERY

Apium graveolens var. *secalinum*

One of China's ancient treasures, Chinese celery is said to have been used in the cuisine since the Han dynasty (206 BCE to 220 CE). It is looked upon as a coolant in traditional Chinese medicine and is used to treat everything from high blood pressure to gastrointestinal and liver ailments. Flavor-wise, it is everything that common celery is not: pungent, bitter, aromatic, herbal, and peppery. It shares the same juicy texture as common celery, though its stalks are much thinner and hollow, with delicate, wispy leaves. Chinese celery, which also goes by *kun choy*, *khuen chai*, *kan-tsai*, and *kinchay*, packs a nutritional punch with vitamins A, B, C, and D and iron and potassium.

VARIETIES GOLDEN LEAF, GREEN QUEEN, TIANJIN GREEN, WHITE STEM

SEASON Summer through early fall

HOW TO CHOOSE The stalks should be firm with no spots or wrinkling; the leaves should be perky with consistent coloring and no spots.

HOW TO CLEAN Rinse quickly under cold running water. Shake off excess water and pat dry.

HOW TO STORE Store in an airtight plastic bin or ziplock bag or wrap in plastic wrap. In the crisper drawer of the refrigerator, Chinese celery will keep for 5 to 7 days.

HOW TO REFRESH Immerse in ice water for 15 minutes. Drain and pat or spin dry.

COOKING METHODS Stir-fry, sauté, simmer in soup, or puree into soup.

PAIRINGS Chile, pork, lamb, chicken, turkey, game meats, tofu.

SAKE-BRAISED CHINESE CELERY

Braised celery with white wine is my favorite European-style way to cook conventional celery, so I wondered how that would work Asian-style. That's where the sake comes in, and I found that braising with sake nicely mellows out this bitter green. I like to serve this dish over broken jasmine rice with sweet, salty, and spicy beef short ribs, braised bok choy, and sesame pickled daikon for balance.

SERVES 4 AS A SIDE DISH

10 ounces [280 g] Chinese celery

½ cup [120 ml] sake (any variety that has a clean, round, and slightly sweet flavor works well)

½ cup [120 ml] water

½ serrano chile, thinly sliced

2 tablespoons toasted sesame oil

Fine sea salt

4 cloves garlic, thinly sliced

1 teaspoon sugar

1½ tablespoons soy sauce

Separate the thinner, leafy tops of the celery from the thicker main stalks. Then, cut the main stalk crosswise into three or four pieces roughly the same length as the leafy tops. You should end up with four or five equal lengths, one with leaves attached and the rest without.

Stack the leafless stalks in a saucepan and add the sake, water, chile, and sesame oil. Lightly season with salt. Cover, bring to a simmer, and simmer for 4 minutes. Place the leafy stalks on top of the others, re-cover, and cook for another 2 to 4 minutes, until the stalks are tender. Stir in the garlic, sugar, and soy sauce and season with salt to taste. Serve warm.

OTHER GREENS TO TRY celery, celtuce

CHRYSANTHEMUM

Glebionis coronaria

Its pretty flowers are just one reason to admire the fair chrysanthemum. Its greens, although not quite as beautiful, certainly stand out on the plate. The Chinese, Japanese, and Koreans have long known about the benefits of ingesting chrysanthemum greens, whether in tea, soups, or stir-fries, as the plants are native to East Asia. The Japanese, who are partial to including the greens (*shunkgiku*) in shabu-shabu, especially revere the plant, which is a symbol of long life. That is not surprising, since the greens of chrysanthemum, as a member of the aster family, hold an abundance of nutrients. Mild, herbal, and grassy in flavor, raw chrysanthemum leaves contain more potassium than bananas do, and they are also rich in vitamin B, carotene, fiber, and flavonoids.

VARIETIES CHOP SUEY GREEN, GARLAND CHRYSANTHEMUM, JAPANESE GREEN, ROUND LEAF, SMALL LEAF, TIGER'S EAR

SEASON Spring through fall

HOW TO CHOOSE Make sure the leaves are bright, perky, and uniformly colored, with no dark spots or yellowing.

HOW TO CLEAN Immerse in cold water and agitate with fingers. Drain; spin or pat dry.

HOW TO STORE Store in an airtight plastic bin or ziplock bag or wrap in plastic wrap. In the crisper drawer of the refrigerator, chrysanthemum will keep for up to 5 days.

HOW TO REFRESH Immerse in ice water for 15 minutes. Drain and pat or spin dry.

COOKING METHODS Serve raw in salads or cook by quickly stir-frying, steaming, or stirring into soups just before serving. Be careful— chrysanthemum greens become slimy when overcooked.

PAIRINGS Lemon, sesame, miso, mushrooms, beef, pork, poultry, fish.

CHRYSANTHEMUM GREENS WITH MISO VINAIGRETTE

The biggest thing to remember about chrysanthemum greens is that they cook really, really fast. So steam them or sauté them very quickly, watching them carefully as they cook. Because they are often found in Chinese, Japanese, Korean, and Southeast Asian dishes, the miso vinaigrette makes the perfect dressing. Pair the greens up with slow-roasted pork loin (page 274) or a roasted fish for a complete meal.

SERVES 4 AS A LIGHT MEAL OR SIDE DISH

> 12 ounces [340 g] chrysanthemum greens, tough stems discarded
>
> 4 cups [630 g] cooked Japanese sushi rice, warm
>
> Miso vinaigrette (page 300)
>
> 2 tablespoons mustard green furikake (page 297) or toasted white sesame seeds

Place a steamer basket or tray over a pot filled with 3 inches [7.5 cm] of simmering water. Put the chrysanthemum greens in the steamer and cover the pot. Steam for 20 to 30 seconds, until the greens have brightened in color and are tender but not slimy.

Divide the rice among four bowls, then top with an equal amount of the chrysanthemum greens. Drizzle the vinaigrette over the greens and top with the furikake.

OTHER GREENS TO TRY amaranth, spinach

BEEF TENDERLOIN, MAITAKE MUSHROOM, AND CHRYSANTHEMUM GREEN MISO SOUP

Chrysanthemum greens are really tender, so they are great to throw into soup raw while the soup is really hot. They have a good flavor on their own, and if they are not cooked ahead, they retain a little bit of crispiness, wilting as you eat your soup. Enjoy the experience as the greens go from slightly crispy to fully cooked once you reach the bottom of the bowl.

SERVES 4

> ½ cup [120 ml] toasted sesame oil
>
> 4 whole maitake mushrooms, broken into 10 to 12 pieces
>
> 2-inch [5-cm] piece fresh ginger, peeled and finely grated on a Microplane
>
> 8 cups [2 L] double chicken stock (page 299)
>
> 12 ounces [340 g] beef tenderloin, sliced ¼ inch [6 mm] thick
>
> ½ to ¾ cup [140 to 205 g] red miso
>
> 4 ounces [115 g] chrysanthemum leaves
>
> Kosher salt

In a small pot, warm the sesame oil over medium heat. Add the mushrooms and cook gently until tender but not browned, 3 to 4 minutes. Decrease the heat slightly, add the ginger and chicken stock, and bring to a simmer.

Add the beef and simmer gently for 1 minute. Turn the heat off and whisk in the miso, starting with ½ cup [140 g] and adding more to taste, until fully dissolved. Add the chrysanthemum leaves, then season with salt to taste. Serve immediately.

OTHER GREENS TO TRY nettles, spinach

Beef Tenderloin, Maitake Mushroom, and Chrysanthemum Green Miso Soup

COLLARD GREENS

Brassica oleracea var. acephala

A relative of cabbage and broccoli, leafy collard greens have been cultivated and eaten for millennia. Some documentation puts them on the tables of the ancient Greeks; other scholars suggest that collards may have been consumed in prehistoric times. Today, the large, deep green leaves are cultivated in South America, Africa, Europe, northern India, Southeast Asia, and in the American South, where they have a long history. The Southern style of slow-cooking collards arrived with African slaves. Earthy, slightly bitter, and mineral in flavor, they are a traditional New Year's Day dish in the South, accompanied by black-eyed peas and corn bread. The greens are also an essential part of everyday cuisine and a staple of soul food. Collards are a part of Southern folklore, too: a fresh collard leaf hung over a door ostensibly prevents evil spirits from entering, and a leaf on the forehead is thought to have the power to relieve headaches. A great source of vitamins A, C, and K and of calcium, iron, manganese, and fiber, collards have been studied for their cholesterol-lowering ability and as a digestive aid, perhaps stemming from the legend that Julius Caesar binged on collards to prevent indigestion after royal banquets.

VARIETIES ALABAMA BLUE, CHAMPION, EVEN STAR LAND RACE, GEORGIA GREEN, GREEN GLAZE, HEN PECK, MORRIS HEADING, VATES, WHITE MOUNTAIN, YELLOW CABBAGE

SEASON Winter through spring

HOW TO CHOOSE Leaves should be sprightly and a deep, vivid green, with no yellowing or dark spots.

HOW TO CLEAN Immerse in cool water. Agitate with fingers. Drain; spin or pat dry.

HOW TO STORE Trim oxidized or damaged areas. Store in an airtight plastic bin or ziplock bag or wrap in plastic wrap. In the crisper drawer of the refrigerator, collards will keep for 3 to 5 days.

HOW TO REFRESH Immerse in ice water for 15 minutes. Drain and spin or pat dry.

COOKING METHODS Sauté, steam, boil, braise, or stew.

PAIRINGS Red pepper flakes or fresh chile, soy sauce, tofu, soybeans, fish sauce, sesame, garlic, vinegar, onions, pork, turkey, ham, black beans, fish, mushrooms, eggs, other greens such as kale, turnip greens, spinach.

SIU MAI WITH COLLARD GREENS

Siu mai are traditionally served without a dipping sauce, but I feel like they need one to complement the meat and greens.

These take some time to make, but the time is well spent because they are so beautiful and satisfying. Using collard greens and pork here speaks to both Asian cuisine and to the cuisine of the American South, though any leafy Asian greens can be substituted for the collards.

MAKES ABOUT 50 DUMPLINGS, SERVES 10

3 tablespoons canola oil

4 ounces [115 g] shiitake mushrooms, stemmed and quartered

4 ounces [115 g] collard greens, stemmed and leaves sliced into 1-inch [2.5-cm] ribbons

½ cup [120 ml] water

Kosher salt

2 ounces [55 g] fresh ginger (about 2 inches/ 5 cm), peeled and finely chopped

1 large clove garlic, finely chopped

1 pound [455 g] ground pork

2 teaspoons fish sauce

1 teaspoon toasted sesame oil

1 package round wonton wrappers (about 50)

Soy dipping sauce (page 296)

Over medium high-heat, warm the canola oil in a large sauté pan. Add the mushrooms and cook, gently stirring, until tender, 3 to 4 minutes. Add the collard greens and water. Bring to a gentle simmer, then decrease the heat to medium. Cook gently until the greens are tender and the water has evaporated, 3 to 4 minutes. Lightly season with salt and set aside to cool.

Line a large sheet pan with parchment paper.

Combine the ginger, garlic, pork, fish sauce, sesame oil, and 2 teaspoons salt in a large bowl. Gently stir to mix, making sure not to overmix, which would make the texture pasty. Finely chop the cooled vegetables and gently mix into the pork mixture.

To wrap the siu mai, place a wonton wrapper in the palm of one hand. Place about 1 tablespoon of the filling in the middle of the wrapper. Bring two opposite edges toward each other and press gently to adhere them to the filling. Repeat with the remaining two edges to form a little cup around the filling, gently squeezing to hold the wrapper in place. Try to form flutes on the edges of the dumpling, making the dumpling look like a flower. Pat the top of the filling flat and squeeze the bottom of the dumpling, making sure to fill any gaps in the wrapper. Place the formed siu mai on the prepared sheet pan. Continue wrapping the remaining siu mai filling. The siu mai can be cooked immediately or frozen.

To steam the dumplings, line a steamer basket or tray with parchment paper (napa cabbage leaves will also work). Pour enough water into the steaming pot or wok so the water is about 1 inch (2.5 cm) below the bottom of the steamer basket or tray. Bring to a boil.

Working in batches, arrange the siu mai in the prepared steamer basket or tray, leaving room around each dumpling. Steam fresh siu mai until cooked through, about 7 minutes. If frozen, steam for about 12 minutes. To test for doneness, pierce the filling with a metal skewer and hold it there for a few seconds. Then, touch the skewer to your lip to see how warm the center is.

Transfer to a plate and serve with the dipping sauce.

OTHER GREENS TO TRY chard, mustard greens, spinach, bok choy leaves

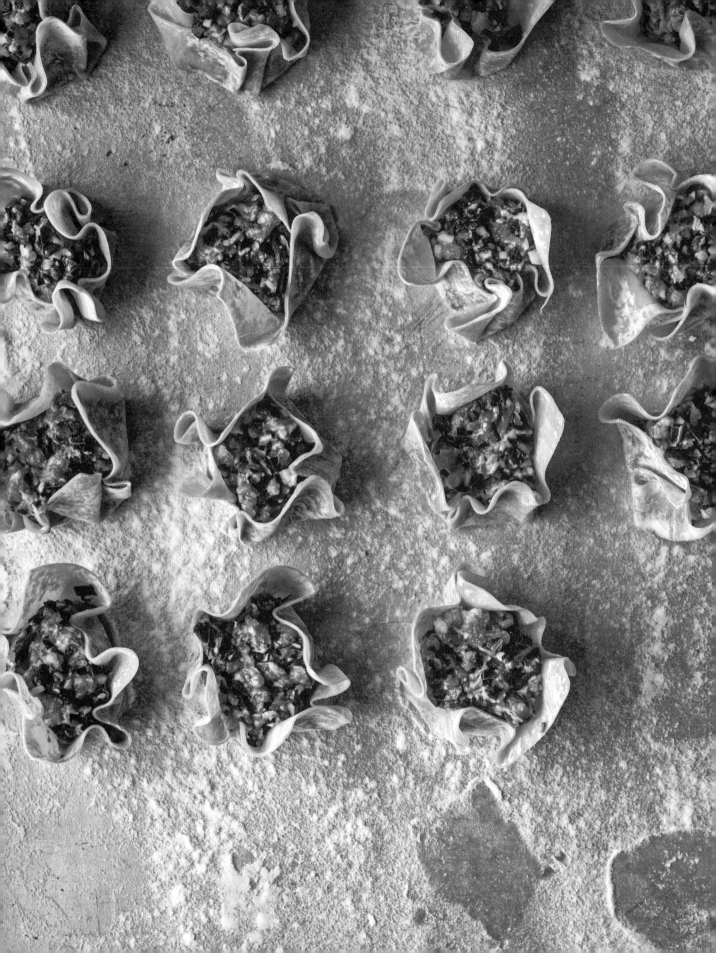

SUMMER VEGETABLE MINESTRONE

I have always wondered why people seem to prefer pasta instead of rice in minestrone. Both are traditionally used in Italy, but in the United States, you are more than likely to find small pasta—like *ditalini*—in a minestrone. I prefer rice in mine, particularly Arborio rice, which is exceedingly absorbent and gets nice and puffy in a soup. Collard greens play the role of broccoli rabe or escarole in this recipe, with just a touch of bitter. And the fresh herbs really come to the fore in this light, summery version. Feel free to add eggplant, green beans, or whatever seasonal vegetables you might have on hand. Adding a rind of Parmigiano-Reggiano or a heel of prosciutto, if on hand, deepens the flavor.

SERVES 4 TO 6

3 tablespoons olive oil, plus ¼ cup [60 ml] for drizzling

½ yellow onion, minced

2 cloves garlic, minced

1 large sweet bell pepper, diced

½ teaspoon dried red pepper flakes

4-inch [10-cm] sprig rosemary

4 fresh sage leaves

2 sprigs thyme

1 teaspoon fresh or dried oregano leaves

3 bay leaves

1 teaspoon fennel pollen or toasted and ground fennel seeds

1 small zucchini (6 ounces/170 g), diced

1 cup [175 g] fresh corn kernels

1 pound [455 g] tomatoes, pureed and strained (about 2 cups/480 ml)

4 to 6 cups [960 ml to 1.4 L] double chicken stock (page 299) or vegetable stock

2-ounce [55-g] piece Parmigiano-Reggiano rind (optional)

½ cup [100 g] Arborio rice

1 pound [455 g] collard greens, stems discarded and leaves cut into ½-inch [12-mm] ribbons

Kosher salt and freshly ground black pepper

½ cup [15 g] lightly packed finely grated Parmigiano-Reggiano, for garnish

In a large pot, warm the olive oil over medium-high heat. And the onion, garlic, bell pepper, pepper flakes, rosemary, sage, thyme, oregano, bay leaves and fennel pollen, and cook until the onion is translucent, about 4 minutes. (If the garlic or onion begins to brown, decrease the heat.) Add the zucchini and corn and cook just until the zucchini begins to soften, 3 to 4 minutes. Add the tomato puree, 4 cups [960 ml] of the chicken stock, and the Parmigiano-Reggiano rind. Bring to a gentle simmer, then stir in the rice. Cook, stirring occasionally, until the rice just starts to become tender, 10 to 12 minutes.

Add the collard greens to the soup and continue cooking until the greens are tender, about 5 minutes. Add additional stock, as needed, to thin the soup. The rice will absorb some liquid and the soup can become too thick.

Remove the bay leaves, Parmigiano-Reggiano rind, and herb stems from the soup and season with salt and pepper.

Ladle the soup into bowls and garnish with the Parmigiano-Reggiano and a drizzle of olive oil.

OTHER GREENS TO TRY kale, spinach

BAKED TURKEY EGGS WITH MOREL MUSHROOMS AND PANCETTA

A trip to the farmers' market inspired this recipe. I simply walked through, picked up a bunch of ingredients, and came up with this wonderful combination where each ingredient was at the seasonal height of its flavor. I think the collard greens are what especially make this work. Their mineral flavor brings some earthiness into the rich, creamy turkey egg.

SERVES 6

1 green garlic

3 tablespoons olive oil, plus more as needed

8 ounces [230 g] pancetta tesa (flat pancetta), regular pancetta, or bacon, cut into lardons

4 ounces [115 g] small morel mushrooms or your favorite mushroom, cut into pieces if large

1½ pounds [680 g] collard greens, trimmed of tough ribs and stems, blanched, and cut into 1-inch [2.5-cm] ribbons

Kosher salt and freshly ground black pepper

1½ cups [360 ml] heavy cream

4 turkey or 9 to 12 chicken eggs

Preheat the oven to 400°F [200°C].

Trim off the green tops of the green garlic and reserve for another use. Thinly slice the white part.

Warm the olive oil in a 10-inch [25-cm] cast-iron skillet over medium heat. Add the lardons and sauté until just starting to brown, 3 to 4 minutes. Add the mushrooms and decrease the heat. Add the green garlic and the collard greens and sauté another 4 to 5 minutes. If the mixture is too dry, add more olive oil. Season with salt and pepper, add the cream, and stir until combined. Crack the eggs over the mixture and season the eggs lightly with salt and pepper. Transfer the pan to the oven and bake until the egg whites are set but the yolks are still runny, 4 to 5 minutes. Serve immediately.

OTHER GREENS TO TRY chard, kale

WEST AFRICAN PEANUT STEW WITH COLLARD GREENS AND SWEET POTATOES

Peanut stews are a signature dish of West Africa. This adaptation also beckons to the flavors of the American South because of the earthy, nutritious trio of peanuts, collard greens, and sweet potatoes. I think the blend of flavors demonstrates the deep ties that both cultures share. But what really distinguishes my version: the punch of heat and spice that the ginger and jalapeño add.

SERVES 8

¼ cup [60 ml] neutral vegetable oil

4 cloves garlic, minced

2-inch [5-cm] piece fresh ginger, peeled and minced

½ to 1 jalapeño chile, finely chopped

1 yellow onion, finely chopped

1 teaspoon ground cumin

1 sweet potato, about 1 pound [455 g], peeled and cut into medium-size pieces

1½ cups [360 ml] tomato puree

6 cups [1.4 L] double chicken stock (page 229) or vegetable stock

1 bunch collard greens, about 13 ounces [385 g], stemmed and leaves cut into ½-inch [12-mm] ribbons (about 3 cups/250 g)

1 cup [265 g] chunky natural peanut butter

Fine sea salt

Cooked long-grain white rice, for serving

¼ cup [15 g] coarsely chopped fresh cilantro

1½ cups [210 g] roasted peanuts

2 cups [160 g] unsweetened shredded dried coconut, toasted

Warm the oil in a large pot over medium-high heat. Add the garlic, ginger, chile to taste, onion, and cumin and cook, stirring occasionally, until the onion and garlic are tender, about 4 minutes. Decrease the heat if the vegetables begin to brown.

Add the sweet potato, tomato puree, stock, and collard greens, stir well, and bring to a gentle simmer. Dilute the peanut butter with some of the hot liquid from the pot until it is fluid, then add the diluted peanut butter to the pot and stir until evenly distributed in the hot liquid. Season with salt, adjust the heat to maintain a gentle simmer, and cook until the sweet potato is tender, about 10 minutes. The mixture should thicken slightly, becoming more stew-like.

Spoon the rice into shallow bowls and spoon the stew over the top. Garnish with the cilantro, peanuts, and coconut and serve immediately.

OTHER GREENS TO TRY kale, chard

RYAN'S COLLARD GREENS

This recipe comes from my friend Ryan Harris, an exceptionally talented chef who lives in the Napa Valley. He is an amazing culinary craftsperson, even making his own bacon from heritage pigs, and he puts a lot of passion into everything he does. Ryan is from the South, and I like this recipe of his for collard greens because it reflects his exploration of what it means to be a Southerner. It is also an example of how he takes time to do something thoughtfully, respectfully, and skillfully. I love what the long baking does to the texture of the collards, turning them absolutely velvety.

SERVES 8

6 ounces [170 g] slab bacon, cut into matchstick-size lardons

2 yellow onions, julienned or cut into half-moons ¼ inch [6 mm] thick

Kosher salt

3 bunches collard greens (about 4½ pounds/2 kg total), stems discarded

½ cup [120 ml] cider vinegar, plus more as needed

Preheat the oven to 250°F [120°C].

Place the bacon in a large cold pan and place over medium heat. Cook until the bacon renders some of its fat, 3 to 4 minutes. Add the onions and a pinch of salt and cook, stirring occasionally, just until translucent, 3 to 4 minutes. Add the collard greens and toss until they start to wilt, 2 to 4 minutes. Add the vinegar, turn the heat to high, and cook for 1 to 2 minutes.

Remove the pan from heat, cover the top with parchment paper, and then cover the parchment with aluminum foil. Transfer the pan to the oven and bake for 3½ hours.

Remove from the oven and remove the foil and the parchment, being careful the escaping steam does not burn you. Toss the collards, cut them if you like, and then adjust the seasoning with salt and with additional vinegar. Serve immediately.

OTHER GREENS TO TRY chard, kale

DANDELION GREENS

Taraxacum officinale

Often looked upon as a scourge to the suburban lawn, dandelions—especially their greens—are healthy and delectable in the kitchen. The word *dandelion* derives from the French *dent de lion*, or "lion's tooth," which alludes to the serrated greens around the flower head. The greens have an intense and bitter flavor when raw that mellows somewhat when cooked, and either way, they have the power to break up overly rich dishes. Dandelions have been used medicinally since the tenth century in the Middle East, and today are still considered to have properties that support a healthy liver, digestive system, and blood. The US Department of Agriculture cites that dandelion greens have more nutritional value than spinach and broccoli, as they are rich in vitamins A, B, C, E, and K and in potassium, protein, omega-3 and omega-6 fatty acids, calcium, iron, manganese, magnesium, phosphorus, and copper.

VARIETIES AMÉLIORÉ A COEUR PLEIN, BROAD LEAVED, VERT DE MONTMAGNY

SEASON Early to midspring

HOW TO CHOOSE Look for vibrant green, firm leaves without any wilting, brown spots, or discoloration. Choose younger, smaller leaves for salad; choose older, larger leaves for cooking because they are less tender and more bitter.

HOW TO CLEAN Immerse in cold water and agitate with fingers. Drain; spin or pat dry.

HOW TO STORE Store in an airtight plastic bin or ziplock bag or wrap in plastic wrap. In the crisper drawer of the refrigerator, dandelion greens should keep for 3 to 5 days.

HOW TO REFRESH Immerse in ice water for 15 minutes. Drain and pat or spin dry.

COOKING METHODS Serve raw in a salad or cook by blanching, baking, sautéing, stir-frying, or simmering in soups or stews.

PAIRINGS Garlic, lemon, olive oil, shallots, chiles, apples, pears, peaches, plums, beets, dairy, white beans, chickpeas, tomatoes, pork, bacon.

DANDELION GREENS, PROSCIUTTO, AND OLIVE PICNIC CAKE

The British love to picnic, and they have this great dish called "picnic cake" in which they include all of the elements of a square meal: meat, egg, vegetables. It is cleverly portable and a great vehicle for spinning out new dishes from leftovers, which can include turning the cake into French toast or just toasting it in a pan with butter. This is my Italian version of picnic cake.

MAKES ONE 9 BY 5-INCH [23 BY 12-CM] LOAF, SERVES 10

3 ounces [45 g] grated Pecorino Romano cheese (about ¾ cup)

2 tablespoons olive oil

2 shallots, sliced

1 large clove garlic, sliced

4 ounces [115 g] dandelion greens, thick stems discarded, cut into ½-inch [12-mm] pieces

4 ounces [115 g] prosciutto, cut into ¼-inch [6-mm] pieces

10 ounces [280 g] assorted olives (about 1 cup), pitted and coarsely chopped

Kosher salt and freshly ground black pepper

1 cup [240 ml] whole milk

¼ cup [55 g] unsalted melted butter

1 egg

¾ cup [180 ml] crème fraîche

2 cups [280 g] all-purpose flour

1 tablespoon baking powder

¼ teaspoon ground cayenne pepper

6 ounces [170 g] Fontina Val d'Aosta or Gruyère, cut into ¼-inch [6-mm] pieces

¼ cup [10 g] loosely packed fresh, coarsely chopped flat-leaf parsley

Preheat the oven to 350°F [180°C]. Line the bottom and sides of a 9 by 5-inch [23 by 12-cm] loaf pan with parchment paper, leaving an overhang of about 1 inch [2.5 cm] on the long sides. Sprinkle half of the Pecorino Romano evenly along the bottom of the pan. Set aside.

Warm the olive oil in a small sauté pan over medium-high heat. Add the shallots, garlic, greens, and prosciutto and cook, stirring often, until the vegetables are tender, about 3 minutes. Add the olives and season lightly with salt and pepper. Cool to room temperature.

In a small bowl, whisk together the milk, butter, egg, and crème fraîche. In a larger bowl, whisk together the flour, baking powder, cayenne, 1 teaspoon salt, and 1 teaspoon pepper. Mix in the Fontina, parsley, and the cooked greens mixture. Using a large rubber spatula, fold the wet ingredients into the dry and stop when they are just combined. The mixture is meant to be wet and loose. Pour the batter into the pan and sprinkle the remaining Pecorino Romano on top. Bake for 45 to 50 minutes, until a skewer inserted in the center comes out clean.

Cool in the pan for 10 to 15 minutes. Using a paring knife, release the cake from the short ends of the pan and then lift the cake out of the pan with the parchment liner. Slice with a serrated knife and serve warm. This cake is best stored in a couple layers of plastic wrap and reheated before serving, but it tastes great at room temperature, too.

OTHER GREENS TO TRY mixed chicories

PANISSE WITH DANDELION GREENS

Hailing from the Provence region of France, these are the real French fries, made with chickpea flour and immersed in hot oil. They are also popular in Sicily, where they are known as *panelle*. In both countries, they are a portable snack that is easy to make.

I added dandelion greens to this recipe to break up the richness of the fritters. In turn, the greens lose some of their harshness when dressed with olive oil and lemon. Here, the greens are a raw accompaniment to give a little bit of bitter structure to something so earthy.

SERVES 8 AS AN APPETIZER OR SNACK

1 tablespoon olive oil, plus more for the baking dish

2¼ cups [270 g] chickpea flour

1½ ounces [40 g] Pecorino Romano, grated, plus more for garnishing

Fine sea salt

½ teaspoon ground cayenne pepper

¼ teaspoon freshly grated nutmeg

1 small clove garlic

4 cups [960 ml] water

About 1½ cups [360 ml] neutral vegetable oil, for frying

4 ounces [115 g] dandelion greens, thick stems discarded

1 lemon, cut into wedges

Lightly coat a 13 by 9-inch [33 by 23-cm] baking dish with olive oil. Set aside.

Combine the chickpea flour, Pecorino Romano, 1 teaspoon salt, cayenne, nutmeg, garlic, and water in a blender. Process on high speed for about 2 minutes, until the batter is smooth.

Transfer the mixture to a large, heavy saucepan and cook over medium-high heat, whisking constantly, until bubbling and very thick, 8 to 10 minutes. Switch to a wooden spoon when the dough is no longer whiskable. If dough is not cooked long enough, it will not hold together when fried. Make sure that you can see the bottom of the pan when stirring, and that the dough is not collapsing back on itself. The dough should be very thick, like wet sand, and should not retreat too fast when stirred.

Pour the chickpea mixture into the prepared baking dish and smooth the top with a rubber spatula. Press plastic wrap directly onto the surface and refrigerate until firm, at least 3 hours or up to 2 days.

Turn the chilled chickpea mixture out onto a cutting board and cut into 3 by ½-inch [7.5-cm by 12-mm] pieces, like fat French fries.

Pour the vegetable oil into a large skillet to a depth of ¼ inch [6 mm] and heat over medium-high heat. Line a plate with paper towels. To test if the oil is hot enough, toss in a small piece of the chickpea mixture; if the oil bubbles up around it on contact (350°F/180°C), it is ready. Working in batches to avoid crowding the pan, add the cut chickpea pieces and fry, turning once, until deep golden brown and crisp, about 2 minutes per side. Transfer to the paper towel–lined plate and season with salt.

Cut the dandelion greens into thirds, season with salt, and dress with the juice from half of the lemon wedges and with the olive oil. Serve the greens alongside a pile of panisses and garnish with a sprinkling of Pecorino Romano and the remaining lemon wedges.

OTHER GREENS TO TRY frisée, puntarelle

SIMPLE DANDELION GREENS SALAD

It's amazing what you can build with a green, a squeeze of lemon, a drizzle of olive oil, and a little salt. This is a prime example.

SERVES 1

1½ ounces [40 g] dandelion greens, thick stems removed and discarded

1 fig or apricot, fresh or grilled, quartered

Fresh lemon juice

Olive oil

Aged balsamic vinegar

Fine sea salt

Put the greens and fruit in a bowl and add a squeeze of lemon and a drizzle of olive oil and vinegar. Season with salt, toss together, and serve.

OTHER GREENS TO TRY mixed chicories, chickweed

DEVILED EGGS WITH DANDELION GREENS AND CORNICHON

This is a companion recipe to Deviled Eggs with Vietnamese Coriander and Chile (page 142). It's a more traditional deviled egg and another example of how greens and eggs make such a great pair. These are marked by sharpness because of the combo of dandelion greens, cornichon, and mustard.

MAKES 12 HALVES

8 eggs

2 teaspoons Dijon mustard

¼ cup [60 ml] crème fraîche or sour cream

6 tablespoons [30 g] finely chopped dandelion greens, thick stems discarded

4 cornichons, minced

1 teaspoon fine sea salt

Place the eggs in a bowl and cover with hot water from the tap. Set aside for 15 minutes to temper the eggs.

Fill a large bowl with ice water. Fill a large pot with water and bring to a simmer. Remove the eggs from the tempering water and add to the simmering water. Cook for 10 minutes, then remove and place in the ice water to stop the cooking. Allow to chill for 15 minutes in the ice water.

Remove the eggs from the ice bath and gently peel. Rinse off any shell that may still be attached.

Cut the eggs in half and put the yolks in a bowl. Mix in the mustard, crème fraîche, dandelion greens, cornichons, and salt and stir until smooth and combined. Using a small scoop or teaspoon, fill the egg whites with the yolk mixture. The yolks of 8 eggs should fill 12 egg-white halves, with 4 white halves leftover for another use. Enjoy immediately or refrigerate for up to 12 hours.

OTHER GREENS TO TRY mixed chicories

DANDELION SALAD SANDWICH

I originally made this sandwich with kale, which is delicious, too. But I started to wonder what other greens would work as the centerpiece, not just as a garnish, of a sandwich. Dandelion greens shine because of their intensity, and when dressed with lemon juice and olive oil, they are mellowed out just enough and still have a satisfying amount of crunch. What especially appeals to me about this sandwich is the notion of making a salad completely portable.

SERVES 1

2 slices seeded whole-grain bread

¼ cup [60 g] butternut squash puree (page 298)

1 medium-boiled egg (page 293), cut into 8 slices

Flaky sea salt

1 ounce [30 g] dandelion greens, thick stems discarded and leaves cut into ¼-inch [6-mm] ribbons

A few pieces of shallot or red onion, cut paper-thin with a knife or shaved on a mandoline

Fresh lemon juice

Olive oil

Lay the bread slices on a work surface and spread one slice with a good slathering of butternut squash puree. Line up the slices of egg across the puree, then season the egg with the flaky salt. (This sandwich works just as well you if reverse the layers of egg and greens.)

In a bowl, toss the greens and shallot with a squeeze of lemon and a drizzle of olive oil. Season with salt and toss to coat evenly. Place the greens on top of the egg and close the sandwich with the remaining bread slice. Using a serrated knife, cut in half and enjoy immediately.

OTHER GREENS TO TRY head lettuces, kale

GAI LAN (CHINESE BROCCOLI)

Brassica oleracea alboglabra

Though labeled as "Chinese," gai lan was introduced to China by Portuguese traders in the sixteenth century, and its popularity spread to the cuisine of other Asian nations, especially Vietnam, Myanmar, Thailand, Laos, and Cambodia. The fact that it is also known as Chinese kale betrays the flavor of the thick-stemmed, dark-leaved green: it tastes like a cross of broccoli and kale and is often described as a stronger, more bitter broccoli. In fact, gai lan and broccoli were paired to create the hybrid known as broccolini. Gai lan is rich in vitamins A, C, and K and in iron and calcium, and recent studies have suggested that it possesses nutrients beneficial to the cardiovascular system.

VARIETIES BIG BOY, BLUE STAR, CHINA LEGEND, CRISPY BLUE, FLOWER KALE, GREEN DELIGHT, HYBRID BLUE WONDER, HYBRID SOUTHERN BLUE, SOUTH SEA, THICK STEM WINNER

SEASON Spring through fall

HOW TO CHOOSE Leaves and stems should be firm and perky. Make sure the stem ends are not dried out or shriveled. Pass up stems with brown spots or white circles.

HOW TO CLEAN Cut the leaves from the stems, then wash thoroughly under cold running water. Pat dry. Thick stems should be peeled with a vegetable peeler before cooking.

HOW TO STORE Store in an airtight plastic bin or ziplock bag or wrap in plastic wrap. In the crisper drawer of the refrigerator, gai lan will keep for up to 1 week.

HOW TO REFRESH Immerse leaves and stems in ice water for 15 minutes. Drain and dry.

COOKING METHODS Stir-fry, steam, sauté, boil, blanch, grill, or roast.

PAIRINGS Ginger, garlic, chiles, oyster sauce, fish sauce, anchovies, pork, poultry.

MISO SOUP WITH TURMERIC, WHEAT NOODLES, AND GAI LAN

When I went to Vietnam, I was floored by how many different varieties of greens there were—greens I've never seen before. Gai lan, however, is pretty accessible in the United States, and palatable and approachable for Americans. It is not pungent and bitter, like a chicory, and it has this innate sweetness, so I look on it as a gateway green. The leaves are distinctly intense and chlorophyl-rich in flavor. Gai lan is typically steamed, with the leaves and stems together. I started to think how interesting gai lan might be in a soup if the stems were cut really thin and the leaves were wilted at the last minute, so they didn't overcook. It works great in this colorful mix of miso, turmeric, and thin Chinese wheat noodles.

SERVES 4

½ cup [120 ml] toasted sesame oil

2 large shallots or 8 small Asian shallots, sliced ⅛ inch [3 mm] thick

4-inch [10-cm] piece fresh turmeric, peeled and finely grated on a Microplane

8 cups [2 L] double chicken stock (page 299) or vegetable stock

12 ounces [340 g] gai lan, stems cut into ¼-inch [6-mm] pieces, leaves cut into 2-inch [5-cm] ribbons

½ cup [140 g] red miso

9 ounces [255 g] fresh thin Chinese wheat noodles

2 tablespoons white vinegar

4 eggs

Shichimi togarashi, for sprinkling

Bring a pot of water to a gentle simmer.

In a separate large pot, warm the sesame oil over medium heat. Add the shallots and cook until translucent but not brown, 3 to 4 minutes. Decrease the heat slightly, add the turmeric, and cook for 2 more minutes.

Add the chicken stock and bring to a simmer. Add the thicker gai lan stems and cook for 2 minutes, until tender. Whisk the miso into the stock to fully dissolve, add the gai lan leaves, and stir to wilt. Turn the heat down to low to keep soup warm; do not allow to simmer.

Add the noodles to the pot of simmering water and cook for about 3 minutes, until they are al dente and retain a snappy texture. Scoop out the noodles with a fine-mesh skimmer or sieve and add to the soup.

Add the vinegar to the simmering water and poach the eggs in the acidulated water as directed on page 293.

Divide the soup among four large bowls, top each bowl with an egg, and then sprinkle with shichimi togarashi. Serve immediately.

OTHER GREENS TO TRY bok choy, chard

STEAMED GAI LAN

I always keep this quick, basic, go-to preparation in my back pocket for when I have an abundance of gai lan on hand.

Pour 1 inch [2.5 cm] of water into a pan and season with salt. Bring to a simmer. If the gai lan stalks are especially long, cut them in half crosswise. If small, use whole. Put the gai lan in the pan and steam until the stems are tender and the leaves have wilted, 4 to 5 minutes. Serve with a drizzle of soy sauce or oyster sauce.

TIP: Add a piece of fresh ginger and a garlic clove to the water for more flavor.

Curry leaves

Lovage

Nasturtium leaves

Sawtooth coriander

Pandan

Lemon balm

HERBS

The following herbs are ones I really love, and ones I think are unique and will provide a basis for understanding a wider variety of herbs without being intimidated when encountering them at the Asian grocery or at the farmers' market. When it comes down to it, herbs are small, flavor-packed leafy greens; they can be used like greens and are just as versatile as some of the vegetables in this book, which means you can go beyond just tossing them in as seasoning at the last minute. It is fun to grow herbs that you cannot typically buy and to learn how to use them. In the following recipes, the herbs are a major component, adding a lot of flavor. My goal with this chapter is also to demonstrate how to use herbs intentionally and deliciously and how to cross different cultures through their use.

CURRY LEAF
Murraya koenigii

Native to South Asia, curry leaves are powerfully flavored, though very different from curry powder. Curry leaves actually come from the thin-stemmed curry tree. Their flavor is complex, and their aroma is pungent and exotic to Westerners. Curry leaves are known for adding depth to Indian and Sri Lankan cuisine. Curry leaves are also used widely in Ayurvedic medicine, and their abundance of nutrients—vitamins A, B, C, and E and folate and iron—are believed to aid in digestion, and to treat anemia, diabetes, and high cholesterol.

NASTURTIUM LEAVES
Tropaeolum majus

Its spicy, peppery flavor is often compared to watercress, so it is no surprise that nasturtium belongs to the same family, Brassicaceae, as the cresses. Its most common use is in salads, though the sturdy nature of nasturtium leaves allows them to be stuffed, à la grape leaves (page 225). A rich source of vitamin C and iron, nasturtiums were traditionally used to prevent scurvy and as a salve, expectorant, antiseptic, and pest repellent among indigenous communities in the Andes.

LOVAGE
Levisticum officinale

Though the flavor of lovage is often compared to celery—it is also called "false celery"—it is not quite as mild. Its similarity, however, makes it a natural as a soup flavoring. Like celery, it is also a great way to jazz up a potato or chicken salad. The feathery leaves are high in vitamin C and quercetin, a plant pigment used as an immunity booster. Scotch lovage is a different genus (*Ligusticum scoticum*) but still something I love and sometimes use with mint to make Butter Lettuce Panna Cotta (page 157).

PANDAN
Pandanus amaryllifolius

The leaves of the tropical screwpine might not be considered an herb per se, but pandan is often used like an herb because of its aromatic quality, and its licorice-like sweetness makes it a fitting companion for desserts. In savory dishes, the leaves are used to wrap meats or fish before grilling or steaming. Pandan has a high content of vitamin C and beta-carotene.

SHISO

Perilla frutescens var. *crispa*

A common sight at Japanese restaurants—as a garnish on a sushi platter, perhaps, or battered and deep-fried on a tempura plate—powerfully flavored, perfumey shiso, also called perilla, comes in green, red, and purple varieties. Leaf size varies—the larger ones are often used in Vietnamese cooking as a wrap, like lettuce. Shiso is a rich source of vitamins A, B, and C and of dietary fiber, calcium, iron, and potassium and is thought to have anti-inflammatory properties.

VIETNAMESE CORIANDER

Persicaria odorata

Also known as hot mint, *daun laksa*, *daun kakok*, *daun kesum*, *laksa lef*, and *rau ram*, this popular Southeast Asian herb has a potent, flavor some-where between tarragon and chives. In Vietnam, it is often used in soups, salads, sandwiches, and as a companion to fried and grilled foods. Vietnamese coriander is rich with vitamins A, E, K, and folate.

SEASON Most herbs grow best spring through fall. Hearty herbs (such as bay leaf or rosemary) can last all year long in temperate areas.

HOW TO CHOOSE Herbs should be aromatic with sprightly green leaves. Avoid herbs with yellowing, wilted leaves and any brown or dark spots.

HOW TO CLEAN Immerse in cool water. Agitate with fingers. Drain; spin or pat dry.

HOW TO STORE Store in an airtight plastic bin or ziplock bag or wrap in plastic wrap. In the crisper drawer of the refrigerator, herbs should keep for 4 to 7 days.

HOW TO REFRESH Immerse in ice water for 15 minutes. Drain and pat or spin dry.

23 THINGS TO DO WITH HERBS

1 Combine delicate herbs for an herb salad to accompany fish.

2 Chop herbs with garlic and a fresh chile for an overnight marinade on meat.

3 Use to make pesto for a soup garnish.

4 Whip herbs into soft butter with sea salt to put on everything: pasta, baked potato, steak.

5 Garnish scrambled eggs with chives and chervil.

6 Muddle herbs into a cocktail.

7 Top your bagel, lox, and cream cheese with dill.

8 Add mint, cilantro, Vietnamese coriander, fresh chile, and a poached egg to congee for a Vietnamese breakfast.

9 Add herbs to any vinaigrette when tossing a salad.

10 Add herbs to fish and bake in parchment.

11 Add fresh oregano and Parmigiano-Reggiano to tuna salad.

12 Hang bumper crops of herbs from your garden to dry them, then package them airtight to use all winter.

13 Infuse basil, mint, sage, or lemon verbena into cream when making ice cream.

14 Add herbs to fruit for summer fruit crisps.

15 Top yogurt or ricotta with herbs, honey, and nuts for breakfast.

16 Stir pesto or an herb puree into risotto just before serving.

17 Warm honey with rosemary, cool, strain, then drizzle over oatmeal or peanut butter toast.

18 Add chopped herbs to a bread dough when mixing.

19 Add epazote to beans when cooking. Toss epazote with cabbage and pineapple to garnish tacos.

20 Stir thyme leaves into pound cake batter, bake, then garnish with thyme leaves cooked in a lemon simple syrup.

21 Toss warm potatoes with pesto or chopped herbs.

22 Add sage leaves when making brown butter.

23 Fry thyme and parsley leaves for an edible garnish on vegetables or meat.

LAMB RAGÙ WITH LOVAGE LEAVES

Lovage adds an herbal quality that nicely contrasts with the richness of the lamb in this sauce. Many liken the flavor of lovage to celery leaves, but I feel the flavor goes beyond that. Think of celery, parsley, and a tiny kick of curry— it is a flavor rarely experienced in American cuisine. This is an example of the power that herbs can bring to a dish. Serve over pasta or soft polenta and garnish with grated Pecorino Romano.

MAKES 6 CUPS [1.4 L]

½ cup [120 ml] olive oil

3 ounces [85 g] pancetta or prosciutto, finely chopped

2¼ pounds [1 kg] boneless lamb shoulder, cut into ¾-inch [2-cm] dice

1 yellow onion, diced

2 cloves garlic, thinly sliced

2 bay leaves

½ teaspoon dried red pepper flakes

½ cup [140 g] tomato paste

¾ cup [180 ml] red wine

10 cups [2.4 L] double chicken stock (page 299), plus up to ½ cup [120 ml] more as needed

Kosher salt and freshly ground black pepper

2 cups [20 g] loosely packed lovage leaves, coarsely chopped

In a large pot, warm the olive oil over medium heat. Add the pancetta and lamb shoulder and cook, stirring occasionally, until the meat is browned and browned bits are sticking to the bottom of the pot, 8 to 10 minutes. If the drippings on the bottom of the pot become too dark or look like they will burn, decrease the heat.

With a slotted spoon, transfer the meat to a bowl, leaving about 3 tablespoons fat in the pot and discarding any excess. Add the onion, garlic, bay leaves, and red pepper flakes and sauté over medium heat until the onion is translucent but not brown, about 4 minutes. The moisture from the onion will help deglaze the pan (dislodge the browned bits).

Add the tomato paste and cook until the tomato caramelizes (it will begin to stick to the bottom of the pot and turn dark red), 4 to 6 minutes. If the tomato paste gets too dark, decrease the heat. Add the wine, increase the heat to medium-high, and bring to a simmer. Use a wooden spoon to scrape up the browned bits from the bottom of the pot and then simmer until the wine has almost completely evaporated, 5 to 7 minutes.

Add the chicken stock and bring to a gentle simmer. Return the meat to the pot, turn the heat to medium-low, and simmer gently—the liquid should bubble lazily—until the meat is tender and the sauce is reduced and rich. Be patient; this will take about 3 hours. Be careful not to let the sauce boil. If the sauce becomes too thick, add up to ½ cup [120 ml] additional chicken stock. Season lightly with salt and pepper and discard the bay leaves. Stir in the lovage leaves just before serving.

To store, transfer to an airtight container and refrigerate for up to 2 days or freeze for up to 1 month. To thaw, place in the refrigerator overnight or until fully thawed.

OTHER GREENS TO TRY rosemary, basil, mint, spinach

CURRY LEAF DOSA

A dosa is a fermented rice and lentil crepe. And what curry leaves do to an otherwise simply flavored dosa in this recipe is amazing—it amps up an herbal flavor. These light, crispy crepes are very nutritious and very simple to make. Soaking the lentils and rice overnight is essential to making them soft enough to puree without any chunks. Serve with your favorite Indian dishes: basmati rice, raita, vegetables, or eggs.

SERVES 4

½ cup [100 g] basmati rice

½ cup [100 g] yellow or red lentils or split peas

1 cup [240 ml] water, plus more as needed

30 curry leaves, or ½ bunch cilantro (with tender stems)

½ cup [120 ml] peanut or neutral vegetable oil

Put the rice and lentils in a 1-quart [1-L] container and cover with cool water by 2 inches [5 cm]. Cover and leave out overnight to soak. Change the water one or two times.

The following day, drain the rice and lentils and puree in a blender with the 1 cup [240 ml] water and the curry leaves until smooth. Add additional water, 1 tablespoon at a time, until the puree is thinned to a cream-like texture.

Warm a 12-inch [30.5-cm] nonstick skillet over medium-high heat. Add 2 tablespoons of the oil, warm, then add one-quarter of the batter and swirl to make a thin crepe. Decrease the heat to medium and cook until the edges of the crepe begin to crisp and the dosa releases from the bottom of pan. Swiftly flip the dosa when the underside is lightly golden and cook briefly on the second side. Repeat with remaining batter to make three more dosas.

Lay the dosas on serving plates and top with preferred accompaniments.

OTHER GREENS TO TRY cilantro, spinach

CLAMS WITH CHILES AND SHISO BUTTER

Using shiso butter in a sauce always adds another dimension to whatever you are cooking. In this recipe it adds a counterpoint to the clams, fish stock, and fish sauce. It also adds a minty element that jumps right out from all of that fishy flavor.

SERVES 4 AS AN APPETIZER OR 2 AS AN ENTRÉE

¼ cup [60 ml] olive oil

A few slices of fresh hot chile

2 cloves garlic, thinly sliced

1 tablespoon finely chopped preserved lemon (page 294)

½ cup [120 ml] white wine

1 cup [240 ml] fish stock

1 tablespoon fish sauce

¼ cup [55 g] shiso butter (page 292)

2 pounds [900 g] Manila or other small clams, well rinsed

½ cup [100 g] fregola, or other small pasta or broken jasmine rice, cooked and warm

Kosher salt and freshly ground black pepper

Lemon wedge (optional)

Crusty artisanal bread, for serving

In a large sauté pan over medium-high heat, warm the oil. Add the chile, garlic, and preserved lemon and cook just until the garlic is tender and loses its raw garlic smell but is not browned, about 1 minute. Add the white wine and cook until reduced by three-quarters. Add the fish stock, fish sauce, shiso butter, and clams, cover, and cook until the clams open, about 5 minutes. Stir in the fregola and season with salt and pepper. Add a squeeze of lemon, if desired, to brighten the flavors. Serve with the bread.

OTHER GREENS TO TRY mint, cilantro

Curry Leaf Dosa

BRAISED FLANK STEAK WITH NASTURTIUM LEAVES AND GREEN OLIVES

This combination of beef, tomato, cheese, herbs, olives, and chile braised in wine and stock is comfort in a pan. Add nasturtium leaves and the flavor profile gets a whole new element: a mild, natural tenderness in a lush combination. I like to serve this braise with soft polenta, which sops up all the juices from the meat and gives the dish the hearty bed it deserves.

SERVES 10

6 tablespoons [90 ml] olive oil, plus more for drizzling

4 ounces [115 g] prosciutto or bacon, minced

1 large yellow onion, finely diced

3 large cloves garlic, sliced

2 bay leaves

2-inch [5-cm] sprig rosemary, leaves only

½ teaspoon dried red pepper flakes

2 teaspoons sweet smoked paprika

2 cups [40 g] loosely packed nasturtium leaves, coarsely chopped

¼ cup [45 g] pitted green olives, coarsely chopped

Fine sea salt and freshly ground black pepper

3 pounds [1.4 kg] flank steak, butterflied (about 2 flank steaks)

8 ounces [230 g] Italian provolone picante, grated or sliced

½ cup [115 g] tomato paste

1 cup [240 ml] white wine

4 cups [960 ml] double chicken stock (page 299)

Preheat the oven to 325°F [165°C].

Warm 4 tablespoons [60 ml] of the olive oil in a large pot over medium-high heat. Add the prosciutto, onion, garlic, bay leaves, rosemary, red pepper flakes, and paprika and cook until tender, 3 to 5 minutes. If the meat and vegetables start to brown, decrease the heat, and cook slowly until tender. Add the nasturtium leaves and cook until wilted. Add the olives, stir, and season with salt and pepper. Transfer the mixture to a flat plate and cool completely. Set the pot aside without washing.

Open the butterflied flank steaks, like a book, and lightly season inside and out with salt and pepper. Divide the cooked filling evenly between them, spreading it on the cut side. Arrange the cheese evenly on top of the cooked filling. Roll up each flank steak into a tight cylinder, making sure to eliminate any gaps. They should be rolled evenly and tightly. Tie with kitchen string at 2-inch [5-cm] intervals.

Add the remaining 2 tablespoons olive oil to the reserved pot, or enough to lightly cover the bottom, and sear the flank steaks over medium-high heat until nicely golden, 3 to 4 minutes per side. Reserve the steaks on a plate.

Add the tomato paste to the same pot, decrease the heat to medium, and cook until the paste turns a darker shade of red, 2 to 3 minutes. Add the wine and scrape up any darkened bits of tomato from the bottom of the pan. Gently simmer until the wine has reduced to ¼ cup [60 ml], 3 to 4 minutes. Add the chicken stock and cook until slightly reduced, 3 to 4 minutes. Stir to combine and season with salt and pepper.

Return the flank steaks to the pot, decrease the heat to low, cover, and braise until meat is tender when pierced with a wooden skewer, 2 to 3 hours.

Let the flank steaks cool to room temperature for at least 1 hour, or chill overnight, so they do not lose their shape. Snip the strings and cut the rolls into slices 1 to 2 inches [2.5 to 5 cm] thick. Serve with a drizzle of good olive oil and a few spoonfuls of braising broth.

OTHER GREENS TO TRY amaranth, lamb's-quarters

PANDAN ICE CREAM

My friend Chef Anita Lo, who owns Annisa restaurant in New York City, made this at an event with her partner and chef de cuisine Mary Attea. When I tasted it, my mind was blown. It has this amazing coconutty, herbal flavor with a cool richness. She kindly lent me this recipe for one of the most refreshing ice creams you'll ever enjoy.

MAKES 1 QUART [960 ML]

2 cups [480 ml] heavy cream

2 cups [480 ml] whole milk

1 (7-ounce/200-g) package frozen pandan (pandanus) leaves (found at any Asian grocery; fresh leaves are hard to find, but if you find them, use them!)

5 egg yolks

1 cup [200 g] sugar

Generous pinch of fine sea salt

Set a large container in a bowl filled with ice.

Scald the cream and milk together over medium heat until small bubbles form around the sides. Coarsely chop the pandan leaves and combine in a blender with a little of the hot cream mixture (just enough to make a liquidy puree with a nice soft texture) and puree. Add to the rest of the cream mixture and remove from the heat.

Whisk the egg yolks with the sugar and salt for a few minutes until the mixture lightens in color, then slowly whisk in a little of the cream mixture to temper, so that the egg yolks don't curdle. Whisk the egg mixture back into the cream mixture and cook over medium heat, stirring, until thickened— the result should coat the back of spoon. Immediately strain into the container nested in the bowl of ice. When cool, transfer to an airtight container and refrigerate. Allow to sit overnight, then churn per your ice-cream maker's instructions.

OTHER GREENS TO TRY lovage, shiso

PANDAN WATER

When you want an alternative to the usual lemon or cucumber water, consider using pandan leaves. The result tastes like a lovely, light coconut water.

Simply take a handful of pandan leaves. Wash them well. Tear them into pieces. Boil about 2 quarts [2 L] water. Pour into a pitcher, add the pandan leaves, and allow to infuse for at least 1 hour. Strain, chill, and serve over ice.

OTHER GREENS TO TRY mint, shiso

DONBURI OF SEARED YUZU KOSHO SKIRT STEAK AND SHISO LEAVES

In the summertime, when I don't like to heat up the house too much, I like to make donburi, which is basically Japanese for a bowl of rice with some meat and vegetables. It is a very fresh, light meal, in which I make use of the abundant shiso growing in my garden. Sometimes I will make it with some grilled Oregon albacore, which happens to be perfectly in season, instead of skirt steak. Even raw albacore is great in this dish. The key is the *yuzu kosho*, a Japanese seasoning paste made from chiles, yuzu peels, and salt, all fermented together, which adds a powerhouse of flavor.

SERVES 4

3 tablespoons yuzu kosho (available at most Asian groceries)

1½ pounds [680 g] skirt steaks

¼ cup [60 ml] soy sauce

¼ cup [60 ml] mirin

¼ cup [60 ml] rice wine vinegar

¼ cup [60 ml] sambal oelek

2 tablespoons sugar

2 tablespoons toasted sesame oil

2 carrots, peeled

4 radishes

Kosher salt

Continued

Donburi of Seared Yuzu Kosho Skirt Steak and Shiso Leaves

Salted Herbs with Vietnamese Coriander

Donburi of Seared Yuzu Kosho Skirt Steak and Shiso Leaves, continued

3 tablespoons neutral vegetable oil

8 green onions, green and white parts

2 cups [400 g] Japanese short-grain rice, white or brown, freshly cooked

Mustard green furikake (page 297), or store-bought shichimi togarashi or furikake

24 large shiso leaves

Rub the yuzu kosho all over the steaks. Marinate, refrigerated, for at least 4 hours or up to 24 hours.

In a small bowl, combine the soy sauce, mirin, rice wine vinegar, sambal, sugar, and sesame oil. Set aside. This sauce can be stored, refrigerated, for up to 1 week.

Using a mandoline or a sharp knife, julienne the carrots and then thinly slice the radishes. Place both vegetables in a bowl with ice water for 15 minutes to crisp. Drain and lightly dry with a clean towel.

Place a heavy pan, preferably cast iron, over high heat. Season the steak with salt. Add the oil to the pan, then the steaks. Cook until the first side is caramelized, about 4 minutes. Add the green onions to the pan and turn the steaks to cook the second sides. Flip the onions when charred, after 2 to 3 minutes, and season with salt. Cook the steaks to medium-rare, about 2 minutes more. Remove the steaks and onions from the pan when cooked. Let the steaks rest for about 10 minutes, then cut across the grain into strips.

To serve, divide the rice among four bowls. Add the carrots and radishes to each bowl along with 2 green onions. Place the slices of steak on top of the rice and sprinkle with the furikake. Set the shiso leaves, to be used as wraps, and the reserved sauce alongside.

To eat, hold a shiso leaf in hand, fill with a tablespoon or so of rice, then add a slice of steak and some vegetables and top with little sauce.

OTHER GREENS TO TRY head lettuces, spinach

SALTED HERBS WITH VIETNAMESE CORIANDER

Salted herbs are popular in Québec, where they can be found in just about every grocery store. They are easy to make, pack a lot of flavor, and can be used in a variety of ways: as a marinade, as a seasoning in soups and stews, or as a garnish.

MAKES 2 CUPS [50 G]

2 carrots, peeled and finely chopped

2 celery ribs, finely chopped

1 head Belgian endive, halved, cored, and thinly sliced into half-moons

3 green onions, green and white parts, thinly sliced

¼ cup [10 g] Vietnamese coriander leaves, coarsely chopped

½ cup [20 g] finely chopped fresh chives

⅓ cup [80 g] fine sea salt

In a food processor, combine the carrots and celery and pulse until the size of corn kernels (or chop by hand with a sharp knife). In a bowl, combine the carrots, celery, endive, and green onions. Add the Vietnamese coriander, chives, and salt and stir to combine. Cover and refrigerate the salted herbs for at least overnight before using. They will keep in an airtight container up to 1 month.

OTHER GREENS TO TRY cilantro, shiso

---

5 THINGS TO DO WITH SALTED HERBS

1 Use a spoonful in fried rice.

2 Sprinkle into scrambled eggs.

3 Use as a dry marinade on grilled meats.

4 Stir into mayonnaise and spread on sandwiches.

5 Use as a seasoning to finish a braise.

DEVILED EGGS WITH VIETNAMESE CORIANDER AND CHILE

Eggs and greens go together like caviar and crème fraîche. Deviling them is a fun way to make use of small, pungent leaves that impart a lot of flavor. Vietnamese coriander is one of those powerful little greens. Instead of mayo, fish sauce aïoli makes perfect sense in this deviling. Sesame seeds are another small ingredient that can add a lot of texture and flavor.

MAKES 12 EGG HALVES

8 eggs

2 tablespoons fish sauce aïoli (page 293)

4 teaspoons sambal oelek

40 large Vietnamese coriander leaves, finely chopped

2 teaspoons fine sea salt

1 teaspoon white sesame seeds, toasted

Place the eggs in a bowl and cover with hot water from the tap. Set aside for 15 minutes to temper the eggs.

Fill a large pot with water and bring to a simmer. Remove the eggs from the tempering water and add to the simmering water. Cook for 10 minutes, then remove and place in a bowl of ice water to stop the cooking. Allow to chill for 15 minutes in the ice water.

Remove the eggs from the ice bath and gently peel. Rinse off any shell that may still be attached.

Cut the eggs in half and put the yolks in a bowl. Mix in the aïoli, sambal, coriander, and salt and stir until smooth and combined. Using a small scoop or a teaspoon, fill the egg whites with the yolk mixture and garnish with the sesame seeds. The yolks of 8 eggs should fill 12 egg-white halves, with 4 white halves left over for another use. Enjoy immediately or keep refrigerated for up to 12 hours.

OTHER GREENS TO TRY minutina, shiso

FRIED RICE WITH VIETNAMESE CORIANDER AND SALTED HERBS

Use your leftover rice to make this umami-packed meal. It is a great vehicle for the superfragrant Vietnamese coriander, but other herbs can steer the dish to the flavors of other ethnicities. For example, for an Italian twist, combine Arborio or Carnaroli rice with basil, oregano, Parmigiano-Reggiano, and black pepper. For a Spanish flavor, use Valencia rice with chorizo, smoked paprika, and piquillo peppers. For Indian, basmati rice with lentils, curry leaves, chopped tomato, coconut milk, and lime. Mexican? Long-grain rice, tomato, ancho chile, avocado, and lime. Just be sure to tweak the herbs in the salt to correspond with the flavor profile you are playing up (use epazote for the Mexican blend, for example, or rosemary for Italian).

The texture of the rice is what makes this dish. Avoid stirring too quickly—wait about 1 minute before stirring so the rice has a chance to crisp up. After that, stir in 2-minute intervals. For the best results, be sure not to overcrowd the pan, which can reduce the crispiness of the rice.

SERVES 4

2 cups [400 g] jasmine rice

¼ cup [60 ml] fish sauce

¼ cup [60 ml] sambal oelek

¼ cup [50 g] sugar

6 tablespoons [85 g] schmaltz (chicken fat), or 6 tablespoons [90 ml] neutral vegetable oil

8 cloves garlic, thinly sliced

4 teaspoons white sesame seeds, toasted

1 cup [20 g] Vietnamese coriander leaves

4 egg yolks

¼ cup [50g] salted herbs with Vietnamese coriander (page 141)

Fill a large pot with salted water and bring to a boil. Add the rice and simmer over medium-high heat until almost fully cooked, about 15 minutes. Drain through a fine-mesh sieve and spread the rice on a sheet pan to cool completely. The rice is best when chilled overnight, lightly covered. Do not rinse the rice before or after cooking. The cooked rice should yield about 8 cups (1.5 kg).

In a small bowl, mix together the fish sauce, sambal, and sugar. Set aside. (This sauce can be stored, refrigerated, for up to 1 week).

Heat a 12-inch [30.5-cm] nonstick skillet or wok over high heat and melt the schmaltz (or heat the oil). Add the rice and, using a spoon, tap gently to flatten. Let the rice crisp on the first side, about 2 minutes, then gently stir. Let the rice crisp on the second side for another 2 minutes and stir again. Add the garlic and sesame seeds, stir well, and then let the rice cook, undisturbed, for 1 minute; the outer grains will crisp up. Add the Vietnamese coriander leaves, stir, and let the rice crisp for 1 to 2 minutes longer.

Add two-thirds of the reserved sauce and stir well, then let the rice crisp for 1 to 2 minutes. If the rice begins to clump, use the side of a spoon in a chopping motion to break up the clumps. The sugar in the sauce will quickly caramelize, so decrease the heat if the rice becomes too dark. Give the rice a good stir, then divide among four plates, top each serving with a raw egg yolk, and garnish with the salted herbs. Enjoy immediately.

OTHER GREENS TO TRY cilantro, shiso

PLUM, CUCUMBER, AND SHISO SALAD WITH RED ADZUKI BEAN VINAIGRETTE

The shiso leaf acts as a little wrap in this fresh salad. Just pile the salad on top, pick up the leaf, fold it over, and eat. Repeat. Here, the shiso really does become the star, because when wrapped around the other elements, its intensity dominates.

SERVES 2

⅔ cup [110 g] cooked red adzuki beans (page 294), drained

¼ cup [60 ml] cider vinegar

2 tablespoons canola oil

1 large clove garlic, thinly sliced

½ small shallot, thinly sliced

Kosher salt and freshly ground black pepper

2 large shiso leaves

4 ounces [115 g] cucumber, thinly sliced

1 plum, pitted and cut into 12 slices

To make a vinaigrette, combine the beans, cider vinegar, canola oil, garlic, and shallot in a bowl. Mix well, season with salt and pepper, and set aside at room temperature for 30 minutes.

Place a shiso leaf on each plate. Set aside.

Add the cucumber and plum to the vinaigrette, toss to coat with the dressing, and season with salt and pepper. Spoon the salad over the shiso leaves and serve immediately.

OTHER GREENS TO TRY mint, cilantro

Curly

Russian

White Russian

Lacinato

KALE

Brassica oleracea var. *sabellica*

A descendant of cabbage, kale's history stretches back to the Stone Age, when it was an important form of nutrition, valued for its ability to withstand cold temperatures. Historical documentation shows that kale was cultivated by the ancient Romans and Greeks. Cato and Pliny the Elder wrote about its health benefits, and the ancient Greeks used it to snap Bacchanalian revelers out of drunkenness. In more modern times, the Scots grew so much of it that they even created their own variety (we have them to thank for that beautiful curly kale). In fact, kale was the most important vegetable in the country until the potato came around. It was so abundant in the Highlands that the term *kailyard* was used to label Scottish writers who were nostalgic for rural life—J. M. Barrie, the author of *Peter Pan*, was a kailyard. Kale spread to become a staple in the rest of Europe, especially in Italy, France, and the colder climes of Germany, Denmark, and the Netherlands. Kale is loaded with vitamins A, B, C, E, and K and with calcium, potassium, manganese, iron, phosphorus, and fiber.

VARIETIES BABY, BLUE SCOTCH, CAVOLO NERO, CURLY, FIZZ, IMPROVED DWARF SIBERIAN, LACINATO (AKA TUSCAN, DINO, DINOSAUR), NAPUS, PURPLE, RAINBOW, RAPE, RED CHIDORI, RED RUSSIAN, RED URSA, RIPBOR, RUSSIAN, SAVOY, SCOTCH CURLED, SIBERIAN, SPIGARELLO LISCIA, WINTER BOR, WHITE RUSSIAN, WINTER RED

SEASON Fall through winter

HOW TO CHOOSE Leaves should be firm and perky, not at all wilted, and bright and deep in color, with no brown or yellow spots. If the stem is dark brown where it was cut, it has oxidized, which means it was cut a while ago and perhaps is not so fresh. Look for cut tips that are whitish or light green. Fresh kale should have an earthy, vegetal, not pungent odor.

HOW TO CLEAN Immerse in cool water. Agitate with fingers. Drain; spin or pat dry. Remove the stem and central rib before cooking. Raw kale must be massaged to attain an agreeable texture. To do this, take kale leaves, cut into ribbons, and, with both hands, work the leaves, as if scrunching paper, until the texture becomes softer.

HOW TO STORE Store in an airtight plastic bin or ziplock bag or wrap in plastic wrap. In the crisper drawer of the refrigerator, kale will keep for up to 1 week.

HOW TO REFRESH Immerse in ice water for 15 minutes. Drain and pat or spin dry.

COOKING METHODS Use raw in salads or cook by braising, roasting, sautéing, stir-frying, or steaming.

PAIRINGS Lemons, olive, anchovies, eggs, pork, sturdy, sweet vegetables like winter squash.

COLCANNON

The Irish know their potatoes, and this creamy peasant dish is among the most comforting recipes to come out of the Emerald Isle. I love the salty depth that the ham brings; I always use *sopressata* because I always seem to have it in the fridge, and it adds some nice spice. But any ham, salami, bacon, or leftover lunchmeat works here. My recipe uses more greens than traditional recipes, and I particularly like using Russian kale—its large leaves give the dish more structure and texture.

SERVES 4 TO 6 AS A SIDE DISH

½ cup [115 g] unsalted butter

½ large yellow onion, cut into ½-inch [12-mm] dice

4 ounces [115 g] sopressata or bacon, coarsely chopped into ¼-inch [6-mm] pieces

8 ounces [230 g] green or Savoy cabbage, trimmed and finely shredded

8 ounces [230 g] Russian kale without stems, cut into ¼-inch [6-mm] ribbons

1 cup [240 ml] whole milk

A few gratings of nutmeg

Kosher salt and freshly ground black pepper

1¾ pounds [800 g] russet potatoes

Preheat the broiler.

In a saucepan, melt the butter over medium-high heat. Add the onion and sopressata and stir to combine. Add the cabbage and kale and cook until both are tender, 6 to 8 minutes. Add the milk and season with nutmeg, salt, and pepper. Cook over medium heat, stirring occasionally, until the greens are soft but not browned, about 15 minutes.

While the greens are cooking, peel the potatoes and cut into 1-inch [2.5-cm] cubes. Put the potatoes in a saucepan, add enough cold water to cover, and bring to a boil over high heat. Decrease the heat to a simmer and cook until the potatoes are tender when pierced with a fork, about 15 minutes. Drain the potatoes and place in the bowl of a mixer fitted with a paddle attachment. Add the kale and cabbage mixture and gently mix on low speed until the potatoes are mashed and evenly mixed with the greens. Season with salt and pepper.

Spread the mixture in a broiler-proof baking dish and place under the broiler until lightly browned on top, about 5 minutes. Remove from the broiler and serve immediately.

OTHER GREENS TO TRY chard, radicchio

FETTUCCINE WITH CAYENNE, FENNEL, AND KALE

Though this recipe takes a little time to make, it is easy and approachable because fresh fettuccine is widely available in most grocery stores. The kale is braised, which yields a tender and slightly chewy green, standing up to the pasta well, and the flavor becomes nice and sweet, with the cayenne adding a layer of heat.

SERVES 6

½ cup [120 ml] olive oil

1½ large yellow onions, diced

1½ large fennel bulbs, diced

6 dried cayenne chiles, finely ground

6 cloves garlic, thinly sliced

1¼ pounds [570 g] kale (any type), stemmed and cut into 1-inch [2.5-cm] pieces

Kosher salt and freshly ground black pepper

18 ounces [500 g] fresh fettuccine

Fresh lemon juice

2 ounces [55 g] Parmigiano-Reggiano, shaved

In a large sauté pan, heat the olive oil over medium-low heat. Add the onions and fennel and cook, stirring ocasionally, for about 30 minutes, until translucent and tender. Add the chiles and garlic, stir, and cook over low heat for another 10 minutes, stirring occasionally. Add the kale and continue to cook until the kale is tender and sticky, about 30 minutes, stirring occasionally. Season with salt and black pepper.

Bring a large pot of salted water to a boil. Drop the fresh pasta in the boiling water and stir immediately so the noodles do not stick together. Cook the pasta for 30 seconds, remove from the water, and add to the kale mixture. Reserve a little of the pasta water and add to the sauté pan, tablespoon by tablespoon, until a light sauce is created. Cook for up to 1 minute but be careful not to overcook the pasta. Season to taste with salt, pepper, and a few drops of lemon juice. Divide among six bowls and top with shaved Parmigiano-Reggiano.

KALE SALAD WITH MINNEOLA TANGERINES, OIL-CURED OLIVES, AND PRESERVED LEMON

Minneola tangerines, aka tangelos, are amazingly intense—juicy, sweet, and delicious. A cross between a grapefruit and a tangerine, they have a unique bell shape. Pair them up with kale for a powerful, bittersweet combination. If you can't find Minneola tangerines, use an orange—better yet, a mandarin orange.

SERVES 4

2 bunches lacinato kale (about 1 pound, 6 ounces/620 g total), stemmed and cut into ¼-inch [6-mm] ribbons

1 shallot, thinly sliced

Kosher salt and freshly ground black pepper

12 oil-cured black Moroccan olives, pitted and torn in half

¼ cup [30 g] almonds, toasted and coarsely chopped

Citrus-tangerine vinaigrette (page 300)

1 Minneola tangerine, peeled and sliced into ¼-inch [6-mm] wheels

Combine the kale and shallot in a large bowl. Season with salt and pepper and massage the greens to soften the texture. Toss in the olives and almonds and lightly dress with the vinaigrette. Place the salad on plates and garnish with the tangerine slices.

OTHER GREENS TO TRY chard, roasted radicchio

KALE WITH ANCHOVY, GARLIC, AND LEMON, SOUS VIDE

I prefer traditional cooking methods, but I wanted to learn how to use a sous vide machine because I think it is important to understand modern methods and technology. The sous vide technique captures the innate freshness in vegetables while sealing in the seasoning. Kale takes particularly well to this method. I was surprised at how quick the process is and just loved how the intense flavor gets completely packed into the green.

SERVES 2 AS AN APPETIZER

8 ounces [230 g] lacinato kale, stemmed

6 tablespoons [90 ml] olive oil

¼ teaspoon kosher salt

2 anchovy fillets packed in oil

2 cloves garlic, halved

4 strips lemon zest, about 4 inches by 1 inch [10 cm by 2.5 cm]

¼ teaspoon dried red pepper flakes

2 eggs

Parmigiano-Reggiano, for garnish

Preheat the sous vide machine to 185°F [85°C].

Divide the kale, olive oil, salt, anchovies, garlic, lemon zest, and red pepper flakes into two plastic bags. Vacuum seal and cook in the sous vide machine for 50 minutes. When finished, shock the bagged kale in ice water until fully chilled. Refrigerate until ready to use.

Decrease the heat of the sous vide machine to 150°F [65°C]. When that temperature is reached, add the eggs and cook for 1 hour. While the eggs are cooking, bring the kale packets to room temperature.

To assemble, empty the packets of kale into a bowl. Remove the lemon zest and garlic cloves. Fluff the kale so that the leaves are not matted. Remove the eggs from their shells and nestle them in the kale. Shave Parmigiano-Reggiano over the eggs and serve.

OTHER GREENS TO TRY chard, collard greens

KALE MALFATTI WITH BROWN BUTTER AND PUMPKIN

Malfatti are Italian pasta dumplings. I love the name: it translates to "poorly formed," which takes off the pressure of shaping them perfectly. Here, the kale is worked right into the pasta dough. The kale gives the dumpling so much flavor, in fact, that just a simple butter and sage sauce is all that's needed to complement them. The pumpkin adds a sweet flourish. *Malfatti* were part of my first book, *Pasta by Hand*; I still enjoy making them, whether back in Italy or at home.

SERVES 4

1 pound [455 g] kale, stemmed

1 cup [240 g] plus 1 tablespoon fresh ricotta

2 eggs

Freshly grated nutmeg

⅔ cup [40 g] lightly packed finely grated Pecorino Romano, plus more for garnish

1½ tablespoons all-purpose flour

Kosher salt and freshly ground black pepper

Semolina, for dusting

¾ cup [170 g] unsalted butter

4 fresh sage leaves

1 lemon

1½ cups [175 g] peeled, seeded, and finely diced pumpkin

Blanch the kale (see page 6), then wring out completely until the greens are in a dry ball. Finely chop. In a bowl, combine the greens, ricotta, eggs, a grating of fresh nutmeg, Pecorino Romano, and flour and mix well. Season with salt and pepper. Generously flour a sheet pan. Scoop the mixture into small balls (approximately 1 tablespoon) and place on the floured sheet pan.

NOTE: The texture of the mixture may vary depending on the size of the eggs and moisture of the ricotta. It should have the consistency of spreadable cheese, with no pooling. If pooling, allow to drain in a sieve for a while, then add cream or milk, tablespoon by tablespoon, until the desired consistency is achieved.

Pour 1 inch [2.5 cm] of semolina into a large red wine glass or a plastic pint container. One at a time, swirl each ball in the semolina until an imperfectly shaped round is formed. Place the balls on the floured sheet pan, and let sit for 4 hours, or overnight, covered with a clean kitchen towel in the refrigerator. Rotate after 2 hours to make sure the semolina evenly encases the dumplings.

Chop the butter into small pats and brown slowly with the sage leaves over medium to medium-low heat. As soon as the butter melts, add a squeeze of lemon and the pumpkin and cook until tender, about 5 minutes; be careful to adjust the heat as needed so the butter doesn't get too dark. Season with salt and pepper.

Cook the malfatti in gently simmering salted water for about 4 minutes. When done, remove from the water with a slotted spoon and gently place in dishes. Garnish with the pumpkin and brown butter. Sprinkle Pecorino Romano over the top of the malfatti and serve.

OTHER GREENS TO TRY chard, spinach

Butterhead

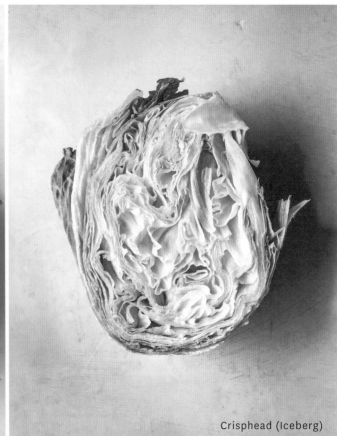

Crisphead (Iceberg)

Romaine

Looseleaf

LETTUCES
Lactuca sativa

It is one of the most ancient of greens: a lettuce hieroglyph has been found in an Egyptian tomb dating back to 4500 BCE. The ancient Greeks and Romans cultivated lettuce, and today there are countless varieties available. Though it is the most recognizable category of greens, it is all too often used the least creatively. Sure, we have lettuce to thank for the existence of the salad. But lettuce can be used in many other ways. The following types of lettuce are among the most common.

BUTTERHEAD

The name refers to the soft texture of the leaves of this head lettuce, with pale green outer leaves and cream-colored hearts. Its silken texture and sweet flavor make it a salad favorite, whether the looser Boston lettuces or more compact Bibb varieties. Its nutritional value is also a winner, with high amounts of vitamins A, C, and K.

ROMAINE

Also called cos, the long, sturdy, frilled leaves of romaine are known for playing a starring role in Caesar salads. Its texture makes it a go-to sandwich topping, as well as the perfect grilling green. Romaine is rich in vitamins A, B, C, and K and in calcium, magnesium, phosphorus, copper, iron, potassium, and manganese.

CRISPHEAD (ICEBERG)

Other lettuce types may blow it away in terms of nutrients, but that doesn't mean that the ubiquitous iceberg is completely lacking. It contains vitamins A, B, C, and K and manganese, potassium, and iron. Crisphead lettuce ships well and keeps well and is not prone to wilting, which accounts for its grocery-store popularity. It has a satisfying crunch, which makes it a nice textural addition to a salad, and it stands up well to dressing.

LOOSELEAF

Named as such because they do not have hearts and do not form tight heads, looseleaf lettuces are clusters of individual leaves. Its colorful, sometimes frilly varieties are often named for their tints. Looseleaf lettuces share a sweet, mild flavor and softly crisp texture. Often used as "bed" garnishes, there is more to this type of lettuce than its looks; it is a good source of vitamins A, B, C, and K and of calcium, dietary fiber, iron, potassium, magnesium, phosphorus, and manganese.

SEASON All of the above are widely available year-round, though spring brings the best crops.

HOW TO CHOOSE Choose lettuce with crisp, sprightly leaves that have uniform coloring and no yellowing or dark spots. Avoid lettuces that are wilted or have a slimy texture.

HOW TO CLEAN Trim any oxidized ends. Immerse greens in cool water. Agitate with fingers. Drain; pat or spin dry.

HOW TO STORE Store in an airtight plastic bin or ziplock bag or wrap in plastic wrap. In the crisper drawer of the refrigerator, most lettuce will keep for 5 to 7 days.

HOW TO REFRESH Immerse in ice water for 15 minutes. Drain and pat or spin dry.

COOKING METHODS Serve raw or cook by braising, simmering in soups, or pureeing as a soup or a sauce; romaine can be grilled.

PAIRINGS Anchovies, garlic, lemon, mustard, mayonnaise, olive oil, avocadoes, cheese, eggs, tomatoes, nuts—basically anything!

"THE ICEBERG THEORY," BY GERALD LOCKLIN FROM *THE ICEBERG THEORY*

all the food critics hate iceberg lettuce.
you'd think romaine was descended from
orpheus's laurel wreath,
you'd think raw spinach had all the nutritional
benefits attributed to it by popeye,
not to mention aesthetic subtleties worthy of
verlaine and debussy.
they'll even salivate over chopped red cabbage
just to disparage poor old mr. iceberg lettuce.

I guess the problem is
it's just too common for them.
It doesn't matter that it tastes good,
has a satisfying crunchy texture,
holds its freshness
and has crevices for the dressing,
whereas the darker, leafier varieties

are often bitter, gritty, and flat.
It just isn't different enough and
it's too goddamn american.

of course a critic has to criticize;
a critic has to have something to say
perhaps that's why literary critics
purport to find interesting
so much contemporary poetry
that just bores the shit out of me.
at any rate, I really enjoy a salad
with plenty of chunky iceberg lettuce,
the more the merrier,
drenched in an Italian or roquefort dressing.
and the poems I enjoy are those I don't have
to pretend that I'm enjoying.

LETTUCE JAM

Chef Trevor Kunk first made this for me. It is like a salsa verde but served like a dip. Use it on sandwiches, as a dip for vegetables, as a garnish for a charcuterie plate, or as a sauce for roasted or grilled pork, fish, chicken, or beef.

MAKES 1½ CUPS [360 ML]

6 tablespoons [90 ml] neutral vegetable oil

10½ ounces [300 g] assorted lettuces (about 1 packed heaping quart/L), including outer leaves and damaged leaves

2 large shallots, sliced into ¼-inch [6-mm] pieces

1½ tablespoons drained capers

8 cornichons

3 tablespoons Dijon mustard

Fine sea salt

Place a large pan over high heat. When very hot, add 4 tablespoons [60 ml] of the oil. When the oil shimmers, add the lettuce. Let the lettuce cook, undisturbed, until the moisture has evaporated, about 2 minutes, then stir to redistribute. Do not burn the lettuce, but cook through and make sure the leaves become dry. This should take 3 to 4 minutes total. The greens will absorb the oil. Using a plastic spatula, scrape the lettuce onto a plate and chill in the refrigerator until very cold.

While the lettuce is cooling, return the large pan to medium-high heat and add the remaining 2 tablespoons oil. Add the shallots and cook until translucent, 2 to 3 minutes. Scrape onto the same plate as the lettuce and cool both completely.

Combine the capers, cornichons, and mustard in a food processor and pulse to chop, leaving the mixture chunky. Add the greens and process until a creamy paste or dip consistency forms. Season to taste with salt. Store in an airtight container in the refrigerator for 2 to 3 days.

OTHER GREENS TO TRY mixed chicories, head lettuces

POACHED ALBACORE TUNA WITH CHARTREUSE LETTUCE SAUCE

I like to think of lettuce as an herb. And just like herbs, lettuces run the gamut from sweet to bitter. Even within the same head, the flavor profile can vary. For example, the inner leaves, known as the "heart," can have a much more tender texture and sweeter flavor than the outer leaves. So depending on what you are looking for in a lettuce sauce, use the inner or outer leaves accordingly. In this recipe, I use an oily fish, so I like to have a bit of bitterness in my green sauce to break up some of that oiliness. The acid in the tomatoes and the kick of the Chartreuse act as a bridge between both.

SERVES 4

Kosher salt

2 heads lettuce, cored, leaves separated,

3 tablespoons olive oil

2 small yellow onions, finely diced

½ cup [120 g] canned tomatoes

1 tablespoon fresh thyme leaves, chopped

1 bay leaf

¼ cup [60 ml] white wine

¼ cup [60 ml] double chicken stock (page 299)

Zest of ½ lemon, finely grated on a Microplane

2 tablespoons Green Chartreuse

Freshly cracked black pepper

4 cups [960 ml] neutral vegetable oil, for poaching

4 (6-ounce/170-g) fillets albacore tuna, about 3 inches [7.5 cm] thick

Freshly ground black pepper, plus more to taste

1 tablespoon thinly sliced green onion, green and white parts

Continued

Butter Lettuce Panna Cotta

Bring a large pot of water to a boil and add 1 tablespoon salt. Blanch the lettuce leaves until just limp, about 30 seconds. Transfer to an ice bath until chilled through. Gently squeeze out the water and let dry in a colander or over towels.

Heat 1 tablespoon of the olive oil in a saucepan over medium-low heat. Add the onions and a pinch of salt. Decrease the heat, cover, and cook gently until the onions are soft and sweet but not browned, 10 to 15 minutes. Remove the lid, add the tomatoes, thyme, bay leaf, and a pinch of salt and cook at a low simmer until almost all of the liquid has evaporated. Add the wine and stock and, once again, cook at a low simmer until almost all of the liquid has evaporated.

Transfer the mixture to a food processor and add the lettuce and lemon zest. Pulse, adding the remaining 2 tablespoons olive oil and the Chartreuse to achieve a texture between a pesto and a relish. Season to taste with salt and freshly cracked black pepper. Set aside.

Fill a sauté pan with the vegetable oil and heat to 150°F [65°C]. Liberally season the portioned pieces of albacore with salt and ground pepper and carefully slip into the oil. After about 4 minutes, check the tuna and pull the pieces out as soon as they become fully opaque on both sides. The oil should never reach a simmer—it's very gentle cooking. Remove the tuna and serve immediately, covered with the sauce and garnished with the green onions.

OTHER GREENS TO TRY Little Gem, green leaf lettuce

BUTTER LETTUCE PANNA COTTA

Dessert is probably the best way to eat your greens. The herbaceousness of butter lettuce lends itself perfectly to *panna cotta*. There is a gentle bitterness that cottons to the fat in the cream here. Then come the strawberries and their bright sweetness. A finish of olive oil, and this truly wows. Use the outer leaves for

this recipe. They are often larger, and they are not as pretty on salads. The inner leaves are a little bit more gentle and often don't have quite the flavor.

SERVES 12

3⅓ sheets gelatin (see Note)

4 cups [960 ml] heavy cream

2 fresh sage leaves

4 strips lemon zest, each ½ by 1 inch [12 mm by 2.5 cm]

½ cup [100 g] sugar

6 ounces [170 g] red or green butter lettuce leaves

18 strawberries, sliced into thin rounds

Olive oil, for drizzling

Put the gelatin in a small bowl, cover with cool water, and set aside.

Combine the cream, sage, lemon zest, and sugar in a small saucepan over medium-high heat and warm just until it starts to simmer. Turn off the heat and allow the flavors to infuse for 5 minutes. Then, using a tablespoon or fork, remove the lemon zest from the pan and puree the lettuce leaves into the cream using an immersion blender or regular blender. Remove the gelatin sheets from water, squeeze the water from the sheets, and whisk the gelatin into the cream. Strain the mixture though a fine-mesh sieve and pour into twelve ramekins (3¼ ounces/95 ml each). Chill until set, about 8 hours.

To unmold, run a knife around the sides of the molds and invert onto plates. Decorate the tops with the strawberries and drizzle with olive oil.

NOTE: To substitute powedered gelatin for gelatin sheets, soften with 1½ teaspoons plain gelatin powder in 1 tablespoon water for about 5 minutes. Whisk the softened gelatin and soaking water into the cream.

OTHER GREENS TO TRY Little Gem, green leaf lettuce

GREENS AND BEANS AND EGGS

Because I always have the ingredients on hand, I make this on the fly when I need something healthy and quick. I shake it up and play with the ethnicity from time to time. Here are two variations on the theme, one Mexican, one Italian.

SERVES 1

½ (15-ounce/430-g) can pinto or black beans with some liquid from can (about 1 cup/240 g)

½ cup [120 ml] salsa

2 to 3 cups [95 to 140 g] loosely packed butter lettuce or other tender leafy greens, coarsely chopped

Kosher salt

1 to 2 eggs

Garnishes: avocado, Jack or Cotija cheese, chopped onion, pickled jalapeños, sour cream, leftover grilled chicken or other meat, tortillas or tortilla chips

In a 7-inch [17-cm] nonstick skillet, combine the beans and salsa. Place over medium-high heat and cook until the sauce begins to simmer. Add the greens and season with salt. Cook, stirring often, until the greens are wilted, 2 to 3 minutes. (Keep at a lazy simmer.) Using a spoon, make a small well in the sauce. Crack the eggs into the well, decrease the heat to medium-low, cover the pan, and cook very gently until the whites are softly set and the yolks are runny, 2 to 3 minutes.

Tip the pan into a bowl, gently emptying the contents of the pan so the eggs remain on top. Serve immediately with any of the garnishes you like.

OTHER GREENS TO TRY any tender head lettuce, spinach

VARIATION: Replace the pinto or black beans with cannellini beans and the salsa with tomato-based pasta sauce. Replace the lettuce with a heartier green, such as escarole or kale (see Note, following). Garnish with Parmigiano-Reggiano, chopped salami or other cured meat, giardiniera (pickled vegetables), good olives, a drizzle of good olive oil, bread crumbs, a piece of rustic bread, cooked bacon.

NOTE: If using kale or a tougher green, remove the stems and thinly slice the leaves, then massage the cut leaves to break down their toughness before cooking.

LETTUCE AND CARROT CAKE

Every year, I host a rabbit dinner. We use all parts of the rabbit, and we make sure we don't waste anything. There was the challenge of the dessert course, however. I didn't think rabbit would go over so well, so I opted for carrot cake to provide an appropriate finish. Rabbits love carrots, after all.

SERVES 10

2 cups [280 g] all-purpose flour

2 teaspoons baking powder

1½ teaspoons fine sea salt

2½ teaspoons ground cinnamon

4 eggs

1½ cups [360 ml] neutral vegetable oil

2 cups [400 g] sugar

3 cups [270 g] peeled and grated carrots

2 cups [145 g] shredded iceberg lettuce

1¼ cups [230 g] drained crushed canned pineapple

Cream cheese frosting (page 160; optional)

Preheat the oven to 350°F [180°C]. Line the bottom of an 8 to 10-inch [20 to 25-cm] round cake pan with parchment paper.

In a bowl, sift together the flour, baking powder, salt, and cinnamon. Set aside. In a separate bowl, mix the eggs, oil, and sugar with a spoon until blended. Sprinkle in the carrots in two batches and mix well each time. Add the lettuce and pineapple and stir to mix. Add the sifted flour mixture and mix again until just combined.

Continued

Lettuce and Carrot Cake

Scrape the cake batter into the prepared pan and bake for 30 to 35 minutes, until the sides of the cake just start to pull away from the pan sides and a wooden toothpick inserted into the middle comes out clean. Remove from the oven and let cool in the pan on a wire rack.

When the cake is cool, flip it onto a plate and lift off the pan. Peel off the parchment paper from bottom of the cake. Invert the cake onto a large plate or a parchment paper–lined sheet pan. Frost the top of the cake, and the sides if you wish, with the frosting.

OTHER GREENS TO TRY butter lettuce

CREAM CHEESE FROSTING

**MAKES ENOUGH TO GENEROUSLY FROST
ONE 10-INCH [25-CM] SINGLE-LAYER CAKE**

> 1 cup [120 g] confectioners' sugar
>
> 8 ounces [230 g] cream cheese, at room temperature
>
> 1 cup [230 g] unsalted butter, at room temperature
>
> 1 tablespoon fresh lemon juice
>
> 1 teaspoon vanilla extract

Sift the confectioners' sugar though a fine-mesh sieve. Set aside.

Using the whip attachment on a stand mixer, whip together the cream cheese and butter until smooth. Scrape down the sides of the bowl using a plastic or rubber spatula and whip again until soft and smooth. Add the confectioners' sugar, lemon juice, and vanilla and mix until blended.

To make spreading easier, keep the frosting at room temperature until you are ready to frost the cake.

WEDGE SALAD

Upon the mere mention of iceberg, the mind automatically goes to the wedge salad. It is a classic, a symbol of steak-house Americana, usually served with blue cheese or Thousand Island dressing. A good wedge salad is clean, crisp, refreshing, and rich all at the same time. One way to achieve that maximum freshness and texture is to make sure that you serve the salad on a cold plate. And it is also important to keep the elements of the salad cold, except for the bacon, of course, which should be room temperature. Make sure to buy the best-quality blue cheese possible—a little crumbly, not too creamy. It will make all the difference for this recipe!

SERVES 4

> 4 thick slices bacon
>
> Blue cheese dressing (page 295)
>
> 1 large head iceberg lettuce, quartered and cored
>
> 2 medium-boiled eggs (page 293)

Warm a skillet over medium-high heat. Lay the bacon strips in the pan and cook until the bacon is golden and crispy, about 2 minutes, then flip and cook the second sides, 1 to 2 minutes. Do not fully crisp the bacon; leave some chew in the texture.

Place 1 heaping spoonful of blue cheese dressing on the center of each of four plates. Place the rounded side of the iceberg wedge atop the dressing, leaving the pointed, cut side, facing up. Drape 1 to 2 large spoonfuls of dressing over the top peak of the wedge. Halve the eggs and press them through a fine-mesh sieve to distribute a snow-like sieved egg over the dressing on each salad. Coarsely chop the warm bacon and sprinkle it over the wedges to garnish. Eat immediately.

OTHER GREENS TO TRY romaine or Little Gem halves

CHOPPED SALAD

French fries on a salad? Why not! They are exactly what make this dish so fun. It reminds me of the delight I felt when discovering French fries snuck into a pita with falafel in Israel or topping a gyro in Greece.

SERVES 4

4 ounces [115 g] baby green or red oak leaf lettuce leaves, cut into ½-inch [12-mm] ribbons

2 ounces [55 g] iceberg lettuce, very thinly sliced

2 ounces [55 g] radicchio, very thinly sliced

2 ounces [55 g] provolone cheese, cut into matchsticks

2 ounces [55 g] salami, cut into matchsticks

1 ounce [30 g] peperoncini, thinly sliced

¼ cup [60 ml] red wine vinaigrette (page 301)

Kosher salt and freshly ground black pepper

French fries (recipe follows)

In a bowl, combine both lettuces, the radicchio, cheese, salami, and peperoncini. Toss with the vinaigrette and add salt and pepper to taste.

Divide three-quarters of the salad mix among four plates. Divide the French fries into four servings and arrange them on top of each salad. Top the fries with the remaining salad and serve.

OTHER GREENS TO TRY Belgian endive, pan di zucchero

FRENCH FRIES

**SERVES 2, ENOUGH FRIES FOR
4 CHOPPED SALADS**

1 pound [455 g] russet or Kennebec potatoes, peeled

8 cups [2 L] neutral vegetable oil

Kosher or fine sea salt

Cut potatoes into batons, roughly ½-inch [12-mm] square and the length of the potato. Soak the potatoes in cool water for 20 minutes, then rinse them four or five times under cool water to release some starch.

Heat the oil to 275°F [135°C]. When hot, add the potatoes in batches and cook for 5 minutes, or until cooked through and limp, not crispy. Make sure not to crowd the pan; the potatoes should be able to swim freely as they cook. Remove the potatoes with a slotted spoon and transfer to a sheet pan to cool to room temperature.

Increase the heat of the oil to 350°F [180°C]. Line a large plate with paper towels. Return the potatoes to the oil and fry until crisp, 3 to 4 minutes, again cooking in batches so as not to crowd the pan. Remove the cooked fries with a slotted spoon and transfer to the paper towel–lined plate. Season with salt and serve immediately.

GRILLED ROMAINE THREE WAYS

Romaine is one of the easiest, tastiest, most grillable greens there is. The resulting char and crunch make it a warm-weather favorite. Preparation requires little more than a slathering of olive oil, a sprinkle of salt, and a hot grill. But why stop there? Garnishes, just as easy to prepare, can make things a lot more interesting. The following topping ideas are three ways to liven up the usual grilled romaine, using Middle Eastern and Mediterranean flavors.

SERVES 4 AS AN APPETIZER

2 large heads romaine hearts, halved through the core

¼ cup [60 ml] olive oil

Fine sea salt

Lemon wedges, for garnish

Desired toppings (see following)

Prepare a medium-hot fire in a grill or preheat a stove-top grill pan or cast-iron skillet over medium-high heat.

In a bowl, toss the romaine with olive oil if grilling, or warm the olive oil in a grill pan or skillet. Cook the romaine, cut side down, until the leaves become dark golden brown but are not fully cooked, 2 to 3 minutes. Lightly season the greens with salt, then flip and lightly season the second side. Cook for 2 to 3 minutes, until the romaine is tender on the outside and barely cooked in the inner leaves.

To serve, place each romaine half on an individual plate or arrange the romaine halves on a platter. Garnish with lemon wedges and one of the toppings.

OTHER GREENS TO TRY Little Gem lettuce, Belgian endive, pan di zucchero

---

TOPPING IDEAS

Try your grilled romain one of three ways:

* With dollops of muhammara (page 299), fresh-leaf parsley, and mint leaves

* With tahini sauce (page 296), small dollops of Lettuce Skhug (page 164), and toasted white sesame seeds

* With drizzled bagna cauda (page 295), Spanish anchovies or sardines, medium-boiled egg (page 293), and baguette

---

LETTUCE SKHUG (ZHUG)

Skhug is a traditional condiment used in Israeli food—a staple that everyone from Jerusalem to Tel Aviv has in his or her fridge. Typically, it wouldn't have lettuce in it. But once, when I tried to make it, I didn't have a lot of cilantro on hand. I did have a lot of Little Gem lettuce, so I just substituted it in with some cilantro and romaine. I loved that the lettuce brought in texture and a little bitterness to the underlying spice. Whether you prefer it chunky or smooth, it is a great companion to falafel, shawarma, *sabich*, or any roasted meat, egg, or eggplant sandwich, especially when tucked in a pita. It is also delicious paired with soft scrambled eggs, tomatoes, and cucumbers.

MAKES 1 CUP [85 G]

1 teaspoon coriander seeds

1 teaspoon cumin seeds

1 head (3 ounces/85 g) Little Gem or romaine lettuce, cored

2 jalapeño chiles, stemmed and quartered

1 bunch cilantro, roughly chopped

2 large cloves garlic

2 tablespoons fresh lemon juice

½ cup [120 ml] olive oil

Kosher salt

Combine the coriander seeds and cumin seeds in a small pan over medium-high heat. Toast until fragrant, about 2 minutes, then remove from the heat and cool. When cool, finely grind in a spice grinder or electric coffee grinder. Set aside.

Combine the Little Gem in a blender along with the jalapeños, cilantro, garlic, lemon juice, and olive oil. Puree until smooth, then season with salt.

Store, in an airtight container in the refrigerator, for up to 3 days.

WHAT IS MESCLUN?

A mesclun salad is a common enough menu fixture. So why don't more people know exactly what it is? Often mistaken for a single variety of lettuce, mesclun, which means "mixture" in Provençal dialect, is actually a mix of lettuces. Frequently comprising anything "baby," such as baby arugula and baby spinach, mesclun is also known to include frisée, romaine, radicchio, mizuna, lamb's-quarters, mustard greens, endive, and red oak leaf lettuce. The purpose of mesclun is to provide a complementary mix of bitter and sweet greens. Always colorful on the plate, the mix is often dictated by greens that are grown and harvested together.

Though the French have been enjoying such a mix for centuries, mesclun salads came into vogue in the United States in the 1980s, when seed companies began to market their own mesclun seed packets and salad-in-a-bag packaging started to populate supermarkets.

GREENS TACOS

Lettuces don't have to be just a garnish for tacos; they can be the main ingredient, too. You need only these few key ingredients.

TORTILLAS

Use a quality corn or flour tortilla. I prefer corn, but I am also a sucker for a warm flour tortilla. Warm the tortillas gently so they are pliable and not crispy. Place the tortillas between two cloths to stay warm.
Then go to town with the fillings!

FILLING

Here are some lettuce recipes that happen to be great stuffed in a taco:

Frisée, Escarole, and Pan di Zucchero Salad with Smoked Lamb Bacon and Poached Egg (page 89)

Carrot Leaves in Cabbage Salad with Dates and Almonds (page 216)

Arugula Salad with Red Grapes, Feta, and Dukkah (page 28)

Tender Bok Choy Salad with Chicken and Orange (page 37)

ADD-ONS

Leftover bacon

Hard-boiled egg (page 293) and frisée with sherry vinaigrette (page 301)

Grilled chicken, salsa, canned pinto beans, and romaine lettuce

Leftover steak, blue cheese, and radicchio.

You can also mix and match! Use whatever salad, cheese, beans, and protein you have in your fridge. Don't forget condiments, such as pickled peppers, salsas, hot sauces, and more.

MÂCHE

Valerianella locusta

Succulent, juicy, delicate, and tender, mâche rosettes are like tiny heads of butter lettuce—just as velvety in texture, and generously flavored. Mâche is also like the popcorn of lettuces because the sweet and nutty clusters pop in the mouth. Also called corn lettuce and lamb's lettuce, the gentle green became popular in the United States via farmer Todd Koons, the lettuce-in-a-bag entrepreneur who included mâche in his salad mix. Mâche is packed with vitamins A, B, and C and with potassium, copper, and iron.

VARIETIES COQUILLE DE LOUVIERS, D'ETAMPES, GROSSE GRAINE, PIEDMONT, VALGROS, VERTE DE CAMBRAL

SEASON Spring through summer

HOW TO CHOOSE Choose mâche with perky leaves that have uniform coloring and no yellowing or blemishes. Avoid leaves that are wilted or have a slimy texture.

HOW TO CLEAN Immerse clusters in cold water. Agitate with fingers. Drain; pat or spin dry.

HOW TO STORE Store in an airtight plastic bin or ziplock bag or wrap in plastic wrap. In the crisper drawer of the refrigerator, mâche will keep for 2 to 3 days.

HOW TO REFRESH Immerse in ice water for 15 minutes. Drain and pat or spin dry.

COOKING METHODS Serve raw in a salad or cook by sautéing, braising, or steaming.

PAIRINGS Nut oils, herbs, garlic, beets, mushrooms, onions, eggs, nuts, grapefruit, blood oranges, fennel, berries, peaches, nectarines, apples, pears, cheese, any meat or fish.

SIMPLE MÂCHE SALAD

The epitome of simplicity, this salad needs little more than a dressing. Mâche is delicate and beautiful, elegant and crisp in its raw state, with pine nuts lending the perfect texture. I love this salad as an accompaniment to scrambled eggs and a piece of toast slathered with goat cheese.

SERVES 4

6 ounces [170 g] mâche

2 tablespoons pine nuts, lightly toasted

Fine sea salt and freshly ground black pepper

Lemon vinaigrette (page 300)

Combine the mâche and pine nuts in a large bowl. Season with salt and pepper and dress lightly with lemon vinaigrette. Toss with your hands, then divide among plates and serve immediately.

OTHER GREENS TO TRY chickweed, dandelion greens

RADISH SALAD WITH MÂCHE AND BUTTERNUT SQUASH PUREE

Crunchiness and creaminess—those are the essences of this recipe. The butternut squash puree brings a lush, velvet sweetness to the sharp flavor and crispiness of the radishes, less intense than usual in this recipe because they are shaved thin. (I suggest using a mandoline to get the radishes to their ultimate slimness.) This recipe includes the magenta, slightly peppery fingerling radishes known as Ostergruss; tangy white daikon; the sweet, supercrisp Misato Rose radish; and the common spicy red. Some mild summer squash mellows it all out, while a simple mustard seed vinaigrette adds a lighly pickled flavor. And then there's the grassy mâche, which really stands out with its green color and flavor. Altogether, it's a really pretty plate.

SERVES 4

2 Ostergruss or other fingerling radishes, thinly sliced

3 ounces [85 g] daikon radish, thinly sliced

2 ounces [55 g] Misato Rose or other radish, thinly sliced

2 ounces [55 g] red radishes, thinly sliced

4 ounces [115 g] heirloom, zucchini or other summer squash, peeled and cut into matchsticks

6 tablespoons [90 g] butternut squash puree (page 298)

6 leaves Belgian endive, cut crosswise into wide matchsticks

2 ounces [55 g] mâche

1 small shallot, thinly sliced

Fine sea salt and freshly ground black pepper

Pickled mustard seed vinaigrette (page 301)

Immerse all the radishes and the zucchini in a bowl of ice water for at least 15 minutes or up to 2 hours to crisp them. Drain and lightly dry on a clean kitchen towel.

Divide the squash puree among four plates or put on a large serving platter by making a swoosh from one end of the plate to the other. Place the radishes and zucchini in a large bowl and add the endive, mâche, and shallot; season with salt and pepper. Dress the salad with the mustard seed vinaigrette and place on top of the squash puree. Eat immediately.

OTHER GREENS TO TRY arugula, spinach

Radish Salad with Mâche and Butternut Squash Puree

MALABAR SPINACH
Basella alba

These greens have a bit of a dual personality. When raw, their flavor is citrusy and peppery; when cooked, the flavor becomes minerally, like common spinach. In terms of texture, raw Malabar is fleshy, juicy, crisp. Cooked, it becomes silken and smooth, but turns downright slimy if overcooked. Eaten all over Asia, particularly in China, the Philippines, and India, Malabar has a slew of pseudonyms, including buffalo spinach, vine spinach, creeping spinach, climbing spinach, Ceylon spinach, *poi choy,* and *chancai.* Nutritionally, it is rich in vitamins A and C, iron, calcium, and fiber.

VARIETIES MONG TOI, PALE GREEN-STEMMED, RED-STEMMED, RUBRA

SEASON Summer

HOW TO CHOOSE Choose crisp, perky, firm greens that have uniform coloring and no yellowing or blemishes. Do not buy if wilted.

HOW TO CLEAN Immerse greens in cool water. Agitate with fingers. Drain; pat or spin dry.

HOW TO STORE Store in an airtight plastic bin or ziplock bag or wrap in plastic wrap. In the crisper drawer of the refrigerator, Malabar spinach will keep for 2 to 3 days.

HOW TO REFRESH Immerse in ice water for 15 minutes. Drain and pat or spin dry.

COOKING METHODS Use raw in salads or cook by stir-frying, sautéing, steaming, simmering in soups or stews, or folding into an omelet, tossing into a pasta, or topping a pizza. Be careful not to overcook, as Malabar develops a slimy texture when heated too long.

PAIRINGS Garlic, chile, curry, ginger, soy sauce, soybeans, tofu, vinaigrette, eggs, dairy, side to any fish or meat.

MALABAR SPINACH SHAKSHUKA

The Israeli breakfast classic of eggs poached in a sauce, *shakshuka* is typically a red dish, meaning that it is tomato based. It is certainly a rich way to start the day. I started to think about how to make it a little lighter and a little greener, and using tomatillos instead of tomatoes came to mind. The tomatillos add a zing of tartness that pairs wonderfully with the creaminess of feta and the egg yolks. Malabar spinach brings a vegetal flavor that cuts through all of that cream. I find myself eating this version any time of the day.

SERVES 2

1 pound [455 g] tomatillos, husks removed and halved

4 ounces [115 g] Malabar spinach leaves and stems, coarsely chopped

1 cup [40 g] fresh cilantro leaves, plus a few sprigs for garnish

1 jalapeño chile, stemmed and cut into thirds

3 tablespoons olive oil

1 small yellow onion, diced

2 cloves garlic, minced

½ teaspoon ground cumin

½ teaspoon ground coriander

½ teaspoon ground caraway

½ teaspoon ground turmeric

Fine sea salt

4 eggs

2 ounces [55 g] sheep's milk feta

Challah toast, for serving

Combine the tomatillos, Malabar spinach, cilantro, and jalapeño in a food processor. Pulse until all of the ingredients are finely chopped. Scrape down the sides of the bowl and process again until the ingredients are well mixed but not fully pureed. The texture of the ingredients should be fine, not chunky. Set aside.

Over medium-high heat, warm the olive oil in a 10-inch [25-cm] skillet. Add the onion, garlic, cumin, coriander, caraway, and turmeric and cook, stirring often, until the onion is translucent, about 4 minutes. If the garlic begins to brown, decrease the heat.

Add the tomatillo mixture, season lightly with salt, and bring the sauce to a light simmer. Cook slowly until the sauce thickens, 8 to 10 minutes. Crack the eggs atop the spinach-tomatillo mixture, turn the heat to low, and cover the pan to allow the eggs to cook gently and steam. Cook the eggs until the whites all set, 4 to 5 minutes.

Spoon into individual bowls with the eggs on top, and garnish with the cilantro sprigs and feta. Serve immediately with challah toast to soak up sauce.

NOTE: If you do not like spicy foods, remove the seeds from the jalapeño before processing the chile.

OTHER GREENS TO TRY chard, spinach

MALLOW

Corchorus olitorius

Used by Middle Eastern cultures as a thickener for soups and stews, mallow, when cooked, emits a thick, slimy substance much as okra does. This quality is no coincidence; it so happens that mallow is a member of the same family as okra. This intensely flavored flowering plant was first cultivated in ancient Egypt (it is sometimes referred to as Egyptian spinach or Jew's mallow), where it was the favorite of pharaohs. It became a source of sustenance for nomadic tribes in Israel, who would forage for it while on the move. Its nutritional value likely helped the tribes to survive desert life, as mallow is rich in vitamin B, iron, protein, calcium, and dietary fiber.

VARIETIES BUSH, GLOBE, MARF, MARSH, POPPY, ROSE, SEASHORE, TREE, TURK'S CAP, WAX

SEASON Summer

HOW TO CHOOSE Choose crisp, perky, firm greens that have uniform coloring and no yellowing or blemishes. Do not buy if wilted or if the texture is slimy.

HOW TO CLEAN Immerse greens in cool water. Agitate with fingers. Drain; pat or spin dry.

HOW TO STORE Store in an airtight plastic bin or ziplock bag or wrap in plastic wrap. In the crisper drawer of the refrigerator, mallow will keep for 2 to 3 days.

HOW TO REFRESH Immerse greens in ice water for 15 minutes. Drain and pat or spin dry.

COOKING METHODS Braise, or simmer in stews and soups as a thickener.

PAIRINGS Meat-based stews and soups.

MULUKHIYA

This nutritious stew was banned in Egypt by a Fatimid Caliphate ruler because it was considered to be a sexual stimulant for women, a ban that was lifted upon the end of his reign in 1021. The key ingredient is mallow, for which nomads would forage. When cooked down, the green's texture becomes like okra and is perfect to thicken stews and soups. The protein used in the stew—rabbit, chicken, beef, or fish—would vary by region. The first time I had this stew was when I was in Jerusalem, and the rich, rustic, comforting texture of the mallow just blew my mind.

SERVES 6

2 whole chicken legs (thighs and drumsticks), or 4 chicken thighs (about 1½ pounds/675 g)

2-inch [5-cm] cinnamon stick

2 bay leaves

8 cups [2 L] double chicken stock (page 299), plus more as needed

2 teaspoons kosher salt

½ cup [120 ml] plus 2 tablespoons olive oil, plus more as needed

8 cups [1.8 kg] packed mallow leaves

1 large yellow onion, chopped

10 large cloves garlic, minced

1 cup [40 g] loosely packed fresh cilantro leaves, finely chopped

½ teaspoon ground cayenne pepper

2 tablespoons fresh lemon juice

Cooked rice, pita, vinegar, finely chopped raw onions, and chopped or sliced tomato, for serving

In a large pot over medium heat, combine the chicken, cinnamon stick, bay leaves, chicken stock, and 1 teaspoon of the salt. Cook for 30 minutes, or until the chicken is just tender when pierced with a fork or knife.

In another large pot over medium heat, warm ½ cup [120 ml] of the olive oil. Add the mallow leaves and cook, stirring, for 10 minutes, or until the leaves are tender. If the pan seems dry, add a tablespoon or two more oil to prevent the leaves from burning. Remove the leaves from the pot and set aside.

Decrease the heat under the same large pot to medium-low. Add the remaining 2 tablespoons olive oil, the onion, and 8 of the minced garlic cloves and cook for 5 minutes, or until the onion is translucent and tender but not gaining any color. If the onion begins to brown, decrease the heat.

Return the cooked mallow leaves to the onion. Remove the chicken from the stock and set aside. Strain the stock, discard the cinnamon and bay leaves, and measure. Add additional stock as needed to make 8 cups [2 L], as some may have evaporated. Pour into the pot with the mallow and onion. Add the remaining 1 teaspoon salt and cook at a lazy simmer for 1 hour, or until the leaves have turned dark green and the stew has become thick.

Meanwhile, shred chicken meat into bite-size pieces, discarding any skin and bones.

After the greens have been cooking in the stock for 1 hour, add the chicken, cilantro, cayenne, and the remaining 2 minced garlic cloves and cook for 20 minutes more. Add the lemon juice and cook for a final 10 minutes. Serve with rice or pita, finely chopped onion, and tomato.

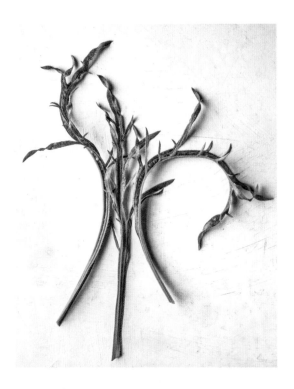

MINUTINA

Plantago coronopus

Going by the alternative names of staghorn, buck's horn, and buck's horn plantain because of the "antlers" protruding from the leaf's edges, minutina is marked by a nutty, minerally flavor and crisp texture. It is also called *erba stella*, or "star herb," and is popular in Italy, from which it originates. Cultivated in the United States since the colonial period, minutina was used in the past as a fever reducer. It is a good source of vitamins A and C, dietary fiber, iron, potassium, and calcium.

VARIETIES BUCK'S HORN PLANTAIN

SEASON Spring through fall

HOW TO CHOOSE Choose crisp, perky, firm greens that have uniform coloring and no yellowing or blemishes. Do not buy if wilted.

HOW TO CLEAN Immerse greens in cold water. Agitate with fingers. Drain; spin or pat dry.

HOW TO STORE Store in an airtight plastic bin or ziplock bag or wrap in plastic wrap. In the crisper drawer of the refrigerator, minutina will keep for 3 to 5 days.

HOW TO REFRESH Immerse in ice water for 15 minutes. Drain and spin or pat dry.

COOKING METHODS Use raw in salads or on a sandwich; cook by sautéing, steaming, or stir-frying; or use as a pizza topping or toss into pasta.

PAIRINGS Butter, eggs, meat, oily fish such as tuna or salmon.

MINUTINA TUNA

Tuna is an oily fish that needs the perfect partner to break up that richness. Enter nutty, bright minutina, which brightens even more with lemon. Lentils make it a little heftier, and the tonnato—that mayo-like sauce in *vitello tonnato*—adds depth. Altogether this is just a nice, fresh, clean yet substantial salad. Even better, put this salad inside a crusty baguette with the tonnato, and add a couple of anchovies and a boiled egg.

SERVES 4 AS A STARTER OR 1 AS A LIGHT ENTRÉE

¼ small red onion, very thinly sliced

4 ounces [115 g] minutina

4 ounces [115 g] tuna canned in oil (preferably Spanish), drained and flaked into small chunks

2 tablespoons cooked green or brown lentils

½ lemon, quartered, seeded, and sliced paper-thin

Kosher salt and freshly ground black pepper

Lemon vinaigrette (page 300)

½ cup [120 g] tonnato (page 275)

Rustic baguette, for serving

Fill a small bowl with ice water, add the red onion slices, and let soak for 5 minutes. Drain and pat dry with a clean towel.

Combine the onion slices, minutina, tuna, lentils, and lemon in a large bowl. Season with salt and pepper and dress with the vinaigrette. Divide the tonnato among four plates, or place a swoosh on the bottom of a large platter. Top with the minutina salad and serve with the baguette. Enjoy immediately.

OTHER GREENS TO TRY agretti, spinach

SWORDFISH WITH SAUTÉED MINUTINA

Swordfish with my crack spice blend is an unbeatable combination: a meaty, mild fish coming to life with the heat of the spice blend plus the brilliance of citrus. The sautéed minutina smoothes it all out. And the best part is this is a really fast dish to put together.

SERVES 4

½ cup [115 g] unsalted butter

2 cloves garlic, minced

8 ounces [230 g] minutina

Zest of 1 lemon, finely grated on a Microplane

Zest of 1 orange, finely grated on a Microplane

Fine sea salt

4 (5-ounce/140-g) swordfish fillets, bloodline removed

4 teaspoons crack spice mix (page 296)

¼ cup [60 ml] olive oil

Freshly ground black pepper

Extra-virgin olive oil, for dizzling

Place a large sauté pan over medium heat and melt the butter. Add the garlic and cook for about 1 minute. Add the minutina and stir until it just starts to wilt. Remove from the heat, add the lemon and orange zests, and season with salt.

Lay the swordfish fillets on a plate and lightly season both sides with the crack spice.

Place a large sauté pan over medium-high heat, add the olive oil and swordfish, and cook until lightly golden, about 3 minutes. Flip to cook the second side, about 2 minutes. The fish should be just barely cooked through.

Divide the minutina among four plates and place a piece of fish next to each pile of greens. Drizzle the fish with extra-virgin olive oil and serve immediately.

OTHER GREENS TO TRY agretti, spinach

MIZUNA

Brassica rapa nipposinica

Mizuna is one of the peppery greens, though somewhat milder than watercress or arugula, and lemony on the palate. The plant, with its deep green and feathery yet sturdy leaves, is native to China, where it has been eaten since ancient times. It was also popular in ancient Japan, where the leaves were often pickled for winter use. In Asia, the green is often treated as an herb because of its agreeable pungency. Mizuna is a good source of vitamins A, C, and folate and of iron and beta-carotene, and other carotenoids.

VARIETIES ALTOR, EARLY, GREEN SPRAY, HAPPY RICH, KOJISAN, KOMATSUNA, KYONA, KYOTO, MANDOVI, MIBUNA, PURPLE, RED AND LIME STREAKS, RED KOMATSUNA, REINHELD, SEMPOSI, SUMMER FEST, TOKYO, VITAMIN GREEN, WAIDO

SEASON Early spring through late summer

HOW TO CHOOSE Choose crisp, perky, bright greens that have uniform coloring and no yellowing or blemishes. Do not buy if wilted or drying.

HOW TO CLEAN Immerse greens in cold water. Agitate with fingers. Drain; spin or pat dry.

HOW TO STORE Store in an airtight plastic bin or ziplock bag or wrap in plastic wrap. In the crisper drawer of the refrigerator, mizuna will keep for up to 5 days.

HOW TO REFRESH Immerse greens in ice water for 15 minutes. Drain and pat or spin dry.

COOKING METHODS Use raw in a salad, on a sandwich, or in a pesto; cook by stir-frying, sautéing, or simmering in soups or stews; or use as a pizza topping or toss into pasta.

PAIRINGS Chile, basil, mint, ponzu, vinaigrette, garlic, ginger, mushrooms, apples, pears, peaches, figs, oranges, bacon, dairy, tomatoes, zucchini, radishes, seafood.

MIZUNA WITH SALMON TARTARE, FENNEL-CURED OLIVES, AND TANGERINE

This is not only a great starter, but also a lovely light meal. It makes a great use for salmon that is left over from cleaning a fish—the meat that you scrape off the bones should not go to waste! The whole dish is raw—raw fish, raw greens—a pure, raw pleasure, especially in the heat of summer.

SERVES 2

6 ounces [170 g] skinless salmon fillet

2½ teaspoons olive oil

1½ teaspoons finely chopped shallot

2 teaspoons finely chopped fennel-cured green olives

1 teaspoon tangerine or orange zest, finely grated on a Microplane

1½ teaspoons lemon zest, finely grated on a Microplane

1 teaspoon fine sea salt

2 ounces [55 g] mizuna leaves

1 medium-boiled egg yolk (page 293)

Bottarga, for topping (optional)

Fresh chervil leaves, for garnish

Fresh tarragon leaves, for garnish

Toasted baguette slices, for serving

Coarsely chop the salmon by hand into very small pieces while keeping the integrity of the texture. Gently mix the salmon with the olive oil, shallot, olives, and tangerine and lemon zests. Season to taste with salt.

Divide the mizuna between two plates, then divide the salmon tartare evenly and place on and alongside the greens. Press the egg yolk through a fine-mesh sieve over the salmon, then lightly grate the bottarga over the egg. Garnish the salmon with the chervil and tarragon and serve with the baguette slices.

OTHER GREENS TO TRY frisée, Belgian endive

MIZUNA, FENNEL, AND DRIED APRICOTS WITH KALAMATA OLIVES

This salad is fun because of its bold and opposing flavors. The olives are salty; the apricots, sweet and tart; and the fennel adds sweetness to mingle with the mizuna, which sits on the lemony side of vegetal. Texturally, the chewy apricots, tender olives, and crunchy fennel make a dreamy combo, especially alongside grilled fish or chicken.

The quality of Kalamata olives can vary greatly. Purchase them at specialty groceries or a great Greek deli and buy them with pits, as pitted olives get soggy. They should be firm and briny but not overly salty, and purple-black.

To pit an olive, lightly crush it with your palm and pull away each side from the pit.

SERVES 4

1 large bulb fennel, trimmed and thinly shaved lengthwise on a mandoline

4 ounces [115 g] small mizuna leaves

¼ cup [5 g] fennel fronds, coarsely chopped

1 teaspoon fennel pollen

¼ cup [40 g] thinly sliced dried apricots

2 tablespoons pitted, torn-in-thirds Kalamata olives

½ shallot, thinly sliced

Fine sea salt

Lemon vinaigrette (page 300)

In a large bowl, combine the fennel, mizuna, fennel fronds, fennel pollen, apricots, olives, and shallot. Season with salt and dress with vinaigrette. Divide among four plates and serve.

OTHER GREENS TO TRY frisée, tender hearts of head lettuces (romaine, Little Gem, red leaf, butter)

Mizuna with Salmon Tartare, Fennel-Cured Olives, and Tangerine

MUSTARD GREENS

Brassica juncea

Quite simply, mustard greens taste like mustard; some even like to say they are the wasabi of salad greens, as they have that certain sinus-clearing quality. Sharply flavored with a lingering bite, mustards are one of the more versatile greens because they can be eaten raw, dried, and cooked in many fashions. They are originally from the Himalayas, with their use dating back over five thousand years, and are now widespread across Asia, Africa, and the United States, especially in the South, where they are as big a staple as collards. And yes, the seeds are used to make that famous yellow condiment. Mustard greens are one of the more nutrient-dense greens, rich in vitamins A, B, C, E, and K and in calcium, copper, manganese, phosphorus, and dietary fiber.

VARIETIES BAMBOO, BLACK, DAI GAI CHOY, DRAGON TONGUE, ETHIOPIAN, GREEN, PURPLE, RED, RUBY STREAK, WHITE, WILD CABBAGE, YELLOW

SEASON Winter through spring

HOW TO CHOOSE Choose crisp, perky, bright greens that have uniform coloring and no wilting, yellowing, or blemishes. The younger, smaller leaves have a more mellow flavor and tender texture.

HOW TO CLEAN Immerse in cool water. Agitate thoroughly with fingers—mustard greens tend to hold on to grit. Drain; pat or spin dry.

HOW TO STORE Store in an airtight plastic bin or ziplock bag or wrap in plastic wrap. In the crisper drawer of the refrigerator, mustard greens will keep for up to 5 days.

HOW TO REFRESH Immerse in ice water for 15 minutes. Drain and pat or spin dry.

COOKING METHODS Use raw in salads or cook by sautéing, boiling, steaming, braising, or stir-frying. Blanching (see page 6) before cooking reduces the sharpness of the flavor.

PAIRINGS Olive oil, sesame oil, soy sauce, tofu, soybeans, bacon, pork, nuts, beef, poultry, lamb, veal, game, firm-fleshed fish such as salmon, swordfish, and sturgeon.

MUSTARD GREEN PANCAKES

These aren't like breakfast pancakes; they are like the green onion pancakes you might find in a Chinese restaurant. If you love the sharp, strong flavor of mustard, you will love these. Or if you don't want so much of a vegetal flavor, consider subbing in a milder green, such as spinach or chard. The dipping sauce drives home the Asian flavor.

MAKES 4 PANCAKES, SERVES 4

Pancakes

2 cups [280 g] all-purpose flour

1 cup [240 ml] boiling water

¼ cup [60 ml] toasted sesame oil

1 ounce [30 g] thinly sliced mustard greens (tender stems are okay)

Dipping Sauce

2 tablespoons soy sauce

2 tablespoons rice wine vinegar

1 tablespoon toasted sesame oil

1 tablespoon thinly sliced green onions (green parts only)

½ teaspoon peeled and grated fresh ginger

2 teaspoons sugar

¼ cup [60 ml] neutral vegetable oil

Kosher salt

To make the pancakes, put the flour in a food processor. With the motor running, slowly drizzle in ¾ cup [180 ml] of the boiling water. Process for 15 seconds. If the dough does not come together, drizzle in more water, 1 tablespoon at a time, until it just comes together. The dough should be neither sticky nor dry. Transfer to a work surface and knead a few times to form a smooth ball. Cover with plastic wrap and allow to rest for 30 minutes at room temperature.

Divide the dough into four equal pieces and roll each into a smooth ball. If sticky, lightly dust each ball with flour. Working with one ball at a time, roll out into a disk about 8 inches [20 cm] in diameter. Using a pastry brush, paint a very thin layer of sesame oil over the top of the disk. Roll the disk up into a cylinder, then start at one end and coil the dough like a snail's shell. Flatten gently with your hand and roll again into an 8-inch [20-cm] disk.

Paint with another layer of sesame oil, top with an even layer of one-quarter of the sliced mustard greens, and roll up into a cylinder again. Again, coil like a snail's shell, flatten gently, and reroll into a 7-inch [17-cm] disk. Repeat with the remaining dough and mustard greens to make three more pancakes.

To make the dipping sauce, combine all of the dipping sauce ingredients in a small bowl, mix well, and set aside at room temperature.

Heat the oil in an 8-inch [20-cm] nonstick or cast-iron skillet over medium-high heat. When the oil is hot, after 2 to 3 minutes, carefully slip one pancake into the hot oil. Cook, shaking the pan gently until the first side is an even golden brown, about 2 minutes. Carefully flip with a spatula or tongs and continue to cook until the second side is an even golden brown, about 2 more minutes. Season with salt and cut into six wedges. Serve immediately with the sauce for dipping. Repeat with the remaining pancakes.

OTHER GREENS TO TRY nettles, spinach, lamb's-quarters, chard

MUSTARD GREENS SALAD WITH PEAR, AGED GOUDA, AND CASHEWS

This salad is weird. But it is a fun, unique kind of weird. I say weird because there is an intense explosion of flavor that you don't often get in a salad. Mustard greens with a mustard vinaigrette alone is a powerhouse for the palate. Add Gouda, cashews, and pears and you've got umami on a plate. Use less-than-ripe pears if you crave crispiness; use ripe pears if you crave sweetness. Both work great in this salad. This salad also works nicely as a filling for my recipe of doubles (page 49) or for lettuce tacos (page 167).

SERVES 4 TO 6

7 ounces [200 g] mustard greens, stems removed and greens sliced into ¼-inch [6-mm] ribbons

2 pears, quartered and cored

2 ounces [55 g] aged Gouda, grated or sliced into small pieces

½ cup [70 g] cashews, toasted

½ shallot, thinly sliced

Fine sea salt and freshly ground black pepper

About 5 tablespoons [TK ml] pickled mustard seed vinaigrette (page 301)

Put the mustard greens in a large bowl. Cut the pear quarters into slices ¼ inch [6 mm] thick and add to the bowl along with the Gouda, cashews, and shallot. Season the salad with salt and pepper, then dress with the vinaigrette to taste. Toss gently and serve immediately.

OTHER GREENS TO TRY head lettuce, arugula

STEAMED BUNS WITH HO-MI Z (DRAGON TONGUE)

A steamed bun: kind of like a taco, kind of like a sandwich. Either way it makes a great container for greens, especially when accompanied by a spread like *muhammara* or butternut squash puree and with meat, vegetables, and salads. Sweet and tender Japanese turnips and Ho-Mi Z, a mildly bitter mustard green variety, are my vegetables of choice for this tasty envelope.

MAKES 16 BUNS, SERVES 8

Steamed Buns

1¼ cups [300 ml] whole milk

2 teaspoons active dry yeast

2 teaspoons sugar

4¾ cups [680 g] bread flour

1 teaspoon fine sea salt

¼ cup [85 g] honey

¼ teaspoon baking powder

1 tablespoon neutral vegetable oil

Salad

32 small Japanese or Harukei (salad) turnips, shaved into rounds on a mandoline

4 ounces [115 g] Ho-Mi Z (dragon tongue) mustard greens

⅓ cup [15 g] pickled chard stems (page 78)

Flaky sea salt

Sherry vinaigrette (page 301)

2 cups [520 g] muhammara (page 299), or 2 cups [480 g] butternut squash puree (page 298)

16 slices slow-roasted pork loin (page 274) or cooked bacon

To make the buns, gently warm the milk to lukewarm in a saucepan. Be careful not to boil; the milk should be warm to the touch—105°F [40°C] or lower—not hot, or it will kill the yeast. Remove from the heat and whisk in the yeast and sugar. Allow the yeast to activate, about 5 minutes.

In a stand mixer fitted with a dough hook, combine the milk mixture, flour, salt, honey, baking powder, and vegetable oil and knead on low speed for 8 minutes. Remove from the mixer, knead a few times to make a ball, cover the dough ball with plastic wrap, and let rest at room temperature until doubled in size, about 2 hours.

When the dough has doubled in size, turn it out onto a clean surface, roll it into a long log, and then cut it into sixteen equal pieces. Shape each piece into a small ball. Working with one at a time, roll out each dough ball into a oblong (think naan) about 3 by 7 inches [7.5 by 17 cm], each with rounded edges. Place a small piece of parchment paper, just larger than the bun, on one-half of the dough, and fold the other half on top, creating a half-moon shape. Repeat with all of the dough balls. Cover the buns with plastic wrap and let rest at room temperature until they begin to puff, about 1½ hours.

Set up a steamer, using a bamboo or other steamer tray, and bring the water to a simmer over medium heat. Working in batches, place the buns in the steamer and cook, covered, for 10 minutes. Cool on a rack until you are ready to fill them.

To assemble, reheat the buns in the steamer until warm, about 2 minutes.

To make the salad, in a bowl, combine the turnips, mustard greens, and pickled chard and season with flaky sea salt. Dress with sherry vinaigrette.

Fill each bun with 2 tablespoons muhammara, a slice of pork, and a good handful of salad. Enjoy immediately.

OTHER GREENS TO TRY New Zealand spinach, red orach

NETTLES

Urtica dioica

Nettles really signify spring because they are the first wild green to surface from the winter chill. Often foraged, they are a fixture in wooded areas, though they are more and more becoming a farmers' market staple. Nettles are native to Europe, Asia, and the North American West. In addition to being prized for their nutty, earthy flavor, they have a long history of medicinal use, with various cultures using them to treat everything from bladder infections to rheumatism to hay fever to gout to MS to PMS to dandruff. Nettles are also useful as a dye, producing a yellow-green color, and have even been used as a cotton substitute in textiles. In literature, Shakespeare employed them as a metaphor for danger in *Henry IV, Part 1*; and in language, the Germans refer to "sitting in nettles" as getting into trouble. These "sticky" comparisons spring from the plant's nature to sting when raw. Therefore, always use gloves when handling raw nettles and always ingest them cooked (though there are some crazy British folk who participate in a raw nettle eating contest each year). Nutritionally, nettles give the body a blast of vitamins A and C, iron, potassium, manganese, and calcium.

VARIETIES BALL, BULL, CAROLINA HORSE, DEAD, DUMB, FALSE, FLAME, HEDGE, HEMP, HIMALAYAN GIANT, HORSE, PAINTED, ROBUST HORSE, ROCK, SILVER LEAF, SMALL-LEAF, SPURGE, STINGING, TEXAS, TREE, WESTERN HORSE, WHITE, WHITE HORSE, WOOD

SEASON Late winter through early spring

HOW TO CHOOSE Nettles should be soft and leafy but not wilted, with a vibrant green color without any brown spots.

HOW TO CLEAN Wear gloves when handling raw nettles to prevent stings, and use scissors to trim the leaves off of the stems. Immerse in cool water. Agitate with (gloved) fingers. Drain; spin or pat dry.

NOTE: Blanching nettles (see page 6) for 2 to 3 minutes, until tender, removes their stinging quality.

HOW TO STORE Store in an airtight plastic bin or ziplock bag or wrap in plastic wrap. In the crisper drawer of the refrigerator, nettles will keep for 3 to 5 days.

HOW TO REFRESH Immerse in ice water for 15 minutes. Drain and pat or spin dry.

COOKING METHODS Always cook nettles before eating. Cook by sautéing, simmering in soup; puree cooked nettles into a pesto, toss with pasta, or use in pasta filling or to top pizza.

PAIRINGS Olive oil, dairy, eggs, poultry, fish, polenta.

YEMENITE BRAISED BEEF SHORT RIBS WITH NETTLES

The nutty flavor of nettles rounds out this Yemenite stew perfectly. The defining component of this dish, however, is *hawaij*, the distinctive Yemenite spice blend composed of turmeric, clove, cardamom, black pepper, cumin, and coriander. The green tomatoes are not traditional, but I like to use them for the tartness that balances the spice mixture and the richness of the beef.

SERVES 6

3 pounds [1.4 kg] boneless beef short ribs or beef chuck, trimmed of any sinew or excess fat and cut into 12 equal pieces

Kosher salt

3 tablespoons olive oil

1 yellow onion, diced

2½ pounds [1.1 kg] green tomatoes, cored and quartered (see Note)

4 cloves garlic, lightly crushed

3 tablespoons hawaij spice mix for soup (page 298), plus more as needed

8 cups [2 L] double chicken stock (page 299)

½ bunch flat-leaf parsley, including tender stems

½ bunch cilantro, including tender stems

Freshly ground black pepper

12 small Yukon gold or creamer potatoes, peeled

4 cups [80 g] raw nettle leaves

Lettuce skhug (page 164) and tahini sauce (page 296), for serving

Generously season the short ribs with salt. Set aside.

In a large pot over medium-high heat, warm the olive oil. Add the onion, green tomatoes, and garlic and cook until tender, about 4 minutes. Add the hawaij and stir to combine. Add the beef and chicken stock and bring to a boil, then decrease the heat to a gentle simmer. Using a spoon or ladle, skim the surface of rendered fat and any foamy impurities.

Add the parsley and cilantro to the pot and season lightly with salt and pepper. Cook for 2 to 2½ hours, until the beef is very tender. Check the doneness of the beef by piercing it with a wooden skewer or fork. The meat should be fall-apart tender, but not shredding, when done.

About 15 minutes before the meat is fully cooked, add the potatoes to the broth. Simmer until the potatoes are cooked, 5 to 8 minutes. Using tongs, carefully add the nettle leaves to the stew, stir, and cook until wilted, 2 to 3 minutes. Season with salt to taste. Serve with the Lettuce Skhug and tahini sauce.

OTHER GREENS TO TRY amaranth, chard, red orach, spinach

NOTE: If you do not have green tomatoes, substitute 3 carrots, peeled and chopped into ½-inch [12-mm] pieces, and 2 celery ribs, chopped into ½-inch [12-mm] pieces.

NETTLE PAKORAS

These fritters are popular in India, where they are usually made with onions or spinach. Nettles are like spinach texturally, so I thought they would take well to this preparation. One thing to note when making this recipe is that the result is supposed to be thin and crispy—not like a typical dense, round fritter—so coat sparingly with the batter. You want just enough batter to hold the fritter together. When done right, the result is an addictively savory, crispy, nutty-flavored treat.

SERVES 4

2 cups [175 g] chickpea flour

1 jalapeño chile, finely chopped

½-inch [12-mm] piece fresh ginger, peeled and finely grated

2 teaspoons white sesame seeds, toasted

1 teaspoon yellow mustard seeds

¼ teaspoon ground turmeric

1 teaspoon curry powder

Generous pinch of asafoetida powder (hing), optional (can be found online or at an Indian grocery store)

⅛ teaspoon baking soda

Fine sea salt

¾ to 1 cup [180 to 240 ml] water, or as needed

4 cups [100 g] medium to large raw nettle leaves

½ yellow onion, halved and thinly sliced

4 cups [960 ml] neutral vegetable oil, for frying

Borani Esfanaaj (Persian Greens Dip; page 28)

In a large bowl, mix together the chickpea flour, jalapeño, ginger, sesame seeds, mustard seeds, turmeric, curry powder, asafoetida powder, baking soda, and 2 teaspoons salt. Add just enough of the water to develop a thick, smooth batter with a consistency that is thicker than cream but thinner than yogurt. Add the nettles and onion and stir to coat them fully with the batter.

In a medium pot, heat the oil to 350°F [180°C]. Line a plate with paper towels or set a wire rack on a sheet pan. Using a spoon, drop clusters of battered vegetables into the oil and fry until golden on the first side, 2 to 3 minutes, then flip and repeat. The vegetable clusters should be thin and fan out so the fritters are crisp rather than dense when eaten. Cook in batches to avoid overcrowding.

Remove the fritters from the oil and drain on the towel-lined plate or cooling rack. Season the fritters with salt and serve with the dip.

OTHER GREENS TO TRY mâche, spinach

NETTLE PUREE

This pesto has so many great uses that I recommend that you make it a pantry basic. It keeps well in the refrigerator or freezer, so it is easy to have on hand for using as directed in the sidebar.

MAKES 1½ CUPS [360 G]

> 3 cups [65 g] raw nettle leaves
>
> 6 fresh mint leaves
>
> 1 clove garlic
>
> ¼ cup [35 g] pine nuts
>
> 2 ice cubes
>
> ¾ cup [180 ml] olive oil, plus more for storing
>
> Kosher salt and freshly ground black pepper

Bring a large pot of salted water to a boil. Add the nettles and mint and cook for 30 seconds. Drain well, wrap the leaves in a clean kitchen towel, and wring out the excess moisture with your hands. Bunch the greens into a ball and cut into four pieces.

Place all of the greens in a blender and add the garlic, pine nuts, and 1 ice cube and pulse until chopped. With the motor running, slowly drizzle in the olive oil and then add the second ice cube and puree until a thin paste forms. (The consistency of the puree can be changed by adding less or more olive oil. Less oil will yield a spreadable paste and more oil will yield a thinner paste.) Season to taste with salt and pepper.

To store the pesto, transfer it to a jar, top with a thin layer of olive oil, cap, and refrigerate for up to 1 week, or transfer it to ice-cube trays, freeze, pop out the cubes, place the cubes in a ziplock plastic freezer bag, and place the bag in the freezer for up to 2 months.

OTHER GREENS TO TRY basil, spinach

10 THINGS TO DO WITH NETTLE PUREE

1 Use in place of tomato sauce on a pizza.

2 Stir into softly scrambled eggs.

3 Spread on a sandwich.

4 Toss with pasta.

5 Drop a dollop into minestrone soup for flavor, use to thicken a pureed vegetable soup, or drizzle into a bowl of chicken soup and garnish with croutons.

6 Thin with fresh lemon juice and olive oil and use as a salad dressing.

7 Spoon on top of plain Greek yogurt and serve as a dip for crudités.

8 Thin with olive oil and spoon over roasted pork.

9 Butterfly a lamb or pork roast, spread with the pesto, then roll up, tie, and roast.

10 Spread on grilled or toasted bread and top with a poached egg and grated Parmigiano-Reggiano.

NEW ZEALAND SPINACH

Tetragonia tetragonioides

This far-flung green originates from Down Under, hence the name. Captain Cook is said to have fed it to his crew to combat scurvy. It came to Europe when botanist Sir Joseph Banks brought it to England in the late eighteenth century. Despite its name, New Zealand spinach isn't technically a spinach, though it does have a similar flavor. It is high in scurvy-fighting vitamin C, as well as vitamin A, calcium, magnesium, phosphorus, and carotenoids.

VARIETIES MAORI

SEASON Summer

HOW TO CHOOSE Choose crisp, sturdy greens that have uniform coloring and no yellowing or dark blemishes. Do not buy if wilted.

HOW TO CLEAN Immerse in cool water. Agitate with fingers. Drain; pat or spin dry.

HOW TO STORE Store in an airtight plastic bin or ziplock bag or wrap in plastic wrap. In the crisper drawer of the refrigerator, New Zealand spinach will keep for 5 to 7 days.

HOW TO REFRESH Immerse in ice water for 15 minutes. Drain and spin or pat dry.

COOKING METHODS Use raw in salads or sandwiches or cook by sautéing, baking, blanching, steaming, stir-frying, braising, simmering in soups and stews, tossing into pasta, or topping pizza.

PAIRINGS Curry, berries, nuts, bacon, pork, cheese, cream, eggs, meats, fish, poultry.

NEW ZEALAND SPINACH WITH CHINESE SAUSAGE

Chinese sausage really stands apart in the sausage arena. Known as *lap cheong*, it has a high fat content and tastes wonderfully salty and savory. The water content of New Zealand spinach makes it a nice wilty green, so when you toss it in at the end of cooking the sausage, it takes on a warm, wilted quality instead of needing a hardcore braise. This keeps this whole dish on the fresher, cleaner side. Serve with medium-grain white rice and roasted pork, roasted or grilled chicken or fish, or fried eggs.

SERVES 4 AS A SIDE DISH

3 tablespoons soy sauce

3 tablespoons mirin

2 tablespoons toasted sesame oil

3 tablespoons neutral vegetable oil

½ yellow onion, finely diced

2 cloves garlic, thinly sliced

4 ounces [115 g] Chinese sausage, sliced into thin rounds

1 pound [455 g] New Zealand spinach, leaves and leaf clusters

Fine sea salt and freshly ground black pepper

Mustard green furikake (page 297)

In a small bowl, combine the soy sauce, mirin, and sesame oil. Set aside.

Warm the vegetable oil in a large sauté pan over medium-high heat. Add the onion, garlic, and sausage and cook until the onion is translucent, about 3 minutes. Turn the heat down if the onion or garlic begins to brown. Add the New Zealand spinach to the pan and stir to combine. Season with salt and pepper, then remove from the heat so as not to wilt the spinach fully. Serve topped with the furikake.

OTHER GREENS TO TRY choys, gai lan

PURSLANE

Portulaca oleracea

Purslane has a distinctive succulent texture that makes it fun to pair with vegetables with a contrasting texture, like cucumbers. Its aliases—pigweed, little hogweed—betray that it is looked upon as a nuisance in the United States, though Europeans, South Americans, Middle Easterners, and Asians have been eating it for millennia. Its unusual sweet and sour taste and succulent quality earned it a place in the Bible as a repugnant food (some say that it may have been a mistranslation of mallow, however). The same cultures that regard it as food have used it medicinally, too. In traditional Chinese medicine, for example, purslane is used for skin ailments. It is known as one of the more nutritious greens, with good amounts of vitamins A, B, C, and E, as well as magnesium, calcium, potassium, and iron.

VARIETIES GOLDBERG GOLDEN, GREEN, GRUNER RED

SEASON Late spring through summer

HOW TO CHOOSE Choose crisp, sturdy greens that have uniform coloring and no yellowing or dark blemishes. Do not buy if wilted.

HOW TO CLEAN Immerse in cool water. Agitate with fingers. Drain; pat or spin dry.

HOW TO STORE Store in an airtight plastic bin or ziplock bag or wrap in plastic wrap. In the crisper drawer of the refrigerator, purslane will keep for 2 to 3 days.

HOW TO REFRESH Immerse in ice water for 15 minutes. Drain and pat or spin dry.

COOKING METHODS Serve raw in salads or cook by stir-frying, sautéing, or simmering in soups and stews.

PAIRINGS Lemon, parsley, legumes, potatoes, chicken, cucumbers, yogurt, feta cheese.

MUJADARA WITH PURSLANE

In the Old Testament, Esau gave away his birthright to his younger brother, Jacob, for a lentil stew. After a hunt, Esau was so hungry, and Jacob's stew was so delicious, that he gave up all rights just to enjoy it. *Mujadara* (lentils and rice with caramelized onions) is believed to have been that memorable stew. My version includes the cool, succulent texture of purslane, along with the traditional caramelized onions, rice cooked in lentil water, and cumin, coriander, and cinnamon. The good news is that you don't have to sacrifice much to enjoy this version.

SERVES 8

1½ cups [300 g] green lentils

1⅔ cups [400 ml] neutral vegetable oil

4 large yellow onions, halved and thickly sliced

Fine sea salt

1 tablespoon cumin seeds

1 teaspoon coriander seeds

2 teaspoons ground cinnamon

1½ teaspoons ground turmeric

1½ cups [300 g] basmati rice or coarse bulgur

Freshly ground black pepper

1 pound [455 g] purslane

Lemon vinaigrette (page 300)

Optional Garnishes

Labneh

Fried flat-leaf parsley

Fried eggs

In a saucepan, cover the lentils with at least 2 inches [5 cm] of water and cook over medium-high heat until just tender but still toothy to the bite, 10 to 15 minutes. Remove from the heat and drain, reserving the liquid. Run the cooked lentils under cool water to stop the cooking and set aside.

Pour the oil into a large, heavy pan and add enough of the onions to make a thin layer on the bottom. Cook over high heat until the onions are a very dark, almost black caramel color, 10 to 15 minutes. Most should be dark and caramelized, though some will stay light. When done, transfer the onions to a sieve and hold the sieve over the pan to drain off any extra oil. Lay the cooked onions on a sheet pan in a single layer to cool and repeat with the remaining onions. Season the cooked onions lightly with salt and set aside.

Drain off all but ⅓ cup [80 ml] of the oil from the pan and return one-third of the cooked onions to the pan. Finely grind the cumin and coriander seeds and add to the pan along with the cinnamon and turmeric. Stir over medium-high heat for 1 minute to toast the spices. Add the lentils, rice, and salt to taste and stir to combine. Add enough water to the reserved lentil cooking liquid to equal 2 cups [480 ml]. Add the liquid to the pan and bring to a simmer. Decrease the heat to low and cover tightly with aluminum foil. Cook gently for 20 minutes, then let rest, off the heat, for 10 minutes. Fluff with the tines of a fork, then stir in the remaining onions.

Toss the purslane in a large bowl with the vinaigrette and season with salt and pepper. Garnish the mujadara with the purslane and with the optional garnishes, if you like, and serve immediately. If not serving right away, store the onions and the lentil mixture separately in the refrigerator for up to 3 days and combine when reheating.

OTHER GREENS TO TRY frisée, mâche

RED ORACH

Atriplex hortensis

Sometimes called mountain spinach or giant lamb's-quarters, this magenta "green" is a member of the amaranth family. Its flavor is often compared to spinach, which makes it a suitable, and colorful, companion and substitute. Thousands of years ago, orach was more commonly eaten than spinach, until the Persians started to cultivate spinach and its seeds more easily proliferated. In Italy, red orach was once used to color pasta; today it is often used to visually dress up salads, pastas, potatoes, and rice. Nutritionally, red orach contains high amounts of vitamins C and K, calcium, magnesium, phosphorus, iron, carotenes, protein, zinc, selenium, and dietary fiber.

VARIETIES GREEN, PURPLE, RED, WHITE, YELLOW

SEASON Spring

HOW TO CHOOSE Choose crisp, sturdy leaves that have bright, uniform coloring and no dark blemishes. Do not buy if wilted.

HOW TO CLEAN Strip leaves from stems. Immerse in cool water. Agitate with fingers. Drain; pat or spin dry.

HOW TO STORE Store in an airtight plastic bin or ziplock bag or wrap in plastic wrap. In the crisper drawer of the refrigerator, red orach will keep for 5 to 7 days.

HOW TO REFRESH Immerse in ice water for 15 minutes. Drain and pat or spin dry.

COOKING METHODS Use raw in salads or cook by sautéing, stir-frying, braising, or simmering in soup.

PAIRINGS Garlic, fennel, fish, lamb.

PIEROGI WITH RED ORACH

When I was in my twenties, I spent some time backpacking in Poland. In Krakow, there was a restaurant off the main square, down a little alleyway. I went to lunch there every day because of its pierogi. I already had a soft spot for pierogi, as I'm half Polish and enjoyed my grandma's version growing up. When creating this recipe, I thought of how a green would be a wonderful addition. Red orach, with its spinach-like flavor that straddles the line between intense and delicate perfectly fits the bill.

MAKES 5 DOZEN PIEROGI, SERVES 8 TO 10

1 egg

2 tablespoons sour cream

1 cup [240 ml] whole milk

1 cup [240 ml] water, at room temperature

5 cups [700 g] all-purpose flour, plus more for dusting

5 pounds [2.3 kg] Yukon gold potatoes (about 12), peeled and quartered

6 ounces [170 g] red orach leaves, coarsely chopped

8 ounces [230 g] cream cheese, at room temperature

¼ cup [55 g] unsalted butter, melted

Kosher salt

Scant 1 teaspoon freshly ground black pepper

Yellow cornmeal, for dusting

To Serve

1 cup [240 ml] melted unsalted butter

Flaky sea salt

2 tablespoons poppy seeds

Whisk together the egg and sour cream, then whisk in the milk and water. Stir in the flour, 1 cup [140 g] at a time.

Turn the sticky dough out onto a floured surface. Using a dough scraper, turn and fold the dough to knead, dusting with flour as needed, until it is elastic and no longer sticky, about 8 minutes. (Be careful not to add too much flour or the dough will be tough.) Cover with plastic wrap and let rest at room temperature for 1 hour.

Put the potatoes in a large pot, cover with water, and bring to a boil. Cook until fork-tender, 25 to 30 minutes. Add the orach 1 minute before the potatoes are done. Drain the potatoes, transfer to a bowl, and mash with a whisk. The potatoes should be mostly creamy, with a few small chunks. Stir in the cream cheese and butter. Season with kosher salt and the pepper.

Divide the dough into four equal pieces and cover with plastic wrap. Line a sheet pan with parchment and dust generously with cornmeal.

On a lightly floured surface, roll out a piece of dough into a round ⅛ inch [3 mm] think. Using a 3-inch [7.5-cm] round cutter, cut out as many rounds as possible. Cover with plastic wrap to prevent drying. Repeat with the remaining dough.

To shape each pierogi, place a 1½-inch [4-cm] oval of the potato filling (about 5 teaspoons) in the center of a round, fold the dough over the filling, and pinch together the edges, sealing well. Place on the prepared sheet pan and cover loosely with plastic wrap.

Bring a large pot of salted water to a boil and then coat a platter with ½ cup [120 ml] of the melted butter. Working in batches, add the pierogi to the pot. They will sink to the bottom and then rise. Once they have risen, allow them to cook through, about 2 minutes. Then using a slotted spoon, transfer the pierogi to the platter. Repeat with the remaining pierogi. Drizzle all of the cooked pierogi with the remaining butter, sprinkle with flaky sea salt and the poppy seeds, and serve immediately.

OTHER GREENS TO TRY beet greens, roasted radicchio (added chopped to drained potatoes)

Beet greens

Broccoli

Carrot greens

Cauliflower leaves

ROOT, FRUIT, AND VEGETABLE GREENS

Part of the ethos of this book is to use all the parts of a vegetable as possible. Tasty, nutritious greens may even occur in vegetables you regularly enjoy, crowning the tops of beets, sprouting from the stalks of broccoli and cauliflower, cradling sweet potatoes. These greens are not garbage! They happen to be great on the plate. As a rule, don't overlook anything green on a root, fruit, or vegetable. Here are several that are especially great to cook.

BEET GREENS
Beta vulgaris

They taste more like chard than beets, but the texture of beet greens, especially when braised, becomes much more tender than other vegetable greens. Beet greens can be eaten raw, boiled, braised, steamed, and sautéed, and the stems are just as good as the leaves. Best in midsummer to late fall and early winter, beet greens are available year-round and are a good source of vitamins A, B, C, and K and of calcium, iron, magnesium, copper, potassium, and manganese. Olive oil, vinegar, lentils, eggs, beans, yogurt, chile, mustard, and nuts pair wonderfully with beet greens. Beet greens are also great cooked like creamed spinach and topped with chopped toasted hazelnuts.

BROCCOLI LEAVES
Brassica oleracea italica

Of course, the florets are the most popular part of broccoli, and their stems are now coming back in vogue. But don't overlook the leaves! They have a mild, slightly sweet flavor and, though not super-abundant on the plant, add a subtle green element to stir-fries and soups and stews. The leaves thrive in the spring and fall—eat them right off the harvested stalks—and contain vitamins A, C, and folate and iron, potassium, and dietary fiber. Broccoli leaves, like their stalks, pair well with bacon, cheese, garlic, chile, citrus, legumes, beans, peppers, potatoes, onions, and any fish, meat, or poultry.

CARROT GREENS
Daucus carota

The leafy tops of the carrot are among those that all too often end up in the garbage. Though very different from their sweet roots, the herbal, parsley-like greens are a useful part of the vegetable. Just as versatile as their root, they can be blanched, sautéed, braised, simmered in soups and stews, eaten raw in a salad, and spun into a pesto, and they also match well with meat, firm fish, pasta, garlic, and chiles. Late spring and fall are when the whole vegetable is at its peak, and the carrot greens share the nutrient value—vitamins A, B, C, and K and manganese and potassium. The greens themselves are sometimes added to mouthwashes because of their antiseptic value.

CAULIFLOWER LEAVES
Brassica oleracea botrytis

Cauliflower thrives from summer into fall, and their greens are often discarded, though they can, and should, be eaten because of their appealing mild, leek-like flavor. They are terrific roasted, sautéed, braised, stir-fried, baked, and tossed into pastas, soups, and stews. Cauliflower greens provide a great source of vitamins B, C, and K and pair well with chile, garlic, soy sauce, any fish, meat, poultry, butter, eggs, and cream.

CELERY LEAVES
Apium graveolens

Certainly more flavorful than their stalks, celery leaves are also much more aromatic and nutritious, providing vitamins A, C, and K, and calcium and potassium. Another great thing about celery leaves is their wide availability. In the grocery, you can find them year-round, though they naturally thrive in fall, winter, and spring. They can be used like any herb for flavoring, especially in stir-fries, stocks, soups, and stews. They pair especially well with lemon, fish, chicken, eggs, potatoes, and white beans, and celery leaf pesto is great in pasta and risotto.

FAVA GREENS
Vicia faba

The flavor of these greens mimic their beans: earthy, with a silken texture. Thriving in late spring through summer, the greens, also like the beans, are a great source of protein as well as folate, manganese, copper, potassium, zinc, iron, and calcium. They pair nicely with pasta, rice, soy sauce, tofu, soybeans, sesame, chiles, and garlic and can be stir-fried, sautéed, steamed, and enjoyed raw in salads. In Asian cultures, they are used to wrap seafood before steaming.

GRAPE LEAVES
Vitis vinifera

Ubiquitous in Middle Eastern and Mediterranean cultures, these tart, sturdy greens are often found stuffed with rice, meat, or both. They are best in late summer through fall, and though they contain ample amounts of vitamins C and K, grape leaves are renowned for their antioxidant properties. Grape leaves are not eaten raw. Steamed, blanched, or sautéed, they go well with rice, any meats, fish,

olive oil, lemon, cream, vinegar, nuts, any grain, cheese, dried fruit, and chiles.

KOHLRABI GREENS
Brassica oleracea gongylodes

These rich greens stand out in stark contrast to their purple or bright green roots. Kohlrabi leaves have a cabbage- or kale-like flavor (kohlrabi itself is actually a variety of cabbage), and can be used similarly: served raw in a salad or cooked by boiling, steaming, sautéing, braising, simmering in soups and stews, and stir-frying. Best in spring and fall, they share their stem's high amounts of vitamins B and C, fiber, copper, manganese, and potassium. Both the stems and the greens are the subject of various studies about cancer prevention.

PEA GREENS
Pisum sativum

The pea plant is much more than a pod: there are pea leaves, shaped like small arrowheads, which grow out of the top of the plant; there are the pea shoots, which are a microgreen—the young, early growth of the plant; and then there are pea tendrils, or *tau miu* in Asian markets, whose light, grassy, stems with tiny leaves taste much like peas, yet lighter. All parts of these pea "greens" are often sautéed, stir-fried, blanched, stirred into soups or stews, or enjoyed raw in salads. Like peas, they are high in vitamins A, C, K, and folate and in dietary fiber, iron, and manganese and are at their best in the spring and early summer. Enjoy them minimally dressed, with a spritz of lemon or with oil and vinegar; paired with a mild cheese, such as goat cheese; or tossed with nuts and salad greens. They also make a fresh garnish for any meat, poultry, or fish.

Celery leaves

Kohlrabi greens

Grape leaves

Pea greens

Radish greens

Squash greens

Sweet potato greens

Tomato leaves

RADISH GREENS

Raphanus sativus

All of the radish varieties—whether French break-fast or daikon—have delicious greens. Pungent and spicy, yet not as sharp as their roots, juicy radish greens are a good source of vitamin C, folate, and potassium and are best in the spring. Radish greens are great for pesto, simmered in soups and stews, roasted, sautéed, stir-fried, braised, steamed, served raw in salads, and even pickled. They pair especially well with braised meats and with sturdy fish such as tuna, swordfish, or salmon. Soy sauce, tofu, soybeans, oyster sauce, fish sauce, garlic, mushrooms, and chiles bring out the best in these greens.

SQUASH GREENS

Cucurbita moschata

Most often eaten in the Koreas, Italy, Bangladesh, and India, this fibrous green has a surprising sweet, mild flavor that some compare to green beans or asparagus. These greens are also packed full of nutrients, such as vitamins A, B, and C and potassium and fiber. Whether cultivated from winter or spring varieties, the leaves should be removed from the stems before cooking. Squash greens make a great companion to pasta, any meat, poultry, or fish and take well to cream, cheese, chiles, soy sauce, tofu, soybeans, sesame, and fish sauce. They are delicious simmered in soups and stews, tossed in pasta, sautéed, stir-fried, boiled, broiled, braised, and steamed. (Use immediately, as some can wilt dramatically soon after harvest.)

SWEET POTATO GREENS

Ipomoea batatas

The best time to use those sweet potato greens is, unsurprisingly, fall—think of all of those sweet potatoes that will be enjoyed on Thanksgiving day. Though the tubers are as all-American as the holiday at which they are enjoyed, the greens are often eaten in China, Polynesia, and the Philippines. They are a rich source of vitamins A, B, C, and K and of manganese, potassium, iron, and calcium. Sturdy to cook, sweet potato greens are great braised, stir-fried, sautéed, broiled, baked, simmered in soups and stews, or tossed with pasta. The greens are wonderful when paired with lemon, olive oil, sesame, soy sauce, soybeans, tofu, garlic, chiles, poultry, firm-fleshed fish such as cod, and any meat.

TOMATO LEAVES

Solanum lycopersicum

Incredibly aromatic, tomato leaves, despite what you may have heard, are not poisonous. Yes, they are part of the nightshade family, but they do not carry the toxic properties often associated with the group. Quite simply, they taste like they smell: intense and slightly perfumy, and they are also packed with nutrients, among them vitamins A, C, and K and dietary fiber, potassium, and manganese. Like the fruit, tomato leaves are best in summer and early fall. They make a wonderful companion to pasta and can be simmered in soups and stews, stir-fried, sautéed, and blanched.

TURNIP GREENS

Brassica rapa rapa

Ask any American Southerner: turnip greens are as important in the Southern culinary lexicon as kale or collards. Slightly bitter, chlorophyll-rich, tender turnip greens are a true cold-weather treat, thriving from fall through winter. Laden with vitamins A, C, K, and folate and with calcium and manganese, turnip greens are best when cooked with any manner of pork, especially ham hocks. They can be used raw in salads or cooked by simmering, sautéing, stir-frying, braising, blanching, boiling, or stewing. They also pair well with chicken, garlic, onions, chile, soy sauce, tofu, soybeans, sesame, vinegar. and olive oil. The varieties Hakurei, Kokabu, and Tokyo can be found at Asian markets.

HOW TO CHOOSE Leaves should be sprightly, not wilted, with no yellowing; they should be free of mold. Roots should look healthy.

HOW TO CLEAN Immerse in cool water. Agitate with fingers. Drain; pat or spin dry.

HOW TO STORE Cut the greens from roots and store in an airtight plastic bin or ziplock bag or wrap in plastic wrap. In the crisper drawer of the refrigerator, most of these greens will keep for 2 to 3 days.

HOW TO REFRESH Immerse in ice water for 15 minutes. Drain and spin or pat dry.

20 THINGS TO DO WITH ROOT, FRUIT, AND VEGETABLE GREENS

1 Add to a vegetable sauté or stir-fry.

2 Chop finely and add to a salad.

3 Puree into a pesto and dollop it in soup, spread on sandwiches, or use as a pasta sauce.

4 Wilt into a brothy soup.

5 Sauté and add to a frittata.

6 Sauté and add to a pasta dish.

7 Cook on the grill with fish and serve together.

8 Steam in parchment packets with butter, herbs, wine, and mushrooms.

9 Cook with other greens and add cream to make creamed greens, like creamed spinach.

10 Cook with rice or add to fried rice (page 142).

11 Cook and puree with beans to make hummus.

12 Eat raw as part of a crudité platter.

13 Roast with chicken and potatoes in the oven, tossing the greens in during the last 15 minutes.

14 Use them in Colcannon (page 146).

15 Cook and chop into egg salad.

16 Add to grain salads, raw and chopped.

17 Use to make salted herbs (page 141).

18 Use in a kimchi pickle (page 81).

19 Combine with other greens or vegetables and serve with bagna cauda (page 295).

20 Cook, then puree into soft butter with garlic and herbs for a compound butter to use on . . . everything!

CARROT GREENS SALSA VERDE AND EGG PIZZA

Jim Lahey is the king of dough. He's a James Beard Award–winning baker and the founder of Sullivan Street Bakery in New York City. His recipe is my go-to pizza dough, always, and is what I use for this remarkably delicious pizza, which is baked with eggs nestled in the greens. I love to finish dishes with eggs, and on this pizza, the yolk is especially rich against the bright and earthy herb puree that adds an unexpected flavor profile. If you're craving a more traditional pizza, feel free to sub in a basil or kale pesto.

SERVES 6

> 1 cup [220 g] carrot greens salsa verde (page 295)
>
> Pizza dough (recipe follows)
>
> 6 eggs
>
> 4 ounces [115 g] provolone, grated
>
> 1½ cups [90 g] lightly packed finely grated Pecorino Romano
>
> Fine sea salt

Preheat the oven to 450°F [230°C].

Gently spread the salsa across the pizza dough, leaving a border of about ½ inch [12 mm] along the edges for a crust. Bake the pizza for 15 to 20 minutes, until the crust begins to brown. Remove the pizza from the oven and crack the eggs onto the areas of the dough that are recessed and will hold them. Sprinkle the provolone over the pizza and return the pizza to the oven. Bake until the egg whites are set and the cheese is melted, about 10 minutes more.

Remove from the oven and sprinkle the Pecorino Romano evenly over the top and then season the pizza with salt. Using an offset spatula, carefully slide the pizza onto a large cutting board and cut into squares. Serve immediately.

NO-KNEAD PIZZA DOUGH FROM JIM LAHEY, CO.

DOUGH FOR 1 HALF SHEET PAN-SIZE PIZZA

> 3¾ cups [525 g] bread flour
>
> 2½ teaspoons active dry yeast
>
> ¾ teaspoon kosher salt
>
> ¾ teaspoon sugar
>
> 1⅓ cups [320 ml] water, at room temperature
>
> ½ cup [120 ml] olive oil

Stir together the flour, yeast, salt, and sugar in a bowl. Add the water and mix until combined. Cover with plastic wrap and set in a warm place to rise for 2 hours. Pour the olive oil onto a half sheet pan and gently scrape all of the dough on top of the oil, using a spatula or plastic bench scraper. Using your fingertips, gently deflate the dough (do not press all of the air out of the dough), then stretch the dough out to the sides to almost fill the pan. It won't quite cover the entire pan. Let rest, uncovered, for 15 minutes before topping.

MOONG DAL AND BASMATI RICE KITCHARI WITH BEET GREENS

Kitchari, popular in Bangladesh, India, Pakistan, and Nepal, is the Sanskrit name for a dish with lentils and rice, a close cousin to—and inspiration for—the dish known as kedgeree. Regional variations feature rice, legumes, spices, vegetables, fish, and egg—all depending on available ingredients and local tradition. Where some regions use coconut oil to sauté and toast the spices, others use ghee (clarified butter). In the Ayurvedic tradition, *kitchari* is used in a popular cleanse. I like to garnish this dish with a poached egg, cilantro, chiles, and toasted cashews, and it is wonderful for breakfast, lunch, or dinner. Purifying and comforting, the beet greens in this dish boost its nutritional factor even more. I tend to use non-red-veined beet greens so the color doesn't bleed into the rest of the dish. If I do use the greens of red beets, I'll often blanch the greens, shock them, and then ring them out really, really well to get rid of some of that redness.

SERVES 4

¾ cup [150 g] moong dal (yellow split mung beans)

⅔ cup [130 g] basmati rice

2 teaspoons coconut oil

2 teaspoons black mustard seeds

1 teaspoon fenugreek seeds

1 teaspoon coriander seeds

½- to 1-inch [12-mm to 2.5-cm] piece fresh ginger, peeled and finely grated on a Microplane

1 teaspoon ground turmeric

1 teaspoon ground cumin

2 bay leaves

4 cups [960 ml] water

4 ounces [115 g] beet greens, stems cut into short lengths, leaves cut into ½-inch [12-mm] ribbons

Flaky sea salt

½ cup [20 g] chopped fresh cilantro

Optional Toppings

Poached eggs (page 293)

Sliced jalapeño chile

Mustard oil

Vadouvan (spice mix; available online at laboiteny.com)

Plain yogurt

Toasted cashews

Rinse the dal and rice together under running cool water until the water runs clear.

In a medium pot, heat the coconut oil over medium heat. Add the mustard seeds and fenugreek seeds and toast until the mustard seeds pop, about 2 minutes Add the coriander seeds, ginger, turmeric, and cumin and cook for about 30 seconds, stirring constantly, until fragrant. Add the dal, rice, and bay leaves and stir until they are coated with the spice mixture. Add the water, stir, bring to a medium simmer, and simmer, uncovered, for 10 minutes. Add the beet greens and stems, stir to combine, and continue to cook until the dal and rice are soft but not mushy, 15 to 20 minutes total. Season with flaky sea salt. Garnish with the cilantro and serve with as many optional toppings as you choose.

OTHER GREENS TO TRY chard, red orach (blanch before adding to rice)

ROASTED TROUT WITH CARROT GREENS SALSA VERDE

I specify ruby trout in this recipe, but the fact is, any really fresh trout works wonderfully with this salsa. For the fish, the trick is to make sure your pan is really hot before cooking the fish on one side until crispy, and then on the other side until just barely cooked through. That way the delicate fish will stay tender rather than overcook. The carrot green salsa verde acts as a fresh, herbal complement to this simple fish dish. Roasted potatoes make a great accompaniment.

SERVES 2

2 (8-ounce/227-g) whole ruby trout, gutted, filleted, and head on

Fine sea salt and freshly ground black pepper

3 tablespoons carrot greens salsa verde (page 295)

6 thin slices lemon, seeds removed, plus lemon wedges, for serving

¼ cup [60 ml] olive oil (enough to thinly cover bottom of pan)

¼ cup [55 g] unsalted butter, cut into 1-tablespoon pats

Preheat the oven to 425°C [220°C].

Dry the trout, removing any excess moisture on the skin, with a clean kitchen towel. Season the fish inside and out with salt and pepper. Spread 1¼ tablespoons of the salsa over the inside flesh of each trout, then lay 3 slices of lemon in each cavity, arranging them to cover the length of the fish. Close the fish.

Place a 12-inch [30.5-cm] cast-iron skillet over high heat and add the olive oil. When the pan is very hot, add the trout and sear until the skin is crisp, about 2 minutes. Using a spatula, carefully turn the trout over in the pan. Open the cavities and place butter pats along the lemon slices. Sear over high heat for 2 minutes.

Place the pan with the fish in the oven and roast just until cooked through, about 3 minutes. Baste with the oil and butter that has melted into the pan.

Serve with lemon wedges.

OTHER GREENS TO TRY herbs such as parsley, dill, tarragon, cilantro

CARROT LEAVES IN CABBAGE SALAD WITH DATES AND ALMONDS

There is nothing like a good crunchy cabbage salad, especially one that includes carrot leaves. The greens from carrots impart a clean and herbal chlorophyll flavor. Red cabbage tastes a bit mustardy, while the cilantro vinaigrette reinforces those carrot greens, and dates and almonds give this salad a Middle Eastern feel. To make it even more Middle Eastern, serve it inside a pita with feta cheese. Otherwise, serve in a lettuce taco (page 167) or over quinoa and grilled chicken in a bowl.

SERVES 4

6 cups [340 g] loosely packed finely shredded red cabbage

6 Medjool dates, pitted and cut into ¼-inch [6-mm] pieces

¼ cup [30 g] chopped toasted almonds

½ shallot, thinly sliced

1½ cups [30 g] clipped carrot greens, in small clusters

Kosher salt and freshly ground black pepper

Cilantro vinaigrette (page 300)

Combine the cabbage, dates, almonds, shallot, and carrot greens in a large bowl. Season with salt and pepper and lightly dress with vinaigrette. Divide among four plates and serve immediately.

OTHER GREENS TO TRY herbs such as parsley, dill, tarragon, cilantro

Roasted Trout with Carrot Greens Salsa Verde

Celery Leaf and Heart Chartreuse Sherbet

CELERY LEAF AND HEART CHARTREUSE SHERBET

Refreshing, delicate, tart, and flavorful, the true flavor of celery—more concentrated in the leaves than in the stalk—comes through in this recipe. This works as either a palate cleanser or as a light, refreshing dessert. Top it with olive oil and dukkah (page 297), or add a scoop of it to a glass of Prosecco. There's something light and festive about it that begs for something frizzante.

MAKES 4 CUPS [960 ml]

    1 teaspoon celery seeds

    1 cup [200 g] sugar

    ⅓ cup [80 ml] hot tap water

    2 cups [480 ml] buttermilk

    ¾ cup [180 ml] whole milk

    ⅔ cup [160 ml] celery heart and leaf juice, from 7½ ounces [215 g] celery leaves and heart, juiced

    2 teaspoons Green Chartreuse

In a small pan over medium heat, gently toast the celery seeds. When fragrant, remove from the heat and cool, then finely grind.

Combine the sugar, water, and ground celery seeds, stirring to dissolve the sugar. Set aside at room temperature for 1 hour to allow the flavors to bloom.

Mix the buttermilk, milk, celery juice, and Chartreuse in a bowl. Using a fine-mesh sieve, strain the celery sugar syrup into the buttermilk mixture, making sure to keep all the celery seeds out of the milk mixture. Chill completely in the fridge.

Freeze the mixture in an ice-cream maker according to the manufacturer's directions. Transfer to a large container and freeze until firm, about 1 hour. The sherbet can be stored in the freezer for up to 5 days.

OTHER GREENS TO TRY Chinese celery leaf, butter lettuce, mâche, cilantro

ROASTED CAULIFLOWER HALVES WITH GREENS

In Israel, there's a wonderful restaurant, Miznon, known for a lot of things, and one of them is whole roasted cauliflower. This recipe reminds me of that memorable dish. I like to cut the head in half and roast it, as you can sear it harder and each half gets a nice, even flavor because of the flat surface area. Ridiculously easy to make, the cauliflower can be served with muhammara (page 299), which adds complex and complementary flavors and creaminess.

SERVES 4

    1 large head cauliflower

    ¼ cup [60 ml] olive oil, plus more as needed

    Kosher salt

Preheat the oven to 425°F [220°C].

Cut the cauliflower head in half through the core, retaining the leaves. Trim away any discolored or oxidized (gray or brown) areas and discard.

Heat the oil in a large cast-iron or other ovenproof pan over high heat. When hot, add the cauliflower halves, cut side down, and cook until golden and charred, about 4 minutes. Turn the halves over to brown on the floret side, about 3 minutes.

Season with salt and drizzle any dry areas with a bit of olive oil. Place the pan in the oven and roast until the core is tender, 15 to 20 minutes.

Remove from the oven and serve.

CARROT SALAD WITH FENNEL AND MUSTARD SEED VINAIGRETTE

This crunchy, quick-and-easy-to-prepare, seasonal salad features one of my favorite vinaigrettes—the mustard seed really causes each element to wake up. This salad is also a winner texture-wise, with the snappy, sweet carrots; the crispy, juicy fennel and apples; and the tender, earthy beets. Carrot greens bring an herbal freshness to the whole array.

SERVES 4

4 carrots (in a variety of colors, if available), peeled

1 apple, quartered and cored

1 small fennel bulb

2 small raw red or golden beets

2 green onions, green and white parts, thinly sliced on the diagonal

¼ cup [5 g] clipped carrot greens, in small clusters

Flaky sea salt

Pickled mustard seed vinaigrette (page 301)

Olive oil, for finishing

Using a mandoline, shave the carrots into thin, but not paper-thin, pieces. Do the same with the apple quarters. Cut any darkened leaves from the fennel bulb and cut the bulb in half lengthwise. Shave the fennel into thin pieces using the mandoline, starting with the cut side so the pieces are large and are connected by the core. Similarly, shave the beets and rinse under running water to reduce the amount of red that will stain the other vegetables. Pat the beets dry using a clean towel or paper towel.

Divide the carrots, appple, fennel, green onions, and carrot greens evenly among four plates, arranging them in a flat pattern. Garnish with the beets. Sprinkle with the flaky salt and drizzle with the vinaigrette and the olive oil. Serve immediately.

OTHER GREENS TO TRY herbs such as parsley, tarragon, cilantro, and dill

CELERY LEAVES AND HEARTS WITH BRUSSELS SPROUTS AND BUTTERNUT SQUASH PUREE

This is a great dish to tuck into in fall and winter. The soft puree, crisp celery, and tart pomegranate combine for a really special salad. Brussels sprouts and almonds enhance the crunchiness.

SERVES 6 AS AN APPETIZER

2 cups [480 g] butternut squash puree (page 298)

3 ounces [85 g] celery hearts and leaves, finely chopped

8 brussels sprouts, trimmed and sliced as thinly as possible

2 tablespoons toasted and chopped almonds

Pomegranate molasses vinaigrette (page 301)

Olive oil, for finishing

Coarse sea salt and freshly ground black pepper

Pita triangles, toasted baguette slices, or cut crisp vegetables, for serving

Spoon the puree onto a large platter or divide among individual plates. Using the back of a spoon, spread the puree thinly to make a circle that covers the bottom of the plate entirely. Scatter the celery and brussels sprouts over the puree and top with the almonds. Drizzle with the vinaigrette and finishing oil, then sprinkle with coarse sea salt and a hefty grind of black pepper. Serve immediately with pita for dipping.

OTHER GREENS TO TRY Chinese celery leaf, butter lettuce, mâche, cilantro

GRAPEFRUIT, ORANGE, AND KUMQUAT WITH FAVA LEAVES

Here is an example of a cusp-season dish: a simple, refreshing salad where the grapefruit, which is just about on the way out, meets the new leaves of spring. The citrus and legume flavors feel very comfortable together on one plate.

SERVES 4

2 ruby grapefruits, peeled and cut into thin wheels

1 orange, peeled and cut into thin wheels

½ small shallot, halved and thinly sliced

5 kumquats, thinly sliced

¼ cup [35 g] cashews, toasted

1 teaspoon white sesame seeds, toasted

1 cup [30 g] loosely packed fava leaves

3 to 4 tablespoons [45 to 60 ml] citrus-tangerine vinaigrette (page 300)

2 to 3 teaspoons flaky sea salt

Lay the wheels of grapefruit and orange on a large platter and scatter the shallot and kumquat slices over them. Top with the cashews and sesame seeds, then tuck in the fava leaves. Dress with the vinaigrette and season with the flaky sea salt.

OTHER GREENS TO TRY frisée, mâche

RABBIT AND PORK POLPETTE WITH FAVA GREENS

Meat and greens love each other. And a meatball is one of those dishes where they mingle best. I happen to love when a meatball is not all meat. Greens are a welcome addition in a meatball: they lighten it up, brighten it up, and they add a bit of moisture, succulence, and, in the case of fava leaves in these *polpette*, a wonderful legume flavor.

SERVES 6 TO 8

4 tablespoons [60 ml] olive oil

1 pound [455 g] fava green leaves (2 pounds/ 900 g fava greens will yield about 1 pound/ 455 g leaves, picked from the stems; discard stems)

8 ounces [230 g] ground rabbit

8 ounces [230 g] ground pork shoulder

3 ounces [85 g] ground prosciutto, bacon, or pork belly

1 cup [240 g] fresh ricotta

½ cup [30 g] lightly packed finely grated Pecorino Romano

2 eggs

7 fresh sage leaves, chopped, plus 3 whole leaves

½ cup [20 g] fresh bread crumbs

Freshly grated nutmeg

Kosher salt and freshly ground black pepper

2 carrots, peeled and finely diced

½ fennel bulb, finely diced

1 yellow onion, finely diced

2 bay leaves

¼ cup [60 ml] dry sherry

3 cups [720 ml] double chicken stock (page 299)

1½ to 2 cups [360 to 480 ml] heavy cream

Cooked polenta or pasta, for serving

Finely grated Parmigiano-Reggiano, grated, for serving

In a large sauté pan over medium-high heat, heat 2 tablespoons of the olive oil. Add the fava greens and sauté until the leaves are wilted and tender, 3 to 4 minutes. Cool the greens completely, then chop finely but do not turn them into a paste.

In a bowl, gently mix the fava greens, rabbit, pork, prosciutto, ricotta, Pecorino Romano, eggs, chopped sage, bread crumbs, a few gratings of nutmeg, 1 tablespoon salt, and 1 teaspoon pepper together. Do not overmix. Scoop up the mixture using a #40 scoop to make balls about the size of a Ping-Pong ball; gently roll the mixture to form cohesive balls without rolling too tightly. Place the balls in a large baking dish in one layer.

Preheat the oven to 350°F [180°C].

In a saucepan, using the remaining 2 tablespoons oil, sauté the carrots, fennel, onion, bay leaves, and whole sage leaves over medium-high heat until the onion is translucent and caramelization starts to form on bottom of pan, 3 to 5 minutes. Add the sherry and increase the heat, scraping bits of caramelization from the bottom of the pan. When the sherry has evaporated, add the stock and bring to a simmer. Season with salt and pepper.

Pour the stock with the vegetables over the meatballs, cover the baking dish with aluminum foil, and bake for 1 to 1¼ hours, until the meatballs are tender.

Place a portion of meatballs and braising sauce into a saucepan and add a few tablespoons of cream. Bring to a simmer over medium heat and cook gently until the balls are warm and the sauce slightly thickens.

Serve over polenta or pasta, garnished with 1½ teaspoons of Parmigiano-Reggiano per serving.

OTHER GREENS TO TRY escarole, mustard greens

STUFFED GRAPE LEAVES

This recipe comes from my friend cookbook writer Adeena Sussman. It was inspired by some stuffed leaves that Adeena enjoyed in Turkey—she describes them as fragrant with warm spices, studded with pine nuts and currants, and cooked until they melted in her mouth. If you live near a farmers' market, you may be lucky enough to find fresh grape leaves during the spring and early summer months. Otherwise, use jarred grape leaves, available in most supermarkets and Mediterranean specialty stores.

MAKES 30 STUFFED LEAVES

½ cup [120 ml] olive oil

1 yellow onion, finely diced

3 cloves garlic, minced

1¼ cups [250 g] long-grain white rice

5 cups [1.2 L] double chicken stock (page 299) or vegetable stock

1 teaspoon kosher salt

1 tablespoon fresh lemon juice

Zest of 1 lemon, finely grated on a Microplane

2 tablespoons pomegranate molasses

6 tablespoons [55 g] currants

6 tablespoons [50 g] pine nuts, toasted

¼ cup [10 g] chopped fresh mint leaves

¼ cup [10 g] chopped fresh curly parsley

½ teaspoon ground cinnamon

¼ teaspoon freshly cracked black pepper

⅛ teaspoon ground allspice

⅛ teaspoon ground cayenne pepper

Pinch of ground cloves

34 fresh grape leaves, stemmed, or 1 (16-ounce/455-g) jar grape leaves, drained and well rinsed

Heat 3 tablespoons of the oil in a saucepan over medium heat. Add the onion and cook, stirring, until translucent, 5 minutes. Add the garlic and cook for 1 minute more. Add the rice and cook, stirring, until the rice glistens and appears to sweat, 2 to 3 minutes. Add 2 cups [430 ml] of the stock and the salt, bring to a boil, decrease the heat, and simmer until the rice is mostly cooked but still has a bit of bite, 14 to 15 minutes. Stir in the lemon juice, lemon zest, and 1 tablespoon of the pomegranate molasses and remove from the heat. Stir in two-thirds of the currants and two-thirds of the pine nuts along with the mint, parsley, cinnamon, pepper, allspice, cayenne, and cloves. Let the mixture cool for 1 hour.

After the mixture is cool, place 1 grape leaf, shiny side down, on a clean work surface. Place 2 tablespoons of the rice mixture toward the stem end of the leaf, fold the sides of the leaf over the filling, then roll up the leaf, cigar style, leaving a little space for the filling to expand while cooking. Set aside, seam side down. Repeat until the filling is used up. You should have 30 stuffed leaves. Line the bottom of a wide, high-sided skillet with the remaining grape leaves, then arrange the rolled leaves, seam side down, in the skillet in concentric circles. Pour the remaining 5 tablespoons [75 ml] olive oil and the remaining 3 cups [720 ml] stock on top of the grape leaves, cover, and cook over very low heat until the grape leaves are very tender, 40 to 45 minutes. Remove from the heat, uncover, and cool for 1 hour.

Arrange the stuffed grape leaves on a serving platter and drizzle with the remaining 1 tablespoon pomegranate molasses. Garnish with the remaining 2 tablespoons each pine nuts and currants and serve.

OTHER GREENS TO TRY chard, fig leaves, squash leaves

SAVORY OAT MUESLI WITH PEA GREENS AND BIRDSEED

This is a great make-ahead breakfast dish that will keep for the whole week in the fridge. I use whole milk for this recipe, but it works well with nut milks, too. The creamy texture makes it very satisfying to eat, and while berries are not unusual for breakfast, pea greens are. It is a revelation how the strawberries and pea greens mingle together—a sweet and herbal representation of spring. Add the crunch and toasty flavor of the "birdseed," drizzle a little maple syrup on the top, and it feels as indulgent as a dessert.

SERVES 4

2 cups [200 g] old-fashioned rolled oats

¼ cup [50 g] black chia seeds

3¼ cups [780 ml] whole milk, plus more for serving

2 tablespoons maple syrup, plus more for serving

Fine sea salt

8 ounces [230 g] strawberries, sliced

¼ cup [40 g] birdseed (page 302)

2 ounces [55 g] pea shoots

Combine the oats, chia seeds, milk, and maple syrup in a bowl and stir to combine. Cover and refrigerate overnight.

Remove from the refrigerator and gently stir. The mixture should have thickened but should still be soft. If it seems dry, add a bit more milk to suit your taste. Season lightly with salt.

Divide the muesli evenly among four bowls and drizzle a bit of maple syrup over the top. Garnish with the strawberries, birdseed, and pea shoots.

OTHER GREENS TO TRY butter lettuce hearts, chickweed, mâche

SNOW PEA GREENS

Common in any Chinatown restaurant, this recipe for snow pea greens is purely traditional. The simple seasonings of garlic, ginger, white pepper, and sesame oil are things that most people have in their pantries, and the combination lets the greens be green. Make sure to cook these over really high heat, and very fast. When overcooked, the greens will turn dark and lose their flavor. Snow pea greens are great with fish, any grilled food, and are even nice on top of rice with an egg.

SERVES 4

3 tablespoons neutral vegetable oil

4 cloves garlic, finely chopped

1 teaspoon peeled and finely chopped fresh ginger

1 pound [455 g] snow pea greens, cut into ½-inch [12-mm] pieces

¼ teaspoon white pepper

1 teaspoon toasted sesame oil

Kosher salt

Heat the vegetable oil in a large skillet or wok over very high heat until it just starts to smoke. Quickly add the garlic, ginger, and pea greens and cook, taking care not to burn them by constantly stirring, for 1 minute. Add the white pepper and sesame oil, season with salt, and mix well.

Put the lid on the wok and cook for 1 to 2 minutes more. Remove the lid, stir briefly, and serve immediately. Opening the lid more than once during cooking will cause the vegetables to lose their bright green color.

OTHER GREENS TO TRY pea shoots or tendrils, mâche, spinach

Savory Oat Muesli with Pea Greens and Birdseed

Radish Green and Mango Smoothie with Curry and Yogurt

RADISH GREEN AND MANGO SMOOTHIE WITH CURRY AND YOGURT

First rule of smoothies in my kitchen: use frozen fruit instead of ice. Ice can make smoothies too watery. I always like to use yogurt in smoothies because it lends the perfect, smooth creaminess and an enjoyable tartness. I started to think of making my own Indian-inspired lassi-type smoothie, so my mind, of course, went to curry powder and ginger. A little bit of honey offsets those big flavors. Radish greens then give the whole mix a gorgeous flavor while not tasting too green—just a tiny bit of bitter to counterbalance the sweet in the fruit and honey. This nutritious mix makes great popsicles when frozen, too!

SERVES 2 TO 4

1 cup [240 g] plain yogurt

Greens from 1 bunch radishes, about 2½ ounces [70 g]

1 tablespoon Madras curry powder

2 tablespoons honey

10 ounces [280 g] frozen mango

½ ounce [15 g] peeled ginger

¼ cup [60 ml] fresh lemon juice

Combine all of the ingredients in a blender. Process on high until very smooth. Serve immediately.

OTHER GREENS TO TRY turnip greens, mâche

GNOCCHI ALLA BISMARCK WITH RADISHES AND THEIR GREENS

Bread crumbs are the base of these *gnocchi alla Bismarck*. Although I'm not certain where they get their name, I'm guessing it is because northern Italy is so alpine and rich with Germanic influences. As I explored in *Pasta by Hand*, I learned that Italian dumplings are regional, reflecting the land and ingredients around them. In different parts of Italy, cooks utilize whatever they have on hand as the foundation of their dumplings. In the north, they would make bread four times a year. They would eat it fresh, then dry the rest to use until the next season. The radish greens add a bit of sharpness and lighten up the denseness of these gnocchi so they don't feel quite as heavy. They act the same way that lettuce does in a meat sandwich.

SERVES 4

8 radishes, cut into quarters

¾ cup [170 g] unsalted butter

2 cups [480 ml] water

2 teaspoons kosher salt

3 tablespoons plus 2 teaspoons fresh thyme leaves

2 ounces [55 g] radish greens (from 4 to 8 radishes)

Gnocchi alla Bismarck (page 230)

½ cup [15 g] lightly packed finely grated Parmigiano-Reggiano

In a large sauté pan over medium-high heat, combine the radishes, ¼ cup [55 g] of the butter, the water, and the salt and bring to a simmer. Cook until the radishes are tender, allowing the water to reduce to create a sauce, 3 to 4 minutes. Add the remaining ½ cup [115 g] butter, thyme leaves, and radish greens and simmer until the sauce has thickened slightly, about 2 minutes more.

In a large pot of salted simmering water, cook the gnocchi; do not boil hard or the dumplings may fall apart. Simmer for about 2½ minutes, until they float, then remove them from the water with a slotted spoon. Add them to the sauce, tossing the gnocchi until coated with the sauce. Serve sprinkled with the Parmigiano-Reggiano.

GNOCCHI ALLA BISMARCK

SERVES 4

¾ cup plus 2 tablespoons [100 g] dried bread crumbs

1½ cups [210 g] all-purpose flour

¾ cup plus 2 tablespoons [80 g] lightly packed finely grated Parmigiano-Reggiano

1 whole egg plus 1 egg yolk

½ cup [120 ml] whole milk, plus more as needed

2 ounces [55 g] prosciutto cotto, pancetta, bacon, American ham, speck, or salami trim, finely chopped

½ teaspoon ground cinnamon

Freshly grated nutmeg

1 teaspoon fine sea salt

Semolina flour, for dusting

In the bowl of a food processor, process the bread crumbs until finely ground.

In a bowl, combine the flour, bread crumbs, and Parmigiano-Reggiano. Add the egg and egg yolk, milk, prosciutto cotto, cinnamon, a few gratings of nutmeg, and the salt and mix with your hands. Add more milk, 1 tablespoon at a time, until the dough is cohesive and soft but not sticky. Transfer to a work surface and knead a few times with your hands, until the dough is a cohesive mass. Cover the dough with plastic wrap and let rest at room temperature for 30 minutes.

Line a sheet pan with parchment paper and dust with semolina. Cut off a chunk of dough about the width of two fingers and cover the rest with plastic wrap. Roll into a log about ½ inch [12 mm] in diameter. Cut the log into ½-inch [12-mm] pieces.

To shape each dumpling, roll a piece of dough on the back of fork tines, applying gentle pressure as you roll to one side and then flick the dough off. This will create a small dumpling with ridges. Put the gnocchi on the prepared sheet pan and shape the remaining dough in the same way. Do not allow the gnocchi to touch on the pan.

Gnocchi can be frozen flat on the sheet pan, then stored in an airtight container for up to 1 month. If frozen, do not thaw before cooking. Cook frozen gnocchi as directed on page 229, but increase the cooking time to 8 minutes, or until the center of the dumpling is no longer cold.

OTHER GREENS TO TRY spinach, turnip greens

BUCKWHEAT PAPPARDELLE WITH SHISO BUTTER AND SQUASH LEAF GREENS

You can cook traditional wheat-based pasta any day, but adding buckwheat to the dough introduces another level of depth to any pasta dish. Though it uses an Italian *papparadelle*, the shiso butter and sesame pull this over to the Asian spectrum of flavors. The squash leaves have a broccoli-like flavor but with a soft, delicate texture. Make sure to salt to taste—the shiso butter is salty, so no additional salt may be needed in this dish.

SERVES 4

1 tablespoon olive oil

2 cloves garlic

4 cups [900 g] loosely packed squash leaves, cut into ½-inch [12-mm] ribbons

4 ounces [115 g] shiso butter (page 292)

Freshly cooked buckwheat pappardelle (recipe follows), plus 1 to 3 tablespoons cooking water

1 tablespoon white sesame seeds

Heat the olive oil and garlic over medium heat and cook gently just until the garlic is fragrant, 1 to 2 minutes. Add the squash greens and shiso butter and cook, stirring gently, until the greens are wilted, 1 to 2 minutes. Add the pappardelle and the pasta cooking water as needed to moisten. Increase the heat and cook for 1 minute to help the butter cling to the noodles.

To serve, divide among four plates and garnish with the sesame seeds.

Gnocchi alla Bismarck with Radishes and Their Greens (page 229)

Tomato Leaf–Egg Pasta

BUCKWHEAT PAPPARDELLE

MAKES 14 OUNCES [400 G], SERVES 4

½ cup [60 g] buckwheat flour

1⅓ cups [185 g] "00" flour

6 tablespoons [65 g] semolina flour, plus more for dusting

3 eggs

1 tablespoon olive oil

Combine the buckwheat flour, "00" flour, semolina flour, eggs, and olive oil in the bowl of a stand mixer fitted with a dough hook. Mix on medium speed for 8 minutes, or until smooth and neither sticky nor dry. The dough should be cohesive, firm, and stiff. If the dough is too dry, add water, 1 tablespoon at a time, until the right consistency is reached.

Wrap the dough in plastic wrap and let rest at room temperature for 1 hour.

To roll the pasta with a pasta roller, place a little pile of semolina on a large cutting board. Unwrap the rested pasta dough and divide it into quarters. Working with one piece at a time, dust the piece of dough in the semolina, then pass it through your pasta roller on the widest setting. Repeat this process with the roller set increasingly narrower until the pasta becomes very thin, but not so thin that it tears. (Usually the setting just before the narrowest is good.) If you find your dough sticking, lightly dust it with semolina before rolling it though the next setting. If it gets too big to handle, cut it in half. If it gets too wide for the machine or becomes irregularly shaped, fold the sides of the dough into the middle, like an envelope; press the dough flat; and run the piece, folded side up, back through the machine on the widest setting. Then, put the dough through all the roller settings again, working your way thinner. This allows the machine to press out any trapped air. Lay the pasta sheet flat on a surface lightly floured with semolina and repeat with remaining pieces.

Once all the pasta has been rolled, cut the sheets into pappardelle: long noodles ½ to 1 inch [12 mm to 2.5 cm] wide.

If you are not cooking the pasta immediately, dry it completely at room temperature or freeze in serving-size bundles. If drying, make sure the pasta is completely dry before storing in an airtight container or mold may develop.

In a large pot of salted boiling water, cook the pasta until al dente, about 1 minute for freshly made pasta or 2 to 3 minutes for dried or frozen pasta (do not thaw first). Drain, reserving a few tablespoons of the pasta water for adding to the sauce.

OTHER GREENS TO TRY chard, mustard greens

TOMATO LEAF–EGG PASTA WITH BUTTER AND FRESH TOMATO SAUCE

Let us put this to rest once and for all: tomato leaves are not toxic and are perfectly fine to eat. They developed a bad rap because tomatoes are part of the nightshade family of plants. And while there are some nightshade leaves we should not be eating—namely, the belladonna herb—tomato leaves are safe to eat, delicious, and nutritious. Now that we are past that, do not throw your tomato leaves away when you harvest them from the garden! They can be gathered throughout the season and cooked like any of the greens defined as "sturdy" in the introduction to this book. Though the leaves have a strong, herbal aroma, it is not an overwhelming flavor in this pasta. And when you serve it with the butter and fresh tomato sauce, think about it: you have the whole plant on the plate.

NOTE: Tomato leaves also make a great pesto when combined with mint and basil, or even a little fresh marjoram or oregano.

Continued

SERVES 4

> 9 ounces [255 g] tomato leaves (about 8 cups)
>
> 2 to 3 large eggs
>
> 15 ounces [420 g] all-purpose flour (3 cups)
>
> Semolina, for rolling
>
> Butter and fresh tomato sauce (facing page)
>
> Olive oil and finely grated Parmigiano-Reggiano, for serving

Fill a large bowl with ice water and set aside.

In a large pot of salted simmering water, submerge the tomato leaves and cook until tender, 2 to 3 minutes. Immediately drain the tomato leaves and transfer to the ice water to cool quickly. When chilled, remove the leaves from the water. Using your hands, wring out the excess water from the leaves, then place the leaves in a clean towel and wring out any remaining moisture.

Put the blanched and squeezed tomato leaves and 2 of the eggs in a blender and process to mix well. Scrape into the bowl of a stand mixer fitted with a dough hook and add the flour. Mix on medium speed for 8 minutes, or until smooth and neither sticky nor dry. It should not be a soft and smooth ball, like bread dough, but it should be cohesive and stiff without being dry. If needed, beat the third egg in a small bowl and drizzle it in, 1 tablespoon at a time, until the right consistency is reached.

Wrap the dough in plastic wrap and let rest at room temperature for 1 hour.

To roll the pasta, place a little pile of semolina on a large cutting board. Unwrap the rested pasta dough and divide it into quarters. Working with one piece at a time, dust the piece of dough in the semolina, then run it through your pasta roller on the widest setting. Repeat this process with the roller set increasingly narrower until the pasta is very thin, but not so thin it tears. (Usually the setting just before the narrowest is good.)

If you find your dough sticking, lightly dust it with semolina before rolling it through the next setting. If it gets too long to handle, cut it in half. If it gets too wide for the machine or becomes irregularly shaped, fold the sides of the dough into the middle, like an envelope; press the dough flat; and run the piece, folded side up, back through the machine on the widest setting. Then, put the dough through all the roller settings again, working your way thinner. Lay the pasta sheet flat on a surface lightly floured with semolina and repeat with the remaining pieces. Once you have finished rolling all the pasta, run each sheet through the fettuccine cutter. You can also cut the pasta sheets by hand on a cutting board into a desired shape.

If you are not cooking the pasta right away, dry it completely at room temperature or freeze in serving-size bundles. If drying, make sure the pasta is completely dry before storing in an airtight container or mold may develop.

Reheat the tomato sauce.

In a large pot of salted boiling water, cook the pasta until al dente, about 1 minute for freshly made pasta or 2 to 3 minutes for dried or frozen pasta (do not thaw first). Drain, add to the pan with the warm tomato sauce, and toss to combine.

To serve, divide among four plates, drizzle with olive oil and sprinkle with Parmigiano-Reggiano.

OTHER GREENS TO TRY chard, nettles, spinach

BUTTER AND FRESH TOMATO SAUCE

SERVES 4

½ cup [115 g] unsalted butter

3 large heirloom tomatoes, cut into large
pieces

Fine sea salt

Melt the butter in a large pan over medium heat
and add the tomatoes to warm. Keep the heat low
to keep tomato pieces from breaking apart. Season
with salt to taste.

FRITELLE DI PANE WITH TURNIP GREENS

Fritelle, aka fritters, are one of the best vehicles for
using up leftovers. Day-old bread, leftover meat,
salami trim, and cheese can all be used here.
I love that not only does this recipe call for those
horseradishy turnip leaves but the stems as well.
These "bread fritters" are fast and hearty; think
of this dish as like a frittata with bread.

Fritelle are sometimes called *fritule* (in Venice),
panzerotti (in Puglia; different from the *panzerotti*
from Puglia on page 89), or *pitticelle* (in Calabria).
No matter what you call them, these delicious
snacks are especially popular at family gatherings
in Italy in the summer.

**MAKES 4 (8-INCH/20-CM) CAKES OR 12 (3-INCH/
7.5-CM) FRITTERS, SERVES 4 AS AN APPETIZER
OR LIGHT MEAL WITH A SALAD**

2 tablespoons olive oil, plus more for frying
the fritters

½ yellow onion, chopped into 1-inch
[2.5-cm] pieces

3 cloves garlic, thinly sliced

4 ounces [115 g] turnip greens and stems,
separated and cut into 2-inch [5-cm] pieces

Fine sea salt

4 ounces [115 g] semidried bread cubes
(about 4 cups/1 L), dried overnight at
room temperature

1 cup [240 ml] whole milk, or more as needed

2 eggs

4 ounces [115 g] feta, crumbled

1 tablespoon coarsely chopped fresh dill

1 tablespoon coarsely chopped fresh oregano

2 tablespoons chopped oil-packed jarred
Calabrian chiles

2 ounces [55 g] salami, prosciutto, or bacon,
chopped (optional)

6 tablespoons [25 g] finely grated
Pecorino Romano

Continued

Warm the olive oil in a large skillet over medium-high heat. Add the onion and garlic and cook, stirring, until the onion is tender and translucent, 2 to 3 minutes. Add the turnip stems, cook for 1 minute, and then add the greens. Season lightly with salt and cook until the greens are tender, about two tosses. Set aside to cool.

Combine the bread cubes, milk, and eggs in a large bowl and stir to mix well. The bread should absorb most of the liquid. Coarsely chop the cooled greens and add to the bread mixture along with the feta, dill, oregano, chiles, salami, and 1 teaspoon salt. Stir gently to mix well.

Place an 8-inch [20-cm] nonstick skillet (for large cakes) or a 12-inch [30.5-cm] nonstick skillet (for smaller fritters) over medium-high heat. Add olive oil to a depth of ¼ inch [6 mm] and heat until hot. To test the temperature, add a small piece of the bread mixture to the pan. If it sizzles on contact, the oil is ready to cook the cakes or fritters. Place one-third of the mixture in the hot smaller pan; if making fritters, add about one-twelfth of the mixture for each fritter to the larger pan, being careful not to crowd the pan. Cook until the first side of the cake or fritters is golden, 3 to 4 minutes. If it becomes too dark, decrease the heat. Sprinkle the uncooked side of the cake or fritters with some of the Pecorino Romano, then flip to cook the second side, 3 to 4 minutes, until lightly golden. If the oil seems to have disappeared, drizzle a bit of additional oil around the inside of the pan's walls and it will spread to cover the bottom. When the cake or fritters are golden on both sides and cooked through, flip and serve with the Pecorino Romano side facing up. Repeat to use all of the mixture and serve immediately, or keep warm in a low oven on a sheet pan lined with a wire rack.

OTHER GREENS TO TRY mustard greens, radish greens

BUTTER-BRAISED HAKUREI TURNIPS AND FRENCH BREAKFAST RADISHES

Hakurei turnips are those adorable little turnips with a mild flavor and crunchy texture. Cooking them in water with a little bit of butter yields a beautiful sauce. The greens aren't nearly as potent; they have a very different vegetal flavor. Overall, this is a dish that is great on its own but especially wonderful with fish.

SERVES 4

2 cups [300 g] Hakurei turnips, quartered, greens separated but reserved

2 cups [115 g] French breakfast radishes, halved, greens separated but reserved

¾ cup [170 g] unsalted butter

2 cups [480 ml] water

Fine sea salt

Lemon, for finishing

Combine the turnips, radishes, butter, and water in a saucepan. Bring to a lively simmer and season lightly with salt. Cook until the vegetables are crisp-tender, about 6 minutes. Remove the vegetables with a slotted spoon and set aside. Increase the heat to high and reduce the liquid for a couple of minutes, or until a delicate, just slightly emulsified sauce is achieved. Add a good handful of the reserved greens (not all or it will become too thick) and stir until wilted. Return the cooked vegetables to the pan, season with a light squeeze of lemon and additional salt to taste, toss to coat, and then serve.

OTHER GREENS TO TRY carrots and their greens

Butter-Braised Hakurei Turnips and French Breakfast Radishes

PASTA CON I TENERUMI (PASTA WITH THE GREEN LEAVES OF SQUASH)

Tenerumi are the young shoots at the tip of the long, pale green cucuzza squash stalk. The word loosely translates as "tenders," which makes sense because of their soft texture. They are so tender, in fact, that they don't require much preparation, they practically melt when heated. This soup with pasta is the Sicilian version of minestrone, taught to me by a Sicilian bartender named Giovanni. (Giovanni prefers *orecchiette* or *ditalini* instead of the spaghetti I use.) Instead of cooking the pasta in a separate pot, the pasta is cooked right in the *tenerumi* sauce. Traditionally water is used, but I prefer a rich chicken stock for more flavor. Keep an eye on the pasta as it cooks, as it will absorb the stock, so adding more might be necessary. And serve and eat immediately, as the pasta will continue to absorb the liquid and become overcooked and mushy if eaten later.

SERVES 6

3 tablespoons olive oil, plus more for finishing

3 large cloves garlic, thinly sliced

3 large tomatoes, diced into large pieces

3 fresh bay leaves

4 sprigs thyme

3 fresh sage leaves

8 ounces [230 g] tender young summer squash leaves, hard stems removed and leaves sliced into ½-inch [12-mm] ribbons

Kosher salt

Dried red pepper flakes

6 cups [1.4 L] double chicken stock (page 299) or vegetable stock, plus more as needed

2 small Yukon gold potatoes, peeled and diced

1 small summer squash, diced

8 ounces [230 g] spaghetti, broken into 2-inch [5-cm] pieces

12 fresh basil leaves, torn into large pieces

1 cup [30 g] lightly packed finely grated Parmigiano-Reggiano

Warm the olive oil in a large pot over medium-high heat. Add the garlic, tomatoes, bay leaves, thyme, and sage leaves and cook until the tomatoes become tender, 4 to 5 minutes. Add the squash leaves, stir, and cook until they wilt, 3 to 4 minutes. The leaves should be dark, not bright, green and very soft. Sprinkle lightly with salt and red pepper flakes, stir, and add the stock. Bring to a gentle simmer and cook until the leaves are very tender, about 5 minutes. Add the potatoes and cook until almost tender, 4 to 5 minutes. Add the squash pieces and broken spaghetti, stir, and cook just until the pasta is al dente, 6 to 8 minutes. Remove any herb leaves and stems with a slotted spoon and season to taste with salt and red pepper flakes.

Spoon into bowls, drizzle with olive oil, and top with the basil leaves and grated Parmigiano-Reggiano. Serve immediately.

OTHER GREENS TO TRY chard, mustard greens

Hijiki

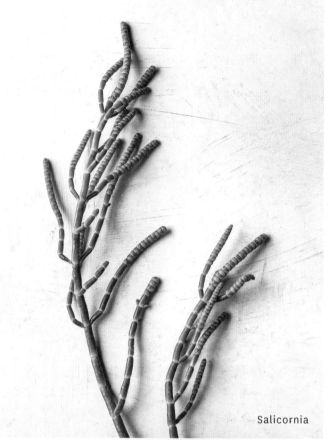

Salicornia

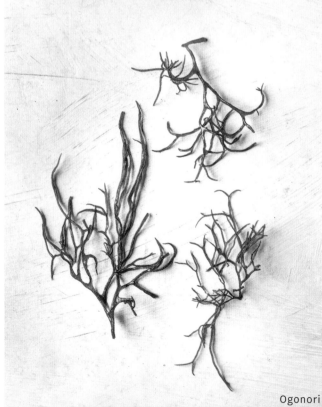

Ogonori

Kombu

SEAWEED

Seaweed is hailed as one of the few plant-based ingredients that has umami, that fifth taste that makes salty, sweet, sour, and bitter come together. It is also exactly what it sounds like: weeds growing underwater. But seaweed also happens to hold a host of nutrients and lend a flavor impact quite unlike any other green. It is considered a nutrient-dense superfood, high in vitamins A and K, calcium, iodine, protein, and fiber, with flavors that range from briny to fresh and textures that vary from slimy to crisp. The following are the most commonly found seaweeds in Asian groceries.

OTHER VARIETIES ARAME, BADDERLOCKS, BLADDERWRACK, CAROLA, CARRAGEEN MOSS (IRISH MOSS), CHANNELED WRACK, CHLORELLA, COCHAYUYO, ECKLONIA CAVA, EUCHEUMA, GELIDIELLA, GRACILARIA, HYPNEA, MOZUKU, OGONORI, SARGASSUM, SEA GRAPES, SEA LETTUCE, SPIRAL WRACK, THONGWEED, WAKAME

DULSE
Palmaria palmata

A brown variety often sun dried. Also called dilisk.

HIJIKI
Sargassum fusiforme

A dark brown to inky dried variety that looks like wiry noodles and is often used as a base for salads.

KELP/KOMBU
Laminaria japonica

This dark green, leafy variety is available dried and less commonly fresh and is used in miso soup, in salads, and to make dashi.

NORI
Poryphyra yezoensis

These are the flat dried sheets used to roll sushi.

SALICORNIA
Salicornia europaea

Small, mild, stem-like greens, also known as glasswort, sea beans, and sea asparagus. Though often grouped with seaweeds for culinary purposes, salicornia is botanically a succulent. Eaten in salads or as a side on their own.

SEASON Though available year-round, most seaweed is harvested in the spring. Nori is harvested from January to March; kombu from July to August.

HOW TO CHOOSE When buying fresh seaweed, look for a firm, lively, not limp texture. When buying dried seaweed, choose specimens with a good, deep color—never gray.

HOW TO CLEAN Dried seaweed (except for nori) should be soaked before eating. Place in a bowl of warm water for 5 to 10 minutes, until tender and pliable. Rinse fresh seaweed to rid leaves of debris, dirt, and sand. Drain and pat dry.

HOW TO STORE Refrigerate fresh seaweed in a ziplock bag or airtight container. Salicornia should be stored with a lightly dampened towel to retain moisture. Fresh seaweed should keep for 1 to 2 weeks. Dried seaweed should be kept in an airtight container with the desiccant packet that came with it. Check expiration date on packaging, but most dried seaweed will keep for up to a year.

HOW TO REFRESH Soak fresh seaweed in lightly salted ice water until it perks up. If it does not, discard.

COOKING METHODS Fresh seaweed can be eaten raw or cooked by simmering in soups and stews, stir-frying, sautéing, boiling, or toasting. Dried seaweed can be used as a seasoning or to wrap rice and fish, sushi-style. It can also be simmered in stews and broths or rehydrated and tossed into salads.

PAIRINGS Soy sauce, tofu, soybeans, rice wine vinegar, lemon, butter, sesame, chiles, fish, shellfish, eggs, mushrooms, most vegetables.

SMOKED FISH SOUP WITH KOMBU AND DASHI

I had a fish soup in Newfoundland from Chef Todd Perrin that inspired me. I used smoked fish instead of fresh and thought, what better than a sea vegetable broth for a smoked fish soup? And there are few better sea vegetables than kombu. Kombu is a really sturdy seaweed that many people use to make dashi—the Japanese stock that is used for miso soup and many other dishes. But when most people make the stock, they strain out the kombu and throw it away. I keep it in this soup, cutting it up really thinly, so as not to miss out on the extra umami and nutritional value. Another cool little spin is that I cook the vegetables in *lardo* before adding the dashi, which gives the soup an extra layer of a subtle porky flavor.

SERVES 4 TO 6

½ cup [110 g] whipped lardo spread (page 299), or ½ cup [120 ml] olive oil (see Note)

3 yellow onions, diced

2 fresh sage leaves

4 sprigs thyme

3 fresh bay leaves

8 small potatoes, cut into quarters

7 cups [1.7 L] dashi (recipe follows)

1 piece kombu, reserved from dashi and cut into thin strips

Kosher salt

1 pound [455 g] smoked cod or mackerel fillet

Warm the lardo spread in a large pot over medium-high heat. Add the onions, sage, thyme, and bay leaves and cook, stirring often, until the onions are translucent and tender, 8 to 12 minutes, stirring often. (The onions and herbs should be lightly coated with fat.) If the onions become dark, decrease the heat to cook them more slowly. Add the potatoes, dashi, and kombu and bring to a very gentle simmer. Season lightly with salt. When the potatoes are almost tender, after 6 to 8 minutes, add the fish and cook until the fish is tender and flaking. The timing will depend on the type of fish used, but it should take 2 to 4 minutes.

Discard the bay leaves and any herb stems and serve immediately.

NOTE: If using olive oil, sauté 4 ounces [115 g] bacon lardons with the onions for a richer flavor.

DASHI

MAKES 6 TO 7 CUPS [1.4 TO 1.7 L]

2 (6-inch/15-cm) pieces dried kombu

8 cups [2 L] water

1½ ounces [40 g] dried bonito flakes

In a large pot, soak the kombu in the water until it softens, about 30 minutes. Bring the water and kombu to a simmer, then remove the kombu. Add the bonito flakes and bring back to a simmer for 5 minutes, then remove from the heat and let steep for 15 minutes. Using a fine-mesh sieve, strain the dashi, but do not press on the bonito to extract more liquid. Use immediately, or store in the refrigerator for up to 1 week or in the freezer for up to 1 month.

NORI AND COCONUT FLOUR BUTTERMILK BISCUITS WITH SESAME SHICHIMI BUTTER

These are not your traditional flaky biscuits; rather, they are soft and tender, thanks to the coconut flour. When making these, I found that the flavors of coconut, seaweed, and sesame go really nicely together. Break a biscuit open when just hot out of the oven, swipe a whole bunch of shichimi togarashi butter on the top of the tender insides, and it becomes a special treat.

MAKES 8 BISCUITS

  5 sheets nori

  2 cups [210 g] coconut flour

  1½ cups [210 g] all-purpose flour, plus more for rolling

  1 tablespoon poppy seeds

  1 tablespoon baking powder

  ¾ teaspoon baking soda

  1 teaspoon kosher salt

  1½ teaspoons sugar

  ¾ cup [170 g] unsalted butter, chilled and cut into ½-inch [12-mm] cubes, plus 2 tablespoons, melted

  1¼ to 1½ cups [300 to 360 ml] buttermilk

  1 tablespoon white sesame seeds

  Sesame shichimi butter (recipe follows)

Preheat the oven to 450°F [230°C]. Line a sheet pan with parchment paper.

Over a gas flame (or over the fire in a grill), toast the nori sheets briefly on each side to crisp up, waving them over the flame for 2 or 3 seconds. Cut into 2-inch [5-cm] pieces.

In the bowl of a food processor, combine the coconut flour, all-purpose flour, poppy seeds, baking powder, baking soda, salt, sugar, nori, and chilled butter and pulse four to five times, until the butter pieces are pea size. Transfer the mixture to a bowl and place in the freezer for 15 minutes.

Remove the flour-and-butter mixture from the freezer. Make a well in the center of the mixture and add 1¼ cups [300 ml] of the buttermilk. Knead gently until the dough comes together and only a few dry spots remain, drizzling in the remaining ¼ cup [60 ml] buttermilk, tablespoon by tablespoon, as needed. The dough should hold together but be neither wet nor sticky.

Gather the dough together and place on a lightly floured work surface. Using your hands, pat the dough into a rectangle, 8 by 8 inches [20 by 20 cm] and about 1 inch [2.5 cm] thick. Using a 3-inch [7.5-cm] round biscuit cutter or overturned glass, cut out eight biscuits. Place the biscuits on the prepared sheet pan and refrigerate for 10 minutes.

Remove the biscuits from the refrigerator and use a pastry brush to coat the tops with the melted butter. Place the biscuits in the oven and immediately decrease the heat to 425°F [220°C]. Bake until golden brown on top, about 15 minutes, rotating the sheet pan back to front midway through baking.

Serve hot with the melted sesame shichimi butter.

SESAME SHICHIMI BUTTER

MAKES ½ CUP [120 ML]

  ½ cup [115 g] unsalted butter

  2 teaspoons shichimi togarashi

  2 tablespoons toasted sesame oil

  2 teaspoons flaky sea salt

In a small pan, melt the butter over medium heat. Remove from the heat and stir in the shichimi togarashi, sesame oil, and salt.

SALICORNIA WITH LEMON BUTTER

There are few things more refreshing than a taste of the ocean. These briny "sea beans" need to be blanched first, but make sure not to salt the water, or you will end up with salt overload. Use them early in the season, when the new growth is most tender. Salicornia pairs wonderfully with fish and sautéed shrimp—combinations that send the palate straight to the seashore.

SERVES 4

1 pound [455 g] salicornia

¼ cup [55 g] unsalted butter

Juice of 1 lemon

2 tablespoons mustard green furikake (page 297) or toasted white sesame seeds (optional)

Place plenty of ice in a bowl and fill the bowl with water. Set aside.

Bring a medium pot of unsalted water to a boil. Add the salicornia and blanch for 20 to 30 seconds. The salicornia should still be bright green and crisp, not limp. Immediately remove the seaweed from the hot water and place in the ice water to arrest the cooking. When cool, drain the salicornia and set aside.

Combine ½ cup [120 ml] water and the butter in a 12-inch [30.5-cm] skillet. Bring to a simmer and add enough lemon juice to brighten the sauce. Add the salicornia and warm through, 1 to 2 minutes. As the sauce cooks it should thicken slightly. If the sauce becomes too thick and not creamy, add more water, tablespoon by tablespoon, to loosen it. Balance out the acidity at the end with a few more drops of lemon juice. Salicornia is salty; seasoning with salt is not necessary. Garnish with the furikake and serve.

OTHER GREENS TO TRY purslane (do not blanch)

SORREL

Rumex acetosa

Tart and tangy, sorrel is a distinctly different green because of its sour green apple, or some say kiwi-like, flavor. One cultural common denominator is that it is used across the globe in soups and stews. In India, it is an essential ingredient in *chukka kura pappu*, a soup made with yellow lentils. In Romania, it is used to make a sour soup. In Nigeria, it is a common ingredient in stews. And in medieval times in Europe, sorrel was made into a soup to be eaten on religious fasting days. Sorrel is said to have eyesight-boosting qualities and is rich in vitamins A, B, and C and in dietary fiber, iron, magnesium, potassium, and calcium.

VARIETIES BROAD LEAF, FRENCH, RED-VEINED

SEASON Early spring

HOW TO CHOOSE Choose crisp, sturdy leaves that have bright uniform coloring and no dark blemishes. Do not buy if wilted.

HOW TO CLEAN Immerse in cool water. Agitate with fingers. Drain; pat or spin dry.

HOW TO STORE Store in an airtight plastic bin or ziplock bag or wrap in plastic wrap. In the crisper drawer of the refrigerator, sorrel will keep for 2 days.

HOW TO REFRESH Immerse in ice water for 15 minutes. Drain and pat or spin dry.

COOKING METHODS Serve raw in salads or cook by simmering in soups and stews.

PAIRINGS Dairy, eggs, poultry, fish.

MANILA CLAMS WITH SORREL AND CREAM

Sorrel is a big mouthful of bright, lemony flavor. The cream in this recipe softens that intensity. The clams take incredibly well to that flavor, and to the creaminess, too. Keep in mind, however, that sorrel's texture can be tricky—it can get slimy when overcooked in warm liquid. Pureeing it in this recipe solves that challenge.

SERVES 2 TO 4 AS AN APPETIZER

Kosher salt

2 ounces [55 g] sorrel

½ cup [120 ml] heavy cream

3 tablespoons olive oil

2 cloves garlic, thinly sliced

¼ cup [35 g] finely diced fennel bulb

¼ cup [35 g] finely diced yellow onion

3 sprigs thyme

¼ cup [60 ml] crisp dry white wine

2 pounds [910 g] Manila clams, well-rinsed

1 cup [240 ml] vegetable stock

¼ cup [55 g] unsalted butter

Freshly ground black pepper

Toasted bread and lemon wedges, for serving

Bring a pan of water to a boil and add 2 tablespoons salt. Meanwhile, prepare an ice bath for the sorrel. Add the sorrel to the boiling water, quickly submerge, and remove immediately. Plunge the blanched sorrel into the ice water bath to cool. The sorrel should have turned an army green. When cool, remove the sorrel from the ice water, wrap in a clean towel, and wring fairly dry.

Cut the blanched, bunched sorrel into four lengths. Combine the sorrel and cream in a blender and blend until smooth. Set aside.

Warm the olive oil in a 10-inch [25-cm] sauté pan over medium heat and add the garlic, fennel, onion, and thyme. Cook until the vegetables are translucent, 3 to 4 minutes. Add the wine and cook until the wine has almost all evaporated, 2 to 3 minutes. Add the clams, vegetable stock, ½ cup [120 ml] of the sorrel cream, and the butter and season with salt and pepper. Cook just until the clams open and the sauce thickens slightly, 2 to 3 minutes.

Serve with the toasted bread and lemon wedges.

NOTE: Use the remaining sorrel cream on pasta, spread on toast, or as a garnish on scrambled eggs.

OTHER GREENS TO TRY dock, spinach, ramp greens

SPIGARELLO

Brassica olevacea var. italica

A leafy variety of broccoli—the English name for it is, after all, "leaf broccoli"—Italians have always prized these greens, especially for tossing in pasta, simmering in soup and stews, baking, roasting, braising, steaming, and sautéing. Though some refer to it as the "parent of broccoli rabe," the gentle, grassy flavor of spigarello could not be more different. The leaves contain vitamins A, C, and folate and iron, potassium, and dietary fiber.

VARIETIES CURLY LEAF, FLAT LEAF

SEASON Midwinter through spring

HOW TO CHOOSE Leaves should be sprightly, not wilted, with no yellowing and they should be free of mold. Roots should look healthy.

HOW TO CLEAN Immerse in cool water. Agitate with fingers. Drain; pat or spin dry.

HOW TO STORE Store in an airtight plastic container or ziplock bag or wrap in plastic wrap. In the crisper drawer of the refrigerator, spigarello will keep up to 5 days.

HOW TO REFRESH Immerse in ice water for 15 minutes. Drain and spin or pat dry.

PAIRINGS Anchovies, pancetta, garlic, chiles, citrus, peppers, potatoes, pasta, onions, and any fish, meat, or poultry.

SLOW-BRAISED SPIGARELLO

Spigarello is particularly nice when long braised, as the leaves become tender and velvety. If you close your eyes, you might feel like you're eating broccoli, as the flavor is so similar.

SERVES 4

½ cup [120 ml] olive oil

1¼ pounds [570 g] spigarello, thick stems removed

½ teaspoon kosher salt

2 cups [480 ml] double chicken stock (page 299) or vegetable stock

In a large, wide pot, warm the olive oil over medium-high heat. Add the spigarello and salt and cook, stirring and turning often, until the spigarello has wilted, about 3 minutes. Add the chicken stock and simmer gently, uncovered, until the stems are tender but not falling apart, 30 to 40 minutes. Serve hot.

OTHER GREENS TO TRY chard, collard greens, kale

RISOTTO WITH SPIGARELLO

The spigarello garnish hidden in this risotto recipe is highly versatile. It can be used in a sandwich, tossed with pasta, or eaten as a side dish. Here, it turns this creamy risotto into a hearty main dish.

SERVES 4 TO 6

1¼ pounds [570 g] spigarello, thick stems removed

7 cups [1.7 L] double chicken stock (page 299)

Kosher salt

5 tablespoons [80 ml] olive oil

½ cup [70 g] minced yellow onion

1 teaspoon rosemary leaves, chopped

1½ cups [300 g] Arborio or Carnaroli rice

4 cloves garlic, thinly sliced

1 cup [240 ml] tomato puree

½ cup [120 ml] dry white wine

Freshly ground black pepper

¼ cup [10 g] fresh basil leaves

8 ounces [230 g] Sungold or other cherry tomatoes, cut in half

¼ cup [30 g] finely grated Parmigiano-Reggiano

½ teaspoon dried red pepper flakes

4 ounces [115 g] Gorgonzola dolce, cut into 4 to 6 pieces

Blanch the spigarello according to the method on page 6 and set aside. Warm the stock in a saucepan over low heat and season generously with salt.

Heat 2 tablespoons of the olive oil in a wide, heavy saucepan over medium heat. Add the onion and rosemary and cook until the onion is tender, about 5 minutes. Add the rice and half of the garlic and cook, stirring, until the rice grains turn opaque, about 4 minutes. Stir in the tomato puree and cook until the tomato coats the rice, 5 to 10 minutes. Add the wine and stir until it has been absorbed by the rice. Add about ½ cup [120 ml] of the hot stock; it should just cover the rice and should bubble gently. Cook, stirring often, until it is nearly absorbed. Continue adding stock, ½ cup [120 ml] at a time, stirring after each addition and adding more only when the rice is almost dry. The rice is done when is just tender all the way through but the center of each grain is still chewy (al dente), 20 to 25 minutes. Season the rice with salt and pepper, then stir in the basil, cherry tomatoes, and Parmigiano-Reggiano and remove from the heat.

In a saucepan over medium heat, warm the remaining 3 tablespoons olive oil. Add the remaining garlic, the reserved spigarello, and the pepper flakes and cook, stirring gently, until the spigarello is reheated through and the garlic is translucent, 2 to 3 minutes.

Divide the risotto among large, shallow soup bowls. Top each serving with a chunk of the Gorgonzola and a mound of the spigarello mixture. Alternatively, chop the spigarello mixture and stir it into the risotto before spooning the risotto into the bowls. Serve immediately.

OTHER GREENS TO TRY broccoli rabe, kale

Slow-Braised Spigarello

SPINACH

Spinacia oleracea

Popeye's favorite should never come out of a can. Fresh from the farmers' market or grocery, spinach is one of the most popular greens in existence. Native to Asia, likely Iran, it has flourished around the world for millennia. And Popeye wasn't its only proponent in history: Catherine de' Medici spread the popularity of the green to France from her native Italy, making sure that any dish made with it was designated as "Florentine." It was so popular in the United States in the early twentieth century that Birds Eye made it one of the initial offerings in its frozen food line in 1930. Spinach is filled with nutrients, particularly vitamins A, B, C, and K and iron, calcium, and potassium.

VARIETIES BABY, BLOOMSDALE, FLAT-LEAF, MERLO NERO, SAVOY, SEMI-SAVOY, SMOOTH, VIROFLAY

SEASON Spring and fall

HOW TO CHOOSE Choose crisp, sturdy leaves that have bright, uniform coloring and no dark blemishes. Do not buy if wilted.

HOW TO CLEAN Immerse in cool water. Agitate with hands, making sure to remove all grit, as spinach tends to hold on to dirt and grit. Drain; pat or spin dry.

HOW TO STORE Store in an airtight plastic bin or ziplock bag or wrap in plastic wrap. In the crisper drawer of the refrigerator, spinach will keep for up to 5 days.

HOW TO REFRESH Immerse in ice water for 15 minutes. Drain and pat or spin dry.

COOKING METHODS Use raw in salads or cook by steaming, braising, sautéing, blanching, boiling, stir-frying, or simmering in soup or stews.

PAIRINGS Anchovies, lemon, chiles, dairy, garlic, sesame, any meat, poultry, eggs, mushrooms, legumes, potatoes.

GREEN PANCAKES

I was talking with my friend Chef Bradley Herron from Miami about how he gets his kids to eat greens, and he told me that throwing any kind of green into a pancake works. His kids never know the difference; to them, a pancake is a pancake. I thought that was both clever and sounded delicious. I started to experiment with greens in pancakes, and this recipe was the result. Adding a lot of mint makes them taste bright, clean, and fresh.

MAKES 16 PANCAKES, SERVES 6 TO 8

2 cups [280 g] all-purpose flour

3 tablespoons sugar

1 teaspoon kosher salt

2 tablespoons baking powder

2 eggs, separated

2 cups [480 ml] whole milk

7 ounces [200 g] spinach

½ ounce [15 g] fresh mint leaves with stems (make sure to use tender leaves and stems; avoid using dark, tough stems)

¼ cup [55 g] unsalted butter, melted

Olive oil

Fresh goat cheese and/or strawberry preserves, for serving

Stir together the flour, sugar, salt, and baking powder in a bowl. Set aside.

Beat the egg whites until they form stiff peaks. Set aside.

Combine the egg yolks, milk, spinach, and mint in a blender and process until fully blended. Add the egg yolk mixture and the melted butter to the flour mixture and stir well. Fold in the egg whites.

Preheat the oven to 200°F [95°C]. Coat the bottom of a nonstick skillet with olive oil and warm over medium-high heat. Scoop up ½ cup [120 ml] of the batter with a measuring cup or ladle and pour into the skillet. Cook until golden on the bottom side and bubbles have formed on the top, 2 to 3 minutes. Flip the pancake to cook the second side, adding 1 tablespoon olive oil to the pan as needed for the second side to become crispy. Transfer to a sheet pan or ovenproof platter and place in the warm oven. Repeat until all the batter is used.

Serve immediately with goat cheese for a savory dish or with strawberry preserves for a sweeter dish.

OTHER GREENS TO TRY chard, mâche

SPINACH AND ARUGULA WITH BEEF KOFTA, OLIVES, AND FETA

A crispy, clean, grilled-meat salad is great in the summertime. In this recipe, it doesn't matter which meat you use—you can substitute chicken or lamb or pork for the beef. No matter which you choose, when a protein is present in a salad, it becomes much more interesting, bringing out flavors of the greens in a whole new way. Plus, the dish is suddenly more than just a salad—it transforms into an entrée. The dates and almonds add a satisfying sweetness and texture. In cold weather, sauté the spinach for a warmer dish.

SERVES 4

1 pound [455 g] ground beef

4 teaspoons pickled chile (page 294), drained

1 egg

½ teaspoon ground cumin

Kosher salt and freshly ground black pepper

4 cups [80 g] loosely packed spinach leaves

1 cup [60 g] loosely packed shaved green cabbage

½ cup [75 g] shaved fennel

⅛ red onion, shaved on a mandoline

¼ cup [30 g] sliced almonds, toasted

8 pitted dates, cut into eighths

1 large dill frond, coarsely chopped

4 ounces [115 g] feta

Red wine vinaigrette (page 301)

Prepare a medium-hot fire in a charcoal grill. Gently mix together the beef, pickled chile, egg, cumin, 2 teaspoons salt, and 1 teaspoon pepper. Divide into eight 2-ounce [55-g] portions and shape into oval patties. Gently place on the grill directly over the fire and grill, turning once, for about 2 minutes per side, until juicy and cooked to medium.

While the kofta are cooking, mix together the spinach, cabbage, fennel, red onion, almonds, dates, dill, and feta in a large bowl. Season with salt

and pepper and lightly dress with the vinaigrette. Divide the salad among four plates and top with the kofta, dividing them evenly. Serve immediately.

OTHER GREENS TO TRY Belgian endive, mâche, red orach, tatsoi

CHALLAH FATTOUSH WITH SPINACH, TOMATOES, CUCUMBER, DILL, MINT, AND OREGANO

Fattoush is a Middle Eastern salad that features toasted pita in the mix. This version uses challah instead of pita, a substitution I came up with because I had some leftover challah from the Jewish holidays. There is a heavy herbal taste in this version, thanks not only to the dill, basil, oregano, and mint but also to the cucumbers. The flavors feel perfectly Middle Eastern, savory and bright and fresh, with a hint of sour from the sumac vinaigrette.

SERVES 2 TO 4

8 ounces [230 g] challah, torn into 1- to 2-inch [2.5- to 5-cm] pieces

8 ounces [230 g] cherry tomatoes, halved

4 ounces [115 g] Persian or English cucumber, quartered lengthwise and thinly sliced crosswise

2 green onions, cut into 1-inch [2.5-cm] batons

1 small red bell pepper, seeded and thinly sliced

2 ounces [55 g] spinach leaves

4 dill fronds, fine leaves coarsely chopped and thick stems discarded

12 fresh basil leaves, cut into ¼-inch [6-mm] ribbons

12 fresh mint leaves, cut into ¼-inch [6-mm] ribbons

3 sprigs oregano, leaves removed and tougher stems discarded

2 ounces [55 g] feta cheese, finely crumbled

Fine sea salt

Sumac vinaigrette (page 301)

Preheat the oven to 350°F [180°C].

Spread the challah pieces on a sheet pan. Bake until mostly dried and lightly golden, about 15 minutes. Remove from the oven and cool completely.

Combine the tomatoes, cucumber, green onions, bell pepper, spinach, dill, basil, mint, oregano, and feta in a large bowl. Season with salt and dress with the vinaigrette. Add the challah and toss until evenly coated, then divide among plates and serve immediately.

OTHER GREENS TO TRY arugula, tatsoi

ASPARAGUS AND SPINACH HUMMUS

Sometimes spinach can be essential to a dish without being the spotlight ingredient. This recipe is the perfect example of using spinach for color and nutrition but not the dominant flavor. It was inspired by an asparagus soup that I make: I cool it down and then add pureed spinach to brighten the color. I use that same approach with this hummus recipe, which tastes like asparagus and is a beautiful green because of the spinach.

MAKES 3 PINTS [1.5 L]

1 rounded cup [230 g] dried chickpeas

6 cups [1.4 L] water

8-inch [20-cm] sprig rosemary

2 bay leaves

14 ounces [400 g] tender parts asparagus or trim from peeling asparagus (after woody bottoms are discarded)

½ cup plus 3 tablespoons [170 g] tahini

3 cloves garlic

5 ounces [140 g] spinach

1 cup [240 ml] olive oil

6 tablespoons [90 ml] fresh lemon juice

1½ tablespoons kosher salt

Put the chickpeas in a large bowl and add water to cover by 3 inches [7.5 cm]. Soak overnight at room temperature.

The following day, drain the beans and transfer to a saucepan. Add the water, rosemary, and bay leaves; bring to a simmer; and cook until the chickpeas are very tender, about 45 minutes. Add the asparagus and continue to cook, stirring often, until the asparagus is tender, about 10 minutes. Remove from the heat and cool completely at room temperature.

Drain the chickpeas and asparagus. Working in batches, transfer the chickpea mixture to a high-powered blender (such as a Vitamix Vita-Prep) and puree with the tahini, garlic, spinach, and olive oil. When each batch is smooth, pass it through a fine-mesh sieve into a large bowl. When all of the batches have been strained, add the lemon juice and salt and stir well to blend the seasonings evenly.

Serve immediately or store in one or more airtight containers in the refrigerator for up to 1 week.

OTHER GREENS TO TRY mâche, New Zealand spinach

SUCCULENTS

A familiar sight throughout the American Southwest, succulents such as various cacti, aloe, and others are not only beautiful natives of the landscape but also lovely additions to a dinner plate. Cacti, for example, are thought to have been part of the terrain for as long as seven thousand years, as evidenced by fossils found in Mexico. The Spaniards, likely thanks to Christopher Columbus, started eating succulents in the late fifteenth or early sixteenth century and then spread the wealth to the Middle East via trade. Today, succulents such as cactus paddles, agave, aloe, and dragonfruit are becoming more common at farmers' markets and groceries. Succulents are distinguished by their fleshy stems and/or leaves, and when cooked, they release a sap much the way okra does. High in vitamin C, fiber, and magnesium, succulents may also contain a fair amount of potassium and calcium.

VARIETIES AGAVE, ALOE, BARREL, DRAGONFRUIT, HENS AND CHICKS, NOPALES, ORCHID, ORGAN PIPE, PRICKLY PEAR, PURSLANE, SAGUARO, SEDUM

SEASON Spring

HOW TO CHOOSE Look for plants that are vibrant green and sturdy, with no black spots. Though the texture will be pliant when squeezed, succulents should not be mushy or limp.

HOW TO CLEAN Wear plastic gloves when handling thorny succulents to prevent being pricked! Rinse thoroughly under cold water. Then, with a vegetable peeler or knife, peel away bumps and thorns. Trim off about one-quarter of the border around the edges, then rinse again. (Thorns are usually, but not always, removed before sold.)

HOW TO STORE Store in an airtight plastic bin or ziplock bag or wrap in plastic wrap. In the crisper drawer of the refrigerator, succulents will keep for 1 week.

HOW TO REFRESH Use as soon as possible after purchase and preparation because most succulents really can't be refreshed once dehydrated.

COOKING METHODS Serve raw in salads or cook by boiling, broiling, roasting, sautéing, grilling, or poaching.

PAIRINGS Citrus, lime, tomatillos, tomatoes, chiles, tropical fruits, meats, poultry, firm-fleshed fish such as tuna.

P.S. I LOVE YOU

I grew up in southern California and we always had aloe growing in a pot. We mostly used the juice in the leaves to quell the pain from sunburns and small cuts or sores. My family spent a lot of time in the desert close to Palm Springs (aka PS), and if it was sunny, I was probably sunburned. Sometimes my mom would buy a large jar of aloe juice and keep it in the fridge. We never really cooked with it then, but today, I like to use it in cocktails. This one is a favorite because I love tequila, and it happens to be made from agave (as is mezcal). Combining tequila with aloe, which is in the same family, is always a good idea. The result is a clean, bright, drink with a little texture thanks to the heft of the aloe vera juice, which also boasts antioxidants is good for digestion.

SERVES 1

2 sprigs cilantro

2 ounces [60 ml] blanco tequila

1 ounce [30 ml] aloe vera juice (recipe follows)

¾ ounce [20 ml] fresh lime juice

½ ounce [15 ml] simple syrup (page 294)

Pinch of kosher salt

Ice

3 ounces [90 ml] celery soda

½ ounce [15 ml] grapefruit juice

Thin strips of young aloe, to garnish

Thinly sliced lime, for garnish

Combine the cilantro, tequila, aloe vera juice, lime juice, simple syrup, and salt in a shaker filled with ice. Shake well and strain into a highball glass filled with ice. Top with the celery soda, then float the grapefruit juice on top and serve garnished with the aloe strips and lime.

ALOE VERA JUICE

MAKES 3½ CUPS [840 ML]

3 large, peeled, halved, and seeded cucumbers

½ cup [120 ml] water

2 aloe vera stalks

In a blender, combine the cucumbers and water and puree until smooth. Pass the puree through a fine-mesh sieve and measure out 3 cups [720 ml] of the resulting cucumber juice. Pour the juice into the blender beaker, add the aloe vera, and blend until smooth. Strain the juice through a fine-mesh sieve. The juice can be served immediately or chilled for up to 1 hour before serving over ice or using in a cocktail.

PUGLIAN FAVA BEANS WITH HENS AND CHICKS SALAD

Despite their name, hens and chicks are vegetarian. These succulents earned their cute moniker because the edible tender offshoots (the "chicks") propagate from their mother (the "hens"). Also known as houseleeks (and botanically as Sempervivum tectorum), these rosette-forming succulents were brought to the United States by early southern European settlers, who planted them outside their kitchen doors for easy harvesting. In the old country, they were also grown on rooftops for insulation and, because they are water-filled succulents, on thatched roofs to keep the roofs from burning. Their taste and texture is similar to cucumber, while their leaves, which can be juiced, are a great substitute for aloe vera (and like aloe vera, can be used to treat burns). This recipe plays up their wonderful raw quality atop a luscious Puglian fava bean puree. They also pair nicely with fish or grilled pork.

SERVES 8 AS AN APPETIZER OR SIDE DISH

2 cups [320 g] peeled dried fava beans

Double chicken stock (page 299) or water, to cover

6 tablespoons [90 ml] olive oil, plus more for finishing

Fresh lemon juice

Fine sea salt

8 ounces [230 g] young, tender hens and chicks offshoots (known as the chicks)

2 tablespoons finely chopped fresh chives

8 fresh mint leaves, cut into ribbons

16 salty black olives, pitted and torn in half

Crusty bread, for serving

Put the beans in a large bowl and add water to cover by 3 inches [7.5 cm]. Soak overnight at room temperature.

Drain the beans, transfer to a pot, and add the chicken stock to cover by about 1 inch [2.5 cm]. Bring to a simmer over medium heat and cook gently, without stirring, until the beans are tender and starting to fall apart, about 15 minutes. Ideally, you do not want to stir the beans until most of the water has been absorbed. By the end of 15 minutes, you should have just enough liquid in the pan to help the beans become a mash when stirred. Remove from heat, add 3 tablespoons of the olive oil and, using a spoon, mash to a rough puree. The consistency should be close to mashed potatoes. Season to taste with lemon juice and salt.

In a small bowl, toss together the hens and chicks, chives, mint, and olives with the remaining 3 tablespoons olive oil, a squeeze of lemon juice, and a sprinkle of salt.

To serve, spoon an equal amount of the puree onto each individual plate. Garnish with the hens and chicks salad and finish with a drizzle of olive oil. Serve immediately with the bread.

OTHER GREENS TO TRY mâche, purslane

BEEF TARTARE TOSTADA WITH NOPALES

In the warm weather, sometimes it is nice to make something that you don't have to turn your oven on for. This is one of those dishes. It is easy, fast, and refreshing and it showcases the wonderful firm and succulent texture of the cactus paddles. A note about using raw meat: Make sure you are using a very fresh product. Talk to your butcher and explain that it is for a raw preparation. Using a lean cut is best, and lamb can be subbed in to mix things up.

SERVES 4 AS AN APPETIZER

1¼ pounds [570 g] beef tenderloin, chopped finely with a knife, or freshly ground through a medium die and then finely chopped

2 ounces [55 g] Cotija cheese, finely grated

Zest of 1⅓ limes, finely grated on a Microplane, plus 4 wedges lime, for garnish

Flaky sea salt

4-ounce [115-g] wedge green cabbage, shaved on a mandoline

4 red radishes, shaved on a mandoline

½ cup [40 g] nopales, spines and thorns removed

1 jalapeño chile, thinly sliced

½ cup [70 g] escabeche (recipe follows)

½ cup [120 ml] neutral vegetable oil

4 (5-inch/12-cm) fried yellow corn tortillas

½ cup [120 ml] Mexican crema or sour cream

24 fresh cilantro leaves

Gently mix the beef tenderloin, Cotija cheese, and lime zest in a small bowl with a spoon. (I always use the thin edge of the spoon to keep it light and not mash the mixture. Do not overmix or it will be pasty.) Season the mixture well with flaky salt and set aside.

In another bowl, mix together the cabbage, radishes, nopales, a few thin slices of jalapeño, and the escabeche. Season the salad with flaky salt and dress with the escabeche pickling liquid and the oil.

Divide the meat among the four fried tortillas and gently spread the beef to the edges. Garnish with the lime wedges, crema, and cilantro leaves.

ESCABECHE

MAKES ABOUT 1 QUART [1 L]

3 tablespoons neutral vegetable oil

½ pound [225 g] jalapeño chiles, stemmed and quartered

1 white or yellow onion, halved and sliced into half moons ½ inch [12 mm] thick

3 carrots, peeled and thickly sliced

8 cloves garlic

2 cups [480 ml] apple cider vinegar

1 tablespoon kosher salt

1 bay leaf

1 teaspoon dried oregano

1 teaspoon dried marjoram

1 tablespoon sugar

Heat the oil in a large, deep skillet over medium heat. Add the chiles, onion, carrots, and garlic and fry, stirring occasionally, for about 10 minutes, until the onion slices are mostly translucent and the vegetables tender.

Add the vinegar, salt, bay leaf, oregano, marjoram, and sugar and bring to a boil. Decrease the heat and simmer for 10 minutes. Make sure the chiles are cooked through. They will be a dull olive color rather than a vibrant green.

Remove from the heat and cool. Store in an airtight container in the the refrigerator for up to 1 month.

TATSOI

Brassica rapa subsp. *narinosa*

This Asian salad green exemplifies the best qualities of various greens. It has a mustardy flavor, but it is not as bitter as mustard greens. Its leaves are attached to juicy stalks that in texture are similar to bok choy, yet are slightly more delicate. Tatsoi is widely available—a fixture at Asian groceries and farmers' markets. When cooked, its flavors become earthy and its texture becomes soft and creamy. Also called spinach mustard, spoon mustard, and rosette bok choy (because of its shape), tatsoi contains vitamins A, C, and K and beta-carotene, potassium, calcium, phosphorus, and iron.

VARIETIES BLACK SUMMER, CHING-CHIANG, JOI CHOI, MEI QING CHOI, TATSOI SAVOY, WIN WIN

SEASON Spring and late summer through early fall

HOW TO CHOOSE Choose sturdy, glossy greens that are a uniform deep green and are free of any dark blemishes, yellowing, and wilting.

HOW TO CLEAN Immerse in cool water. Agitate with fingers. Drain; pat or spin dry.

HOW TO STORE Store in an airtight plastic bin or ziplock bag or wrap in plastic wrap. In the crisper drawer of the refrigerator, tatsoi will keep for 3 to 5 days.

HOW TO REFRESH Immerse in ice water for 15 minutes. Drain and pat or spin dry.

COOKING METHODS Use raw in salads or cook by steaming, briefly stir-frying, or simmering in soup.

PAIRINGS Fish sauce, soy sauce, vinegar, ginger, coconut milk, chicken, fish, mushrooms, braised meats, scallops.

COCONUT MILK RICE PORRIDGE WITH TATSOI

Whenever I am sick, I crave the rich Asian rice porridge known as congee. This porridge is like congee but more luxurious and fragrant because of the coconut milk, not a usual ingredient in the classic version. Tatsoi lends a little bit of texture and brightens up the whole bowl. For this recipe, the young leaves of tatsoi—the ones that are typically smaller and more tender—work best. Overall, this porridge is easy to make, and it holds really well for a week. And being sick is certainly not a requirement for eating it.

SERVES 4

2- to 3-inch [5- to 7.5-cm] piece fresh ginger, peeled and sliced into ¼-inch [6-mm] pieces

1 stalk lemongrass, tough outer leaves removed

1 jalapeño chile, quartered

2 cloves garlic

Juice of 1 lime

2 tablespoons palm or light brown sugar

1 cup [200 g] jasmine rice

½ (13½-ounce/400-ml) can coconut milk, shaken before opening

3 quarts [2.8 L] double chicken stock (page 299) or vegetable stock

2 to 4 bird's eye chiles, cut lengthwise through the center without separating the halves

5 kaffir lime leaves

2 to 3 tablespoons fish sauce

Fine sea salt

4 ounces [115 g] young tatsoi leaves

¼ cup [35 g] chopped roasted peanuts

2 teaspoons white sesame seeds, toasted

Using a mortar and pestle, finely crush the ginger, lemongrass, jalapeño, and garlic until a chunky paste forms. Add the lime juice and crush until combined.

Combine the crushed mixture in a pot with the palm sugar, rice, coconut milk, chicken stock, bird's eye chiles, and kaffir lime leaves. Stir and bring to a gentle simmer. Continue stirring for a few minutes to make sure the rice does not stick to the bottom of the pan. Allow the porridge to cook, uncovered, for 1 ½ to 2 hours, until the rice is extremely tender and breaking apart. The porridge should have a very soft texture. Add water or stock to thin as needed.

When done, remove and discard the bird's eye chiles and kaffir lime leaves. Stir in the fish sauce and season to taste with salt. Ladle into bowls and top each bowl with the tatsoi leaves, peanuts, and sesame seeds, dividing them evenly.

The porridge can be stored in an airtight container in the regrigerator for up to 1 week. To reheat, add water or stock to thin to the original consistency and warm over medium-low heat.

OTHER GREENS TO TRY celery leaves, mâche

WATERCRESS

Nasturtium officinale

A variety of cress, this ultrapeppery, strong-stemmed green is often used in salads or in sandwiches (most famously for British afternoon tea), or pureed as a soup. One of the oldest documented greens, watercress dates back to ancient Greece, Rome, and Persia, where it was typically fed to soldiers to build their strength. Hippocrates reportedly prescribed it to treat blood disease around 400 BCE, and Captain Cook and his crew consumed it to combat scurvy during long voyages. In 2014, researchers at William Paterson University in New Jersey named it the most nutrient-rich vegetable, packed with vitamins A, B, C, E, and K and with calcium, phosphorus, potassium, and manganese.

VARIETIES CRINKLED CRESS, CURLY CRESS, GARDEN WATERCRESS, KOREAN WATERCRESS, UPLAND CRESS, WILD WATERCRESS (SEE PAGE 282)

SEASON Spring and fall

HOW TO CHOOSE Choose crisp, sturdy leaves that have bright uniform coloring and perky stems. Avoid if wilted, blemished, or if the texture is slimy.

HOW TO CLEAN Trim off long and tough stems. Immerse in cool water. Agitate with fingers. Drain; pat or spin dry.

HOW TO STORE Store in an airtight plastic bin or ziplock bag or wrap in plastic wrap. In the crisper drawer of the refrigerator, watercress will keep for 2 to 3 days.

HOW TO REFRESH Immerse in ice water for 15 minutes. Drain and pat or spin dry.

COOKING METHODS Use raw in salads or sandwiches or cook by simmering in soups and stews, sautéing, or steaming.

PAIRINGS Eggs, sausage, any meat, fish, or poultry.

CHICKEN AND PORK BELLY PAELLA WITH WATERCRESS

Peppery and bright, raw watercress is more than a garnish on this dish: it is a clean component that contrasts with the richness of the meat and rice. I find that to be the case when I use watercress in anything, actually—it has the same powerful effect of arugula on pizza, completing the flavor by adding an edge of spiciness and freshness to any rich, heavy, meaty, or starchy dish.

SERVES 4

¼ cup [60 ml] olive oil, plus more for finishing

4 ounces [115 g] thick-cut bacon, cut into 1-inch [2.5-cm] lardons

4 ounces [115 g] boneless chicken thighs, cut into 1-inch [2.5-cm] pieces

1 yellow onion, diced

2 cloves garlic, thinly sliced

2 tablespoons sweet smoked paprika

1 cup [200 g] Calasparra, Valencia, or Bomba rice

Small pinch of saffron threads (about ½ teaspoon)

2 tomatoes, cut into 6 pieces each and most seeds removed

Fine sea salt and freshly ground black pepper

4 cups [960 ml] double chicken stock (page 299) or water, plus more as needed

4 ounces [115 g] roasted pork belly or ham, cut into ½-inch [12-mm] pieces

4 ounces [115 g] watercress, torn into bite-size sprigs

Warm the olive oil in a 13½-inch [34-cm] paella pan over medium-high heat. Add the bacon and cook for 2 minutes, then add the chicken. Cook for 1 to 2 minutes, making sure that the bacon stays tender and does not crisp, then add the onion, garlic, and paprika. Cook until the onion is translucent, about 3 minutes. Add the rice and saffron and stir to evenly coat and toast the rice, 4 to 5 minutes. Add the tomatoes and cook until they become warm and begin to fall apart, about 3 minutes more. Season with salt and pepper.

Evenly distribute and flatten out the rice in the pan and then add the stock. Turn the heat to high, taste the broth, and adjust the seasoning. Bring to a simmer, then decrease the heat to a medium simmer and cook, rotating the paella pan every 2 minutes, for about 20 minutes, until the rice is plump and cooked. Taste and adjust with salt and pepper.

Add the cooked pork to the pan, nestling the pieces into the rice. Keep the paella over high heat and continue to rotate the pan every 2 minutes to create an evenly crispy bottom (known as socarrat). Add additional chicken stock or water as needed to fully cook the rice.

Garnish with the olive oil and watercress.

OTHER GREENS TO TRY chickweed, fava greens, blanched broccoli rabe

SLOW-ROASTED PORK TONNATO WITH WATERCRESS AND TOMATOES

Traditional *vitello tonnato*, which combines cold, sliced veal and a creamy tuna sauce, is a dish from Piedmont in the north of Italy. My version uses pork instead of veal. While it is a bit of a project, the pork will end up with a texture like you've never had before. The watercress salad is the perfect counterpoint to all of that meat and cream and intense fish.

SERVES 4

¾ cup [180 g] tonnato (facing page)

8 ounces [230 g] slow-roasted pork loin (recipe follows), cold (about 12 slices)

Flaky sea salt

2 ounces [55 g] watercress, torn into bite-size sprigs

½ medium cucumber, peeled if skin is thick, thinly sliced

8 Sungold or other cherry tomatoes or small heirloom tomatoes

16 brined green olives, pitted and torn in half

1 small shallot, thinly sliced

8 cornichons, sliced into thin rounds

½ cup [120 ml] pickled mustard seed vinaigrette (page 301)

Freshly ground black pepper

2 medium-boiled eggs (page 293), halved

Using a large platter or four individual plates, smear the tonnato over one-third of the surface. Lay the pork slices on the tonnato and season with salt.

In a bowl, combine the watercress, cucumber, tomatoes, olives, shallot, and cornichons. Dress with the vinaigrette, season with salt and pepper, and toss well. Garnish the pork with the dressed salad. Lay the egg halves around the salad and season the cut sides with salt. Serve immediately.

OTHER GREENS TO TRY chickweed, spinach

SLOW-ROASTED PORK LOIN

MAKES 1 POUND [455 G]

8 cups [2 L] ice cubes

6 quarts [5.7 L] water

¼ cup [75 g] kosher salt

2 tablespoons molasses

1 tablespoon black peppercorns

5 bay leaves

1 pound [455 g] boneless center-cut pork loin

Fine sea salt and freshly ground black pepper

¼ cup [60 ml] olive oil

Put the ice cubes in a large plastic container and set aside.

In a large pot, combine the water, kosher salt, molasses, peppercorns, and bay leaves. Bring to a simmer, then remove from the heat and pour over the ice cubes. When fully cooled, add the pork, submerging it in the brine by weighting it down with a plate. Cover and place in the refrigerator for 24 hours.

After 24 hours, remove the pork from the brine, dry it off with a clean towel, and season with fine sea salt and pepper.

Preheat the oven to 200°F [95°C]. Line a sheet pan with parchment paper and place a roasting rack on the sheet pan.

Warm the oil in a large sauté pan over medium-high heat. Add the pork loin and sear until golden on all sides, 2 to 4 minutes on each side. When done, place the pork loin on the roasting rack. Roast until a thermometer inserted into the thickest part of the pork reads 138°F [59°C], 2 to 2½ hours. Remove from the oven and allow the pork to cool to room temperature. Once fully cooled, wrap in plastic wrap and refrigerate until fully chilled before using. The pork will keep for up to 5 days.

TONNATO

MAKES 2 CUPS [480 G]

1¼ cups [300 ml] mayonnaise, preferably homemade

2 small cloves garlic, finely grated on a Microplane

4 ounces [115 g] good-quality, oil-packed canned albacore or other tuna, preferably Spanish

3 anchovy fillets packed in oil

Zest and juice of 1 lemon, zest finely grated on a Microplane

3 tablespoons drained capers

Kosher salt and freshly ground black pepper

In a food processor, combine the mayonnaise, garlic, tuna, anchovies, lemon zest and juice, and capers and puree until smooth. Season with salt and pepper. The tonnato will keep in an airtight container in the refrigerator for up to 1 week.

WATERCRESS SOUP WITH CRÈME FRAÎCHE AND ZA'ATAR

Serve this soup warm or cold. Either way, it has a nice green flavor. This soup is also the perfect use for watercress stems—so don't throw them away! Here's the opportunity to repurpose something that would typically be thrown out. The spice mixture *za'atar* makes the flavor feel Middle Eastern. You can buy *za'atar* in nearly any specialty grocery store.

SERVES 8

1½ pounds [680 g] Yukon gold potatoes, peeled and cubed

4½ cups [1.1 L] water, or more as needed

1 large clove garlic, cut in half

8 ounces [230 g] watercress stems or wild watercress

½ cup [120 ml] olive oil

1 cup [240 ml] buttermilk

1 cup [240 ml] whole milk

1 tablespoon kosher salt

½ cup [120 ml] crème fraîche

8 teaspoons za'atar

In a stockpot, combine the potatoes, 4 cups [960 ml] of the water, and the garlic. Bring to a simmer over medium-high heat and cook until the potatoes are very tender, about 20 minutes. Add the watercress and cook for 2 to 3 minutes, until the greens are tender. Transfer to a shallow pan to cool faster, then place in the refrigerator and chill completely.

In batches, puree the potato-watercress mixture in a blender until very smooth, drizzling in the olive oil while pureeing. Pour the puree into a large container and stir in the buttermilk, milk, and salt. Thin with the remaining ½ cup [120 ml] water or more as needed to achieve the desired consistency.

The soup can be served cold or warm. Ladle into bowls and garnish each serving with 1 tablespoon of the crème fraîche and sprinkle with 1 teaspoon of the za'atar.

OTHER GREENS TO TRY cilantro, parsley stems, spinach

WATER SPINACH
Ipomoea aquatica

Its crunchy texture, even when cooked, distinguishes water spinach from common spinach. Among its aliases are *kangkong, ong choy*, river spinach, Chinese spinach, Chinese watercress, swamp cabbage, and water morning glory. The origin of water spinach is unknown, though it thrives in tropical and subtropical climates, primarily in Southeast Asia, where it is a fixture in markets in Vietnam and Thailand. A relative of morning glory and the sweet potato, water spinach is marked by lean, hollow stems, and with leaves shaped like arrowheads. Think of it as a crunchy, nutty spinach, packed with hearty doses of vitamins A, B, C, and E.

VARIETIES LARGE LEAF GREEN STEM, LARGE LEAF LIGHT STEM, SMALL LEAF GREEN STEM, SMALL LEAF LIGHT STEM

SEASON Summer

HOW TO CHOOSE Choose crisp, sturdy leaves that have bright uniform coloring and no dark blemishes. Do not buy if wilted.

HOW TO CLEAN Immerse in cool water. Agitate with fingers. Drain; pat or spin dry.

HOW TO STORE Store in an airtight plastic bin or ziplock bag or wrap in plastic wrap. In the crisper drawer of the refrigerator, water spinach will keep for 2 to 3 days.

HOW TO REFRESH Immerse greens in ice water for 15 minutes. Drain and spin or pat dry.

COOKING METHODS Use raw in salads or cook by steaming, stir-frying, sautéing, simmering in soups or stews, braising, or coating in tempura batter and frying.

PAIRINGS Oyster sauce, fish sauce, garlic, chiles, mushrooms, or any meat, fish, poultry.

WATER SPINACH SIDE DISH

I learned this recipe on a trip to Vietnam, after seeing it at all the markets and asking a vendor to make it for me. It is so easy and distinctly Asian—a light, clean, bright accompaniment to many dishes. Soy sauce or fish sauce complements the green's graceful quality while keeping those ethnic flavors in line. (Ginger is also a great addition.) Be sure to cook the greens as quickly as possible so they retain their vibrant green color.

SERVES 4

¼ cup [60 ml] neutral vegetable oil

4 cloves garlic, thinly sliced

4 dried chiles, crushed

6 cups [170 g] water spinach

1 tablespoon fish sauce

Fine sea salt

Place a wok or large sauté pan over high heat and add the oil, garlic, and chiles. When the garlic and chiles begin to sizzle, add the water spinach and stir rapidly, using chopsticks or a fork. Do not cook for more than a minute. The greens are ready when they just start to wilt, and they will continue to cook when removed from the pan. Season with the fish sauce and salt. Serve immediately.

OTHER GREENS TO TRY pea shoots, pea tendrils, spinach

Burdock

Dock

Fiddleheads

Lamb's-quarter

WILD AND FORAGED GREENS

No matter what the calendar says, the real sign of spring is when wild greens start sprouting around tree roots, creeping out between the sidewalk cracks, lining up on riverbanks, cropping up in gardens, and budding in clusters in any grassy or wooded area. You might first think that these are weeds. But upon closer inspection, they may be perfectly edible greens that would add an uncommon diversity to your cooking repertoire. Though you may spot some of these at farmers' markets, wild greens are not commercially grown and the best way to find them is to make friends with your local foraging expert and go out to hunt. Always consult an expert no matter where you are foraging, as some plants may be poisonous and soil can be contaminated in areas, especially in vacant lots. But once you become adept at identifying wild greens, you'll see that all the world can be a bounteous garden. Following are ten that are especially a treat to unearth.

BURDOCK
Arctium lappa

Most know burdock for its edible roots, which are commonly enjoyed in Asian cuisine. In Japan (where it is known as *gobo*), the leaves are also eaten when they are young and tender and their bitter flavor less pronounced. Like the root, the leaves partner well with pork, soups, and rice and are great when stir-fried or sautéed. The leaves are also used for wrapping food. Burdock greens contain vitamins B, C, and E and dietary fiber, calcium, and potassium and are sometimes used as an appetite stimulant. Find burdock in the fringes of parks, in scrubland, and often in urban areas, where they are looked upon as weeds.

DOCK
Rumex crispus

A member of the buckwheat family, these durable leaves—especially the larger ones—have been used by many cultures to wrap and store butter. Notoriously acidic and bitter, the curly edged varieties tend to be the most palatable and are best eaten when they are young and tender, and their flavor is less aggressive. Their sturdiness takes wonderfully to cooking—stir-frying, sautéing, braising—which also helps reduce their innate bitterness. Dock is nutrient rich; full of vitamins A and C, protein, and iron; and when rubbed on the skin is useful for the relief of nettle stings. A keen eye can spot dock anywhere, from vacant city lots to suburban backyards.

FIDDLEHEADS
Matteuccia struthiopteris

Named as such because of its resemblance to the scrolled top of a fiddle, this bright green vegetable is a harbinger of spring, along with its seasonal mates ramps, fava, and morels. The tastiest fiddleheads are the young shoots of ostrich ferns, which are also durable and diverse in the kitchen. Prepared in similar fashion to asparagus (and a nice seasonal substitute for the common vegetable), fiddleheads need to be blanched or steamed first, however, before cooking and consuming, and they take well to sautéing, frying, baking, stewing, and even grilling. They are also lovely when tossed in pasta, with potatoes, in a salad, or just on their own. Fiddleheads are high in vitamins A, C, and niacin and in manganese, iron, and protein. Seek out the ferns alongside rivers, creeks, and streams.

LAMB'S-QUARTER
Chenopodium berlandieri

A hearty and relentless grower, lamb's-quarter is one of the most easily foraged greens around; it can be found creeping everywhere from rural gardens to city tree pits. Its mineral flavor is often likened to chard. Also known as goosefoot (for its shape), pigweed, dungweed, baconweed, and wild spinach, lamb's-quarter is related to beets, spinach, and orach and is popular in Chinese and Korean cuisines. It is high in vitamins A and C, fiber, protein, manganese, calcium, copper, and iron.

LEMON BALM
Melissa officinalis

Also known as common balm, balm mint, or simply "balm," lemon balm is a member of the mint family. Its name is a giveaway to its scent and flavor: akin to the citrus fruit, with a lemony essence that makes it compatible with many other ingredients, especially fish, desserts, fruit and vegetable salads, soups, meat, and poultry. It also works as a prime ingredient in tea, jelly, jam, chutney, dressings, syrups, and sauces. The bug repellent Citronella may have even gained its inspiration from lemon balm, as the leaves are used to repel mosquitoes by rubbing them into the skin. Rich in vitamins B and C, lemon balm is most likely found in woodlands.

MINER'S LETTUCE
Claytonia perfoliata

The California gold rush is responsible for this green's distinctive name: miners ate it in order to get their fill of vitamin C and to prevent scurvy, a trick they learned from Native Americans. The delicate lime-colored leaves weren't much of a chore for the rugged workers to enjoy; their flavor is pleasantly mild and slightly sweet. Its somewhat succulent texture holds a lot of water, like purslane, and in addition to its high vitamin C content, miner's lettuce is also rich in vitamin A and iron.

RAMP GREENS
Allium tricoccum

Ramp season is heartbreakingly fleeting, so grab them when you can in early spring. Their bright, leafy tops share the garlic-like flavor of their white and magenta stalks, yet are not quite as intense. They are wonderful in brothy soups; when sautéed, stir-fried, steamed, or braised; tossed in pasta; used as a pizza topping; made into a pesto; or pickled, for longer-lasting enjoyment. Ramp greens pair well with eggs, mild greens, mild-flavored fish, and poultry.

WILD PEA GREENS
Lathyrus vestitus

Wild pea greens were once thought to be poisonous, which is a bit preposterous since they are nearly identical to common garden pea greens, especially in that nontoxic way. The flavor of wild pea greens tends to be sweeter, and the wild peas themselves are much smaller, but both the greens and the peas are rich in vitamin B, protein, and beta-carotene. Like their cultivated cousin, delicate wild pea greens are best when lightly sautéed or served raw in salads. In the Pacific Northwest, look for wild pea greens in wooded and brush areas.

WILD WATERCRESS
Nasturtium microphyllum

Wild watercress is pretty much a twin to its cultivated partner (see page 271), if with a slightly more intense peppery and piquant flavor. Its cultivated version, as a matter of fact, is one of few that retains the identical appearance and flavor of its wild ancestor. Like conventional watercress, wild watercress is incredibly

Lemon balm

Miner's lettuce

Ramp greens

Wood sorrel

nutritious, high in vitamins A, B, C, and E and in beta-carotene, calcium, potassium, iron, and dietary fiber. Wild watercress is usually found along streams, rivers, lakes, ponds—any watery terrain.

WOOD SORREL

Oxalis acetosella

A dead ringer for a shamrock and frequently called "sour grass," this three-leaved plant has a refreshing lemon-lime taste, is packed with vitamin C, and is known for its diuretic and stomach-soothing properties. It imparts a lightly acidic flavor when added to sauces, soups, or stews; makes a bright garnish on a raw salad; and is a terrific partner to any fish. Wood sorrel is often found in wooded areas, grassy fields, or meadowlands.

SEASON Spring, summer, and fall

HOW TO CHOOSE Practice safe foraging and always consult an expert to properly identify greens.

HOW TO CLEAN Immerse in cool water. Wash thoroughly, agitating with fingers, to rinse off sand and grit. Drain; spin or pat dry.

HOW TO STORE Store in an airtight plastic bin or ziplock bag or wrap in plastic wrap. In the crisper drawer of the refrigerator, wild greens will keep for 2 to 3 days.

HOW TO REFRESH Immerse in ice water for 15 minutes. Drain; pat or spin dry.

WOOD SORREL BUTTER

This recipe reminds me of the magic that happens—the ideal brightness—when you create the perfect balance of fat and sourness in a recipe. Think of lemon bars: they taste great when you combine just the right amount of butter and fat from egg yolks with the right amount of sourness from lemons. That's what happens in this butter recipe. Lemony wood sorrel that has been gently cooked down and then blended with butter strikes that same magic balance of brightness.

MAKES 8½ OUNCES [245 G]

> 1 ounce [30 g] wood sorrel leaves
>
> 1 cup [230 g] unsalted butter
>
> Zest of ½ lemon, finely grated on a Microplane
>
> 1 tablespoon flaky sea salt

Bring a small pot of water to a boil, add the wood sorrel, and blanch for 1 minute. Drain into a large sieve and then hold under cold running water until cool. Wrap the greens in a clean kitchen towel and wring out the excess moisture with your hands. Bunch the greens into a ball and cut into five pieces.

In a food processor, combine butter and wood sorrel and process until well mixed, stopping to scrape down the sides of the bowl as needed. Add the lemon zest and salt and process until evenly blended.

Scoop the flavored butter onto a sheet of plastic wrap or parchment paper and roll it up, forming a log. Refrigerate for up to 2 weeks or freeze for up to 2 months.

OTHER GREENS TO TRY lemon balm, nettles, Vietnamese coriander

MINER'S LETTUCE SOCCA

Socca is the French version of the delicious chickpea pancakes I fell in love with in Italy (page 122), where they are called *farinata* or *cecina*. I think that Chris Bianco of Pizzeria Bianco in Phoenix, Arizona, has the best recipe ever. He includes cheese in his pancakes, and this version is based on his. My twist, of course, is the addition of miner's lettuce, which lends an earthy, wild green flavor.

MAKES 8 PANCAKES, SERVES 4

- 1 cup [90 g] chickpea flour
- 1 cup [240 ml] sparkling water
- ¼ cup [60 ml] olive oil, plus more for cooking
- 1 clove garlic
- ¼ cup [10 g] grated Parmigiano-Reggiano
- ¼ teaspoon smoked paprika
- Zest of ½ lemon, finely grated on a Microplane
- 1 teaspoon fine sea salt
- 4 cups [55 g] loosely packed miner's lettuce, plus more for garnish

In a blender, combine the chickpea flour, water, olive oil, garlic, cheese, paprika, lemon zest, and salt. Blend until combined, then add the miner's lettuce. Blend until very smooth.

Heat a cast-iron or nonstick griddle over medium-high heat. Drop 1 tablespoon olive oil onto the hot surface, then, using a ¼-cup [60-ml] measure, pour ¼ cup [60 ml] of the batter over the oil. Cook until golden with crispy edges, about 2 minutes, then flip using a large spatula. Cook until the edges are crispy and the center is creamy, 1 to 2 minutes. Repeat with the remaining batter. The pancakes do not hold, so serve immediately, garnished with miner's lettuce.

OTHER GREENS TO TRY arugula, spinach

SPAETZLE WITH NETTLES, LEMON BALM, AND GUANCIALE

One of the richer pastas, spaetzle stands up to lush sauces very well. This decadent recipe really puts the pasta's sturdiness to the test, with a hearty earthiness from the nettles, some saltiness from the *guanciale*, and lemon balm to brighten everything up, just like a squeeze of lemon would.

SERVES 4

- 6 tablespoons [90 ml] olive oil
- 1 teaspoon fresh rosemary leaves
- Cooked spaetzle (page 286)
- ¼ cup [55 g] unsalted butter
- ¼ cup [40 g] thinly sliced and chopped guanciale, bacon, or pancetta
- ¾ cup [180 ml] heavy cream
- 1¼ cups [40 g] lightly packed finely grated Parmigiano-Reggiano
- 1 cup [25 g] loosely packed fresh nettle leaves
- ⅓ cup [10 g] loosely packed lemon balm leaves
- Fine sea salt and freshly ground black pepper

Warm the olive oil and rosemary in a small nonstick sauté pan over medium-high heat. Add the spaetzle and butter and cook until the spaetzle is just golden brown and crispy on one side, 2 to 3 minutes, then toss to flip. Add the guanciale and let cook, rendering the guanciale but not crisping it, for about 1 minute. Add the cream and 1 cup [30 g] of the Parmigiano-Reggiano and simmer for 30 seconds, tossing to coat the spaetzle. Toss in the nettle leaves and lemon balm and cook just to wilt, then season with salt and pepper. Add a tablespoon or two of water as needed to soften and thin the sauce. Serve topped with the remaining ¼ cup [10 g] Parmigiano-Reggiano.

OTHER GREENS TO TRY spinach for nettles; flat-leaf Italian parsley, mint, or basil for lemon balm

SPAETZLE

MAKES 1 POUND [455 G], SERVES 4 TO 6

2½ cups [350 g] all-purpose flour

2 teaspoons kosher salt

2 eggs

1¼ cups [300 ml] whole milk, plus more as needed

Olive oil, for tossing

In a large bowl or the bowl of a stand mixer fitted with a paddle attachment, combine the flour, salt, eggs, and milk. Mix with a wooden spoon or on medium speed until just combined, 3 to 4 minutes. Stir more vigorously or increase the speed a notch or two and beat until the batter becomes slightly shiny and elastic, 3 to 5 minutes. Cover the bowl with plastic wrap and let rest at room temperature for 30 minutes.

After 30 minutes, check the texture of the batter. It should be thin and elastic, with more stretch than a typical batter. If it is too thick, add more milk, 1 tablespoon at a time, to achieve this texture.

Line a sheet pan with parchment paper. Bring a large pot filled with generously salted water to a simmer over medium-high heat.

Working in batches, press the dough through a spaetzle maker or colander into the simmering water. Simmer the spaetzle until they float to the surface, about 1 minute. Stir to release any spaetzle that have settled on the bottom of the pot. Simmer for 1 minute more, or until tender. Remove immediately with a fine-mesh sieve and transfer to the prepared sheet pan. Toss the cooked spaetzle with a little olive oil so they don't stick together. Allow to cool to room temperature in a single layer on the sheet pan, then use as directed in the recipe on page 285.

LAMB'S-QUARTERS WITH BROWN BUTTER AND SHALLOTS

This is a favorite recipe of my chef de cuisine, Sara Woods. Anything with brown butter becomes really rich. When you cook the shallots in the butter, the butter browns, the shallots caramelize, and these delicate greens resonate with huge flavor.

SERVES 4 AS A SIDE DISH

½ cup [115 g] unsalted butter

4 shallots, thinly sliced

12 ounces [340 g] loosely packed lamb's-quarters, thick stems removed (16 cups)

Kosher salt and freshly ground black pepper

In a large sauté pan over medium-high heat, melt the butter, swirling the pan until the butter froths, 4 to 6 minutes. Add the shallots and continue cooking until the shallots are golden brown, 3 to 4 minutes (by this time the butter should also be brown and smell nutty). Add the lamb's-quarters and stir just until wilted, about 1 minute. Remove from the heat and season with salt and pepper.

OTHER GREENS TO TRY chicories, spinach

Lamb's-Quarters with Brown Butter and Shallots

Miso Soup Stracciatella with Ramp Greens

MISO SOUP STRACCIATELLA WITH RAMP GREENS

Here is an example of a cross-cultural dish that works on many levels. Ramp greens bridge the Italian and Asian influences in this warming soup. Miso, of course, is commonly used in Asia. And *stracciatella* is a word that you see a lot in Italian cuisine. It means "long strands," and it can be used to describe a string cheese, an ice cream with strands of chocolate, or, in this case, the strands of egg in a soup, which hearkens to Chinese egg drop soup. Ramp perfumes the soup with the flavors of leek and garlic, which pervade both cultures. Since ramps have a very short season, feel free to swap them out for green onion tops.

SERVES 1

2 eggs

2 cups [480 ml] double chicken stock (page 299) or vegetable stock

¼ cup [20 g] loosely packed cut-up ramp greens, cut in ¼-inch [6-mm] pieces

3 tablespoons red miso

Crack the eggs into a small bowl and beat with a fork until fully combined. Set aside.

In a small pot, heat the chicken stock and ramp greens over high heat until the stock boils. Immediately turn the heat to low. There should be no simmer at this point. Using a whisk, stir in the miso until fully dissolved.

Remove the pot from the heat and immediately drizzle the beaten eggs off the fork tines and into the pot of soup, drizzling around the pot to make long strands. The residual heat will cook the eggs to a very tender finish.

Carefully tip the soup pot and pour the soup into a bowl without damaging the soft curds of cooked egg. Enjoy immediately.

OTHER GREENS TO TRY chrysanthemum greens

PICKLED RAMPS

Some ingredients, when pickled and kept for an extended period, lose flavor. Not so when it comes to ramps. They take particularly well to pickling because of their oniony, garlicky flavor—seasonings you would likely add in a pickle brine. What I like to do at the beginning of the season is pickle some, put them away, then ride the season out with the fresh ones. When the fresh ramps are gone, the pickles should be ready to use, to stretch that harvest and enjoy it a little longer.

MAKES 2 QUARTS [2 L]

1 pound [455 g] cleaned wild ramps, ideally small, new growth

½ bunch thyme

4 cups [960 ml] white wine vinegar

3 cups [720 ml] water

¼ cup [50 g] sugar

2 tablespoons fine sea salt

4 teaspoons fennel seeds

4 teaspoons black peppercorns

Put the ramps and thyme in a large glass jar (3- to 4-quart/3- to 4-L capacity).

Combine the vinegar, water, sugar, salt, fennel seeds, and peppercorns in a saucepan over high heat and bring to a boil. Turn down the heat and simmer for 2 minutes. Strain the liquid and discard the spices. Pour the strained liquid over the ramps and weight the ramps down with a small plate to submerge them. Leave at room temperature to cool, then cover and refrigerate. The pickled ramps can be eaten the next day, though they will taste even better in a week. They will keep for 6 months, refrigerated.

OTHER GREENS TO TRY green onions

LARDER

KIMCHI BUTTER

MAKES 4 CUPS [900 g]

> 1 pound [455 g] unsalted butter
>
> ½ cup [75 g] peeled and sliced fresh ginger
>
> 1¼ cups [175 g] kimchi, homemade (page 81) or store-bought, drained
>
> 3 tablespoons kimchi liquid
>
> 2 tablespoons fish sauce

In a pot, melt the butter with the ginger over medium heat. Add the kimchi, kimchi liquid, and fish sauce. Stir to combine, then transfer to the refrigerator and chill until no longer liquid but not quite firm, about 30 minutes. Scrape the butter into a food processor and process until the solids are finely minced. Transfer to two pint containers and store for up to 3 weeks in the refrigerator or for up to 6 months in the freezer.

SHISO BUTTER

MAKES 8½ OUNCES [240 G]

> ½ ounce [15 g] fresh shiso leaves
>
> 1 cup [230 g] unsalted butter, at room temperature
>
> 2 teaspoons flaky sea salt
>
> 1 tablespoon fish sauce
>
> 1 tablespoon ground cayenne pepper

Blanch the shiso leaves in a small pot of boiling water for 2 minutes. Remove from the heat, drain, and run under cool water. When the leaves are cool, wring out any excess water and form into a ball. Cut the ball into five strips.

In a food processor, combine the butter and shiso and process, stopping to scrape down the sides, until well combined. Add the salt, fish sauce, and cayenne and blend thoroughly.

Roll up the butter in plastic wrap or parchment paper, forming a log. Refrigerate for up to 2 weeks or freeze for up to 2 months.

5 THINGS TO DO WITH SHISO BUTTER

1 Spread on toast and serve plain, or spread on toast and top with seared tuna or sliced roasted chicken with peanuts and coconut.

2 Place a pat on fish or potatoes before roasting.

3 Toss braised greens with shiso butter before serving.

4 Add a dollop to finish soft scrambled eggs.

5 Add a pat to finish pasta with sautéed scallops, mint, and fresh chile.

CREAM CHEESE PASTRY DOUGH

MAKES DOUGH FOR TWO 9-INCH [23-CM] PIE CRUSTS

> 2 cups [280 g] all-purpose flour
>
> 2 tablespoons sugar
>
> ¼ teaspoon kosher salt
>
> 1 cup [230 g] unsalted butter, chilled and cut into ½-inch [12-mm] pieces
>
> 6 ounces [170 g] cream cheese, chilled and cut into 8 pieces

In a food processor, pulse the flour, sugar, and salt until combined. Add the butter and pulse until it breaks down into pea-size pieces. Add the cream cheese and process just until incorporated and a mass of dough forms. Do not overmix or the final crust will be tough.

Dump the contents of the processor bowl onto a counter and gather the dough into a cohesive mass. Divide the dough in half and form each half into a flat disk. Wrap in plastic wrap and refrigerate for 45 minutes before using. To freeze the dough, place the wrapped dough in the freezer for up to 6 months. Thaw in the refrigerator overnight and bring to a firm, yet rollable texture to use.

MEDIUM- AND HARD-BOILED EGGS

MAKES 6

6 eggs

Place the eggs in a bowl and cover with hot tap water. Set aside to temper for 15 minutes. Make an ice bath by filling a large bowl with ice water. Set aside.

Remove the eggs from the water. Over medium-high heat, bring a medium pot of water to a simmer. Gently add the eggs to the simmering water with a slotted spoon. Take care to keep the water at a lively simmer without becoming a boil and knocking the eggs around too much. For medium-boiled eggs, cook for 8½ minutes; for hard-boiled, cook for 9½ minutes. Immediately place the cooked eggs in the ice bath to cool completely, about 15 minutes. Remove from the water. Crack and peel to use.

Eggs can be stored in an airtight container in the refregerator for up to 4 days.

POACHED EGGS

MAKES 4

2 tablespoons distilled white vinegar

4 eggs

Over medium heat, bring a 2-quart [2-L] saucepan filled with water to a gentle simmer and add the vinegar. Using 2 of the eggs, crack each egg into a custard cup or small ramekin. Use the handle of a spatula or spoon to quickly stir the water in one direction to create a vortex. Add 1 egg at a time to the swirling water and cook until the white is set and the yolk is soft and runny, 3 to 4 minutes. Using a slotted spoon, remove the eggs from the water and serve immediately. Repeat with the 2 remaining eggs.

CROUTONS

MAKES 8 TO 12 CUPS [320 TO 480 G]

2 loaves pain au levain or other artisanal bread

¾ cup [180 ml] olive oil

Kosher salt

Preheat the oven to 325°F [165°C].

Remove the crust and cut the bread into 1-inch [2.5-cm] cubes. In a bowl, toss the bread cubes with the olive oil and season lightly with salt. Spread the cubes on a sheet pan, then toast in the oven until golden and dry throughout, 20 to 25 minutes. If the bread becomes too dark, decrease the heat. Once the croutons are cool, they can be held for 1 to 2 days in an airtight container.

FISH SAUCE AÏOLI

MAKES 1 CUP [240 ML]

1 egg yolk

2½ teaspoons kimchi liquid, from homemade (page 81) or store-bought

1 cup [240 ml] neutral vegetable oil

½ teaspoon Sriracha sauce

2 teaspoons fish sauce

¼ teaspoon kosher salt

In a medium bowl, whisk together the egg yolk and kimchi liquid. Slowly drizzle in the oil, whisking constantly, until a thick mayonnaise forms. Stir in the Sriracha, fish sauce, and salt. Store in an airtight container in the fridge for up to 1 week.

KIMCHI SYRUP

2 parts kimchi liquid, from homemade (page 81) or store-bought

1 part sugar

Heat the kimchi liquid and sugar in a pan over high heat just until the sugar dissolves. Let cool. Store in an airtight container in the refrigerator for up to 6 months.

SIMPLE SYRUP

1 part water

1 part sugar

Heat the water and sugar in a pan over high heat just until the sugar dissolves. Let cool. Keeps for up to 6 months in an airtight container in the refrigerator.

PICKLED CHILES

MAKES SCANT 2 QUARTS [2 L]

2 pounds [900 g] red Fresno chiles (or red jalapeño, green jalapeño, or serrano chiles), stemmed and halved

4 cups [960 ml] white vinegar

1 teaspoon kosher salt

Put the chiles in a food processor and pulse until chopped into small pieces but not minced. Add the vinegar and salt and pulse once or twice to mix. Store in quart containers in the refrigerator for 1 week before serving. Keeps for up to 6 months in an airtight container in the refrigerator.

PRESERVED LEMONS

MAKES 3 GALLONS [11.4 L]

15 pounds [6.8 kg] lemons

2 cups [75 g] bay leaves

2 cups [270 g] kosher salt

15 cinnamon sticks

2 cups [280 g] juniper berries

3 cups [720 ml] fresh lemon juice, plus more to cover

Carefully wash all the lemons; set aside. Wash and rinse a 3-gallon [11.4-L] glass jar.

Cut all the lemons into quarters lengthwise. Holding a knife at an angle, cut the center membrane from the lemon quarters and gently scrape out the seeds.

Squeeze the juice from the lemon qurters into the jar. Arrange the juiced lemon quarters in layers in the juice, distributing the bay leaves, salt, cinnamon, and juniper berries evenly among the layers. Top with additional lemon juice until all the lemon quarters are covered with juice. Weigh down the lemons with a few small plates to fully submerge them. Cover the jar tightly with plastic wrap. Set aside in a cool or room-temperature spot, out of direct sunlight.

Check the lemons every few days and scrape away any dark film that forms on the surface. If the lemons rise to the top, push them down with clean hands or a spoon so they are submerged, then replace the plastic wrap with a fresh piece.

The lemons will be fully cured when the skins are tender but not mushy. Depending on the temperature where stored, this can take 3 to 5 weeks. The white pith will have broken down, but the yellow zest will be tender and hold its integrity.

Store the cured lemons, submerged in the lemon juice in an airtight container, in the refrigerator for up to 6 months.

To use, remove a lemon quarter from the jar, carefully cut away any white pith, and rinse the yellow zest well.

RED ADZUKI BEANS

MAKES 4 CUPS [640 G]

2 cups [320 g] dried red adzuki beans

½ yellow onion, finely diced

6 cups [1.4 L] water

Kosher salt

Preheat the oven to 325°F [160°C].

Combine the beans, onion, and water in a saucepan and bring just to a simmer. Pour into a baking dish and cover with aluminum foil. Bake the beans until tender, but not soft, about 30 minutes. Season with salt and let cool. Transfer to an airtight container and store the beans, covered with cooking liquid, in the refrigerator for up to 1 week.

BLUE CHEESE DRESSING

MAKES 2 CUPS [515 G]

> 1 cup [240 ml] mayonnaise
>
> 1 cup [240 ml] sour cream
>
> 1 tablespoon Worcestershire sauce
>
> 1½ teaspoons kosher salt
>
> 1½ teaspoons freshly ground black pepper
>
> 1½ teaspoons red wine vinegar
>
> 3 ounces [85 g] buttermilk blue cheese

Mix together the mayonnaise and sour cream in a food processor. Add the Worcestershire, salt, pepper, and red wine vinegar and puree until smooth. Add the blue cheese and pulse until the cheese is broken up and pebbly but not pureed into the dressing. Keeps for 1 week when refrigerated in an airtight container.

BAGNA CAUDA

MAKES ½ CUP [60 G]

> 3 tablespoons olive oil
>
> ¼ cup [55 g] unsalted butter
>
> 1½ teaspoons dried red pepper flakes
>
> 3 small garlic cloves, very thinly sliced
>
> 8 anchovy fillets packed in oil
>
> 2 teaspoons fresh lemon juice
>
> Kosher salt and freshly ground pepper

In a saucepan, warm the olive oil, butter, red pepper, garlic, and anchovies over medium heat. With the back of a fork, break up the anchovies as the mixture warms. The flavors will meld and the anchovies will dissolve. Add the lemon juice and season with salt and pepper. The bagna cauda will keep in an airtight container in the refregerator for up to 1 weetk.

CARROT GREENS SALSA VERDE

MAKES 1 CUP [220 G]

> 1 teaspoon caraway seeds
>
> 1 teaspoon yellow mustard seeds
>
> 1 teaspoon cumin seeds
>
> 1 teaspoon coriander seeds
>
> 2 ounces [55 g] carrot greens, thick, tough stems removed
>
> 2 ounces [55 g] cilantro, including stems
>
> 1 clove garlic
>
> 1 preserved lemon quarter (see facing page)
>
> ⅓ cup [80 ml] olive oil
>
> 1 teaspoon kosher salt

Combine the caraway seeds, mustard seeds, cumin seeds, and coriander seeds in a small sauté pan and toast over medium-high heat for about 1 minute, until the spices are toasted and fragrant; be careful not to burn them. Let cool, then grind finely.

Combine the toasted spices, carrot greens, cilantro, garlic, preserved lemon, olive oil, and salt in a food processor. Process until finely chopped but not pureed.

Using a plastic spatula, scrape the sauce into a storage container, then press a piece of plastic wrap directly onto the surface of the sauce so it will not be exposed to air. Store in the refrigerator for up to 5 days.

5 THINGS TO DO WITH CARROT GREEN SALSA VERDE

1 Spread on any sandwich or in pita bread with falafel.

2 Serve on grilled oily fish or on grilled chicken or seafood.

3 Mash into butter and place under chicken skin when roasting chicken.

4 Dollop into soup.

5 Spread on crostini with shaved Cotija cheese.

SOY DIPPING SAUCE

MAKES 3 CUPS [720 ML]

1½ cups [360 ml] soy sauce

1 cup [240 ml] cool water

3 tablespoons hot sauce, such as Sriracha

1 teaspoon sugar

2 tablespoons rice wine vinegar

1 tablespoon toasted sesame oil

1½ tablespoons peeled and finely chopped fresh ginger

2 teaspoons white sesame seeds, toasted

1 green onion, green and white parts, thinly sliced

Combine the ingredients in a small bowl and stir to mix. Allow to sit for 30 to 60 minutes before serving. Store in an airtight container in the refrigerator for up to 1 week.

TAHINI SAUCE

MAKES ABOUT 3 CUPS [720 ML]

6 tablespoons [90 g] tahini

Preserved lemon quarter (page 294)

½ cup [120 ml] fresh lemon juice

2 cloves garlic

½ cup [120 ml] cool water

2-inch [5-cm] piece fresh ginger, peeled

1½ cups [360 ml] neutral vegetable oil

Fine sea salt

Combine the tahini, preserved lemon, lemon juice, garlic, water, and ginger in a blender (preferably a high-speed blender) and puree until smooth. Slowly drizzle in the oil while blending, until the dressing thickens. Season with salt. Store refrigerated in an airtight container for up to 1 week.

TOMATO SAUCE

MAKES 6 CUPS [1.4 L]

6 cups [1.4 L] tomato puree (pureed and strained whole peeled tomatoes)

3 bay leaves

¾ teaspoon dried red pepper flakes

¾ cup [170 g] unsalted butter

1 tablespoon kosher salt

Combine all the ingredients in a saucepan and bring to a gentle simmer over medium heat. Cook until the sauce thickens slightly and bits of melted butter rise to the top of the sauce, about 30 minutes. Remove the bay leaves and serve the sauce, or let cool and store in the refrigerator for up to 1 week.

CRACK SPICE MIX

I started calling this crack spice because we used this blend to season cracklings at our restaurants. It is also good sprinkled on tortilla chips, Brussels Chips (page 52), or just about anything you like.

MAKES ¾ CUP [220 g]

⅓ cup [55 g] kosher salt

½ teaspoon ground cayenne pepper

3 tablespoons sweet smoked paprika

1 teaspoon freshly ground black pepper

Combine all the ingredients in a bowl and stir to mix. Store at room temperature in an airtight container. The flavors will start to diminish after 1 month.

DUKKAH

MAKES 1 CUP [120 G]

3 tablespoons white sesame seeds

¼ cup [45 g] coriander seeds

2 tablespoons cumin seeds

1 tablespoon black peppercorns

2 teaspoons caraway seeds

1 teaspoon fennel seeds

½ cup [60 g] toasted hazelnuts

1½ teaspoons dried mint leaves

2 teaspoons fine sea salt

Place a heavy skillet over medium-high heat and toast the sesame seeds until lightly golden, 2 to 4 minutes. Transfer to a plate to cool. Combine the coriander, cumin, peppercorns, caraway seeds, and fennel seeds in the same skillet and toast over medium-high heat until slightly browned and fragrant, 2 to 4 minutes, being careful that they don't blacken and burn. (Smell for the fragrances to become enhanced and take off the flame before they become too dark.) Remove from the heat, transfer to another plate, and cool completely.

Pour the toasted spices into a mortar and pound until the mixture is crushed. Make sure that the peppercorns are crushed fairly well, as they will be very pungent. Add the hazelnuts to the mixture and pound until they are broken into very small pieces. Do not allow the mixture to become a paste. Stir in the sesame seeds, mint, and salt.

Store in an airtight container at room temperature for up to 1 month.

MUSTARD GREEN FURIKAKE

MAKES 1 CUP [110 G]

2 lemons

2 oranges

1¼ ounces [35 g] dried mustard green chips (recipe follows)

2 teaspoons white sesame seeds, toasted

1 tablespoon poppy seeds, toasted

1 tablespoon Korean chile flakes (gochugaru; available online)

Preheat the oven to 300°F [150°C]. Line a sheet pan with parchment paper.

Using a Microplane, finely zest the lemons and oranges onto the prepared sheet pan. Bake until fully dry, about 15 minutes. Remove from the oven and cool completely. Alternatively, leave the zest at room temperature, uncovered, overnight to dry.

In a small bowl, gently mix the dried zest, mustard green chips, sesame seeds, poppy seeds, and chile flakes. Store in an airtight container at room temperature for up to 1 week.

MUSTARD GREEN CHIPS

MAKES 1¼ OUNCES [35 G]

8 ounces [230 g] large mustard leaves, thick stems removed (this will yield about 5½ ounces/155 g leaves without stems)

3 tablespoons olive oil

1 teaspoon kosher salt

Preheat the oven to 250°F [120°C]. Line a sheet pan with parchment paper.

Toss the mustard greens in a large bowl with the olive oil and salt. Place in a single layer on the prepared sheet pan and bake until fully dried, 20 to 25 minutes. If the leaves begin to brown, decrease the oven heat to 200°F [95°C].

Once the greens are dehydrated and crisp, remove from the oven and cool completely. If some leaves are soft or have wet spots, leave those in the oven until dry. When cool, gently crush the leaves with your hands and remove any thicker ribs that do not crumble. Store in an airtight container at room temperature for up to 1 week.

HAWAIJ SPICE MIX FOR SOUP

MAKES ¾ CUP [95 G]

1 tablespoon [15 g] black peppercorns

1 tablespoon plus 1 teaspoon [9 g] cumin seeds

2½ teaspoons [6 g] celery seeds

1 tablespoon [8 g] green cardamom pods

1 tablespoon [8 g] caraway seeds

1 tablespoon [5 g] coriander seeds

1 teaspoon [2 g] whole cloves

1¾ teaspoons [4 g] ground cinnamon

3 tablespoons [20 g] ground turmeric

2 tablespoons [20 g] fine sea salt

In a heavy skillet, combine the peppercorns, cumin, celery seeds, cardamom, caraway, coriander, and cloves. Place over very low heat and toast until fragrant and golden, about 10 minutes. Be very careful not to blacken or burn spices. Remove from the heat and cool completely.

Grind the spices finely. Add the cinnamon, turmeric, and salt and sift through a fine-mesh sieve. Store the blend in a tightly sealed container at room temperature for up to 1 month.

BUTTERNUT SQUASH PUREE

MAKES 2 CUPS [480 G]

9 tablespoons [135 ml] olive oil

½ yellow onion, diced

2 large cloves garlic, thinly sliced

2 fresh sage leaves

1 pound [455 g] peeled and seeded butternut squash, cut into small pieces

¼ teaspoon ground cinnamon

Kosher salt

Warm 3 tablespoons of the olive oil in a saucepan over medium-high heat. Add the onion, garlic, and sage and cook until the vegetables are tender, 4 to 6 minutes. Decrease the heat if the vegetables begin to darken. Add the squash and enough water just to cover the vegetables (about 3 cups/720 ml). Cook at a simmer until the squash is tender, about 10 minutes.

Using a fine-mesh sieve, drain the vegetables and discard the cooking liquid or reserve it for another use (it is a great flavored vegetable broth at this point). Transfer the vegetables to a blender or food processor, add the remaining 6 tablespoons [90 ml] olive oil and the cinnamon, and process until finely pureed. Season with salt. Store in an airtight container in the refregerator for up to 1 week.

WHIPPED LARDO SPREAD

MAKES 6 CUPS [1.4 KG]

15 ounces [430 g] lardo, very cold

1 clove garlic

¼ cup [60 ml] extra-virgin olive oil

Zest of 1 lemon, finely grated on a Microplane

Using a paper towel, wipe off any excess seasoning from the lardo, making sure to leave some seasoning on the surface.

Cut the lardo into ½-inch [12-mm] pieces. Transfer two-thirds of the lardo to a food processor and combine with the garlic and olive oil. Process until smooth and soft. Add the remaining lardo and pulse just until combined, with small pieces of lardo suspended in the soft spread. Add the lemon zest and pulse just until evenly combined. Store in an airtight container in the refrigerator for up to 2 months.

MUHAMMARA

MAKES 3 CUPS [560 G]

- 1 tablespoon dried red pepper flakes, or 1 small dried red chile, minced
- ½ teaspoon ground toasted cumin
- ¾ cup [90 g] walnuts, toasted
- ¼ cup [35 g] dried bread crumbs
- ¼ cup [60 ml] olive oil
- 2 tablespoons pomegranate molasses
- ¼ cup [55 g] tomato paste
- 2 large roasted red peppers
- ¼ cup [60 ml] warm water
- ½ teaspoon fine sea salt

Combine the red pepper flakes, cumin, walnuts, bread crumbs, olive oil, pomegranate molasses, tomato paste, and roasted red peppers in a food processor and puree into an even consistency. Mix in the warm water in increments to achieve an easily spreadable consistency similar to a thick yogurt. Season with salt and adjust the seasonings, if needed. Store in an airtight container in the refrigerator for up to 1 week.

CARROT GREEN BUTTER

Have 1 pound [455 g] unsalted butter at room temperature. Using a stand mixer fitted with a paddle attachment, whip the butter until fluffy and soft, scraping down the sides of the bowl a couple of times with a plastic spatula. Add 1 cup [220 g] carrot green salsa verde (page 295) to the butter and mix until combined.

Use the butter as a sauce on hot spaghetti, as a spread on crostini topped with a piece of prosciutto, as a dollop on soft scrambled eggs, as a spread on halibut before roasting, or under the breast skin of a whole chicken before roasting.

DOUBLE CHICKEN STOCK

MAKES 7 CUPS [1.7 L]

- 5 pounds [2.3 kg] chicken bones
- About 4 quarts [3.8 L] homemade chicken stock

Preheat the oven to 450°F [230°C]. Line a sheet pan with parchment paper.

Lay the chicken bones on the prepared sheet pan in a single layer. Roast the bones until nicely browned, about 20 minutes.

Transfer the roasted bones to a 6-quart [5.7-L] stockpot and fill with just enough stock to cover the bones. Bring to a rapid simmer over high heat, then immediately decrease the heat to medium to achieve a gentle, lazy simmer. Simmer for 6 to 8 hours, until the stock is rich, reduced, and flavorful. If the stock simmers too briskly, the fat will emulsify into the stock, rendering the stock greasy. If the stock reduces too quickly, add a bit of additional water. This should not be necessary, and ideally the stock will reduce by one-third to one-half when cooking slowly. As the stock is simmering, use a spoon or ladle to skim off and discard any foamy, dark impurities that rise to the top.

Set a fine-mesh sieve over a large, heavy-duty plastic container. Pour the stock through the sieve into the container and discard the chicken bones and any debris. Transfer the stock to airtight containers and refrigerate until cool. When the stock is cold, remove the fat by carefully scooping it from the top with a spoon.

To store the chicken fat, transfer it to an airtight container and refrigerate for up to 1 month. To store the stock, refrigerate for up to 1 week or freeze for up to 2 months.

CILANTRO VINAIGRETTE

MAKES ABOUT 2 CUPS [480 ML]

- ½ bunch cilantro with tender stems
- 2-inch [5-cm] piece fresh ginger, peeled
- ½ cup [120 ml] fresh lime juice
- ½ cup [120 ml] fresh orange juice
- 1 medium clove garlic
- 1½ cups [360 ml] neutral vegetable oil

Combine the cilantro, ginger, lime juice, orange juice, and garlic in a blender and process until fully combined. With the motor running, drizzle in the oil and process until thickened and emulsified. Store in an airtight container in the refrigerator for up to 1 week.

CITRUS-TANGERINE VINAIGRETTE

MAKES ABOUT 2 CUPS [480 ML]

- 2 preserved lemon quarters (page 294)
- 1 medium clove garlic
- Zest of 1 very large Minneola tangerine or orange, finely grated on a Microplane
- ½ cup [120 ml] white wine vinegar
- 1½ tablespoons honey
- ½ cup [120 ml] fresh Minneola tangerine or orange juice
- ¼ cup [60 ml] fresh lemon juice
- 1 cup [240 ml] olive oil
- ½ cup [120 ml] neutral vegetable oil

Combine the preserved lemon, garlic, tangerine zest, vinegar, honey, tangerine juice, and lemon juice in a blender and puree until smooth. With the motor running, drizzle in both oils and process until thickened and emulsified. Store in an airtight container in the refrigerator for up to 1 week.

LEMON VINAIGRETTE

MAKES ABOUT 2 CUPS [480 ML]

- ¾ cup [180 ml] fresh lemon juice
- Zest from 4 lemons, finely grated on a Microplane
- 1 cup [240 ml] plus 2 tablespoons olive oil

Combine all of the ingredients in a dressing bottle or jar and shake to mix well. Store in an airtight container in the refrigerator for up to 1 week.

MISO VINAIGRETTE

MAKES ABOUT 2 CUPS [480 ML]

- 3 tablespoons red miso
- 3 tablespoons soy sauce
- 3 tablespoons toasted sesame oil
- 1 cup [240 ml] rice wine vinegar
- 3 tablespoons neutral vegetable oil
- 1 clove garlic, thinly sliced

Combine all of the ingredients in a dressing bottle or jar and shake to mix well. Store in an airtight container in the refrigerator for up to 1 week.

FETA VINAIGRETTE

MAKES 2 CUPS [480 ML]

- 3 ounces [85 g] feta
- Zest of ⅓ lemon, finely grated on a Microplane
- ⅓ cup [80 ml] white wine vinegar, plus more if needed
- 3 tablespoons cool water
- 1 small clove garlic
- ¾ cup [180 ml] plus 2 tablespoons olive oil

Combine the feta, lemon zest, vinegar, water, and garlic in a blender. Turn on the blender and then slowly add the oil, processing until all the ingredients are blended. Taste and add more vinegar if needed. Store in an airtight container in the refrigerator for up to 1 week.

PICKLED MUSTARD SEED VINAIGRETTE

MAKES ABOUT 2 CUPS [480 ML]

1 cup [240 ml] champagne vinegar

½ cup [90 g] yellow mustard seeds

1 cup [240 ml] olive brine (from olive jar or can)

½ cup [120 g] olive oil

Combine the vinegar and mustard seeds in a small saucepan over high heat and bring to a simmer. Immediately remove from the heat and allow to cool completely. When cool, add the olive brine and olive oil and whisk to combine. Store in an airtight container in the refrigerator for up to 2 months.

POMEGRANATE MOLASSES VINAIGRETTE

MAKES ABOUT 2 CUPS [480 ML]

½ cup plus 2 tablespoons [150 ml] pomegranate molasses

½ cup plus 2 tablespoons [150 ml] olive oil

¼ cup [60 ml] fresh lemon juice

Combine all the ingredients in a dressing bottle or jar and shake to mix well. Store in an airtight container in the refrigerator for up to 1 week.

RED WINE VINAIGRETTE

MAKES ABOUT 2 CUPS [480 ML]

¾ cup [180 ml] neutral vegetable oil

¼ cup [60 ml] olive oil

¼ cup [60 ml] red wine vinegar

Combine all the ingredients in a dressing bottle or jar and shake to mix well. Store in an airtight container in the refrigerator for up to 1 week.

SHERRY VINAIGRETTE

MAKES ABOUT 2 CUPS [480 ML]

⅔ cup [160 ml] sherry vinegar

1⅓ cups [320 ml] olive oil

Combine all the ingredients in a dressing bottle or jar and shake to mix well. Store in an airtight container in the refrigerator for up to 1 week.

SUMAC VINAIGRETTE

MAKES ABOUT 2 CUPS [480 ML]

2 tablespoons plus 2 teaspoons ground sumac

2 tablespoons fresh lemon juice, plus more to taste

2 tablespoons plus 2 teaspoons pomegranate molasses

2 small cloves garlic, thinly sliced

2 tablespoons plus 2 teaspoons white wine vinegar

2 teaspoons dried mint

1½ cups [360 ml] olive oil

Combine the sumac with 2 teaspoons water in a small bowl and let sit for 10 minutes.

Transfer the sumac mixture to a dressing bottle or jar, add the lemon juice, pomegranate molasses, garlic, vinegar, mint, and olive oil and shake to mix well. Store in an airtight container in the refrigerator for up to 1 week.

TARRAGON VINAIGRETTE

MAKES ABOUT 2 CUPS [480 ML]

> 3 small cloves garlic
>
> ½ cup [15 g] fresh tarragon leaves
>
> 2 egg yolks
>
> Zest and juice of 2 lemons, zest finely grated on a Microplane
>
> 1¾ cups [420 ml] neutral vegetable or olive oil
>
> Kosher salt and freshly ground black pepper

In a blender or food processor, combine the garlic, tarragon, and egg yolks and process to create a creamy blend. Add the lemon zest and juice and blend again. With the motor running, slowly drizzle in the oil to create an emulsified, creamy consistency. Avoid adding the oil too quickly or the vinaigrette will separate. Add water, 1 teaspoon at a time if the emulsion becomes very thick, then continue to add oil. Season to taste with salt and pepper. Store in an airtight container in the refrigerator for up to 1 week.

WHITE BALSAMIC VINAIGRETTE

MAKES ABOUT 2 CUPS [480 ML]

> ⅔ cup [160 ml] white balsamic vinegar
>
> 1⅓ cups [320 ml] olive oil
>
> 2 teaspoons honey
>
> Zest of ½ orange, finely grated on a Microplane
>
> ½ large shallot, thinly sliced

Combine all the ingredients in a dressing bottle or jar and shake to mix well. Store in an airtight container in the refrigerator for up to 1 week.

RULES FOR VINAIGRETTES

1 Keep vinaigrettes refrigerated for longer life, especially if they contain egg, dairy, or raw herbs.

2 Make small batches in a jar—shake them up and use.

3 Every vinegar is different. Some are more acidic and will need to be balanced accordingly with oil. Always taste before you dress!

4 Foods like tomatoes are acidic and need less acid to wake them up.

5 Greens contain iron and chlorophyll and usually need more acid to brighten their flavors.

6 I rarely season vinaigrettes; I would rather season the salad and adjust.

BIRDSEED

MAKES ¾ CUP [120 G]

> 2 tablespoons poppy seeds
>
> 2 tablespoons white sesame seeds
>
> 2 tablespoons flaxseeds
>
> 2 tablespoons millet
>
> 2 tablespoons amaranth seeds
>
> 2 tablespoons red quinoa

Preheat the oven to 425°F [220°C].

Combine the poppy seeds, sesame seeds, flaxseeds, millet, amaranth seeds, and quinoa in a small ovenproof skillet and bake until toasted, about 10 minutes, removing the pan every few minutes to stir the seeds and make sure they are toasting evenly and not burning. Cool, then store in an airtight container at room temperature for up to 2 months.

ACKNOWLEDGMENTS

To the greatest support system in the world, you were there when I needed you and this book is for you. I am totally grateful for you all.

This book would not have been possible without the constant support and love of Kathleen Squires. You have a gigantic heart.

Also, my team on this book: Ed Anderson, George Dolese, David Hale Smith, Ashley Lima, Hannah Rahill, Jim Myers, Emily Timberlake, Sam the photo shoot cat.

Philip Baltz, thanks for letting me keep you on speed dial, and for your wisdom.

Thank you Shannon Flanagan for your loyalty, honesty, and kindness.

Anita Lo, you give the greatest advice; thank you for steering me in the only direction to go.

Adeena Sussman, thank you for letting me lean hard, no matter where in the world we are. Thank you for your generosity.

Thank you Sara Woods for your strength, general awesomeness, and help with this book.

To the most spectacular neighborhood ever, and the #neighborkidhomies: Gina, Matt, Charlie, and Theo Eiben; Negar, Max, Payam, and Arman Heckscher; Lisa Pearlstein; Harrison, Addison, and Cassius Petit; Natasha, Bryan, Hope, and Zane Stanley.

To my people: Mary Attea, Amanda Bishop, Bob Comis, Elizabeth Falkner, Brandon Fernandez, Mollyanne and Patrick Fleming, Betsy and Tom Henning, Erin Janssens, Bruce Kalman, Lissa Kaufman, Dan and Amy Kayon, Keith Kreeger, Susie Lubell, Erin and Bella Marquiss, Emily Powell, Jessica Robinson, Ronnie Rodriguez, Emma Rowland, Tricia San Mateo, Marcia Smith, Rick and Andrea Streedain, Amy Sullivan, Vanessa Vega, Randi Weinstein, Amy Witkop.

Britt Bartels, Mike Caspar, Ethan McMillen, Erin Tewes, Jimmy Traub, Jordan Huston, Kelsey Sweedler-Devlin, Metal Mike Stone, Mike (Linguini) Landauer, Ry Chambliss.

Wasco, Silverado Silverstein, Saul Liebowitz (aka Orange Cat; RIP), Boris Bullyoski (aka White Cat; RIP).

And to my sister, Stacy Louis. I love you.

—J.L.

Jenn Louis, I am so grateful you chose me to be your coauthor and even more grateful to be your friend. I learned so much from you, and not only about cooking. I admire your strength, unending well of positive energy, and your kind and beautiful soul.

The amazing Green Team: Emily Timberlake, Ed Anderson, George Dolese, Ashley Lima, Hannah Rahill, and David Hale Smith.

My ever-supportive family: John and Catherine Squires; Christine Squires, Steve Pashkoff and Emma Pashkoff; John, Mary Lou, William, and Elizabeth Squires. I love you all so much.

Edna Perez and Miguel Juan Rodriguez; Mari Carmen Bosch and Enrique Nieves—who gave me wonderful places to toil while writing this book.

And, as ever, Ronnie Rodriguez. You are my everything. Thank you for always, always believing in me.

—K.S.

ABOUT THE AUTHORS

JENN LOUIS has competed on Bravo's *Top Chef Masters*, was named one of *Food & Wine* magazine's Best New Chefs, and has two nominations for the James Beard Foundation award of Best Chef: Northwest. Her debut cookbook, *Pasta By Hand*, was nominated for an IACP cookbook award. She resides in Portland, Oregon, with her two cats, Wasco and Silverado Silverstein.

KATHLEEN SQUIRES is a food and travel writer based in New York City. Her work has appeared in the *Wall Street Journal, Saveur, Every Day with Rachael Ray,* and many other publications. She is also the coauthor of three cookbooks: *The Coolhaus Ice Cream Book, Stuart O'Keeffe's The Quick Six Fix,* and *The Journey,* for which she was awarded the 2014 IACP prize for best e-Cookbook. In 2016, Les Dames d'Escoffier International awarded Squires first prize in the print category of its M. F. K. Fisher Awards for Excellence in Culinary Writing.

Photo: Hernan F. Rodriguez

INDEX

Published in the United States by Ten Speed Press, an imprint of the
Crown Publishing Group, a division of Penguin Random House LLC,
New York.
www.crownpublishing.com
www.tenspeed.com

Ten Speed Press and the Ten Speed Press colophon are registered
trademarks of Penguin Random House LLC.

Grateful acknowledgment is made to the following for
permission to reprint previously published material:

Gerald Locklin: "The Iceberg Theory" from *The Iceberg Theory*
by Gerald Locklin (San Pedro, CA: Lummox Press, 2000), copyright
© 2000 by Gerald Locklin. Reprinted by permission of the author.

Clarkson Potter/Publishers, an imprint of the Crown Publishing Group,
a division of Penguin Random House LLC: "Pizza Dough" from *My Pizza:
The Easy No-Knead Way to Make Spectacular Pizza at Home* by Jim Lahey
with Rick Flaste, copyright © 2012 by Jim Lahey. Reprinted by permission
of Clarkson Potter/Publishers, an imprint of the Crown Publishing
Group, a division of Penguin Random House LLC.

Library of Congress Cataloging-in-Publication Data

Names: Louis, Jenn, author. | Squires, Kathleen, author. | Anderson, Ed
  (photographer), photographer (expression)
Title: The book of greens : a cook's compendium of 40 varieties, from
arugula to watercress, with over 150 recipes / Jenn Louis with
Kathleen Squires; photographs by Ed Anderson.
Description: First edition. | Berkeley : Ten Speed Press, [2017] |
Includes bibliographical references and index.
Identifiers: LCCN 2016036277 (print) | LCCN 2016048674 (ebook)
Subjects: LCSH: Cooking (Greens) | LCGFT: Cookbooks.
Classification: LCC TX803.G74 L68 2017 (print) | LCC TX803.G74
(ebook) | DDC
  641.6/54—dc23
LC record available at https://lccn.loc.gov/2016036277

Hardcover ISBN: 978-1-60774-984-4
eBook ISBN: 978-1-60774-985-1

Printed in China

Design by Ashley Lima
Food styling by George Dolese

10 9 8 7 6 5 4 3 2 1

First Edition